Judith Bell's

Guide To U.S. Cooking Schools

db
DORN
Books

Copyright © 1979 by Judith Bell
Published by Dorn Books
            7101 York Ave. So.
            Minneapolis, MN 55435

Creative Supervisor: Kenneth M. Nelson
Art Director: Sherry Reutiman
Cover Photo: James Majerus
Inside Art: The Art Directors

First Edition
First Printing 1979
ISBN 0 934070 00 8
Library of Congress Catalog Number 79-84765

To Bob and Elliot for their love and patience and encouragement.

To Simone "Simca" Beck, Julia Child and James Beard. Together they have influenced the daily lives, health and happiness of millions of families and individuals in America. They have nutured creativity, quieted and helped abolish fears in the kitchen and brought joy to the hearts of Americans. It is doubtful that cooking schools would have grown as they have and we might all be "starving" (in more than one way) were it not for their leadership and untiring inspiration.

Thanks

No one is an island and books are really a cooperative venture. Thus it is important to give thanks where they are due. Cynthia MacGarvey helped with preliminary organization. Sharon Lane, my associate, provided invaluable assistance with her innumerable talents of organization. It is doubtful that the book would be a reality without Sharon's help.

On the publisher's side, Charles Mundale, Wayne Christensen, Herb Kent and Bill Dorn deserve special thanks. They have "fathered" the book well beyond the normal obligations for a publishing team and we thank them for their moral support and continuing encouragement. Last, but not least, goes a bushel of appreciation to Susan Mundale who had the nearly overwhelming task of editing this book.

Table of Contents

Introduction

I'm very tempted to close my cooking school this year! I'd like to travel to Chattanooga and East Hampton, to Albuquerque and Portland, to San Diego and Washington, to Little Rock and Fond du Lac—to so many of the schools profiled in this *Guide to U.S. Cooking Schools*.

I'd go for a great variety of reasons, but mostly because of the people and what they are teaching, how they are teaching, and why they are teaching. I could learn something of value from probably every school in this book. Just the uniqueness of people and the wide variety of training and experiences guarantees an interesting learning experience. From the resumes I've seen, the professional qualifications of the staff members at many schools are nearly overwhelming. One has to respect those who have sacrificed time, money, and energy to earn diplomas here and abroad. This hard work and commitment show in their schools and in what they are able to teach.

As with any art, however, you can't overlook those who are simply wonderful, dedicated cooks. They call themselves "self-taught," and yet they may represent some of the best common sense, practical advice, and delicious food this side of heaven. These people have much to offer and much to teach.

The Guide may serve as a stimulus to travel. Just being away from home seems to awaken all the senses, and you are often ready to learn something in another setting that might seem mundane or boring at home. But remember, a prophet is often without honor in his home territory—and the same is true of cooking schools and teachers, so we can also learn from those close to home.

Inspiration for the Guide was twofold. At first it was just a desire to find out who was teaching cooking and where. Then it became an almost insatiable curiosity to know more about the schools and the specialties of the teachers. The research discovered teachers who specialize in breads, pastries, meat, Greek, French, Italian, Mexican and almost every cuisine you can imagine. There are those who teach techniques, others who focus on creative cooking, some who are purists of classical cuisine, and still more who seem to teach the kinds of classes that are best suited to their local students' needs.

The cooking school business isn't new. Some people have been teaching for more than 30 years, and a few schools are more than 15 years old. But the majority of cooking schools are less than 10 years old, and more are probably starting even as this introduction is being written.

Why the boom? Didn't Americans always want to learn to cook? To my knowledge no one, myself included, can give a definitive answer to these questions. But a list of pioneers, those who first began to engage the interest of Americans, would certainly include Julia Child, James Beard, and Simone "Simca" Beck.

Cooking schools, of course, are not the only result of people's heightened interest in good food. Food manufacturers, appliance manufacturers, herb farms, cheese shops, fish stores, and gourmet cookware shops—even clothing and certainly publishing—have all been a part of this phenomenon.

The wide variety of cooking schools means that there is also a wide variety of people teaching. This Guide is in no way an attempt to make judgements about the quality of any school or the qualifications of any individual. The information is presented in as objective a manner as possible.

We asked the schools the questions we thought any potential student would ask. Who is the owner/director? What is his or her professional background? Who are the teachers? What are their professional backgrounds? How do they teach? What kinds of classes are taught? How many students are in each class? Is the school associated with another business? Does it have special classes for out-of-town students? What is the philosophy of the school? Each school had the opportunity to submit a recipe, and the recipes have been changed only to comply with a standard typographical form. Schools that did not respond to our letters or phone calls (or those we discovered too late to include) are listed without description.

No one can predict the future, but I suspect that as long as there is someone to teach and someone to learn, cooking schools will grow better and better. I hope you will read the book and use the book. Maybe we'll meet in Dallas, or Denver, or Philadelphia, or Glenview, Illinois—or maybe in Minneapolis. It's a pleasure to share with you.

Judith Bell

Dear Judith,

First of all, all my very sincere congratulations for all the research you have done to obtain all the information regarding cooking schools.

I take great interest in a work that further stimulates the world of "Cuisine." This anthology offers anyone interested in virtually any area of food a wide selection of talented women and men, offering their culinary expertise. I am both happy and proud to discover graduates of L'Ecole des Trois Gourmandes who entered with very limited knowledge and now have successfully achieved positions of recognition in cooking schools throughout the United States.

Simone "Simca" Beck

Eastern States

Carmen's Cuisine
516 Faraday Road
Hockessin, Delaware 19707
302/239-2996

Carmen I. Jones brings a highly professional background to the series of specialized classes, Carmen's Cuisine, that she presents at The Back Burner, a gourmet cookware shop and luncheon restaurant in Hockessin.

Carmen was trained as a chef at the Culinary Institute of America and in France at Chateau de Trelague in Tangenier, with the Troisgros brothers, Roanne, and with Simone Beck.

Although The Back Burner is a new shop, Carmen has been teaching for nine years in cooking schools in Delaware and Texas. She has written about food for newspapers in Texas, Delaware, and Idaho, and is the author of *Simply Gourmet,* a cookbook for today's new kitchen mixers.

The school's repertoire includes specialty classes such as The 10-Minute Gourmet, Soups of All Lands, and European Tortes, as well as the Cuisine Diplome, a six-week series in preparing classical cuisine. About one-third of the classes are lecture/demonstration with a maximum of 40 students. The remaining classes, including the Cuisine Diplome, are participation, and enrollment is more limited to "give all sufficient time to participate."

Carmen has sponsored study trips to France, and says that accommodations and travel arrangements for out-of-town students "could easily be arranged."

Brochure available   Fees: moderate

Carol Mason's Food Originals
2723 P Street N.W.
Washington, D.C. 20007
202/333-2448

At Carol Mason's Food Originals the emphases are on total menu design, nutrition, presentation, and the use of fresh ingredients whenever possible.

Carol Mason, owner/director, says she "always uses the techniques and principles of

French cooking at all levels."

Carol's food background is exceptional. She graduated with an advanced degree from the Cordon Bleu, London, was an instructor for two years at L'Ecole de Cuisine, Washington, and was a chef for two years in a Boston restaurant. She has been teaching and catering for 10 years. She serves as a food consultant to Fiddler's Restaurant in Washington and with James Beard to the National Gallery of Art in Washington.

Classes at her in-home school are lecture/demonstration with a maximum of 16 students. Classes meet weekly and are about two hours long.

No brochure available   Fees: high

The Renaissance Chefs Cooking School
2450 Virginia Avenue N.W.
Washington, D.C. 20037
202/659-5735

The Renaissance began in Italy, and it is no coincidence that Mario Cardullo's Renaissance Chefs Cooking School has both the flavor and savor of this rich period of history.

Mario, who has been cooking "seriously" for at least 20 years, traces his family back to the 15th Century and says that generation after generation, it was associated with cooking and baking.

A bit of a Renaissance man himself, Mario not only teaches cooking but is also an energy expert, a television performer, and a history buff. He often, it seems, brings all these talents into play with his classes.

His school offers in-depth total participation classes in a 20-session course, The Essentials of Northern Italian Cuisine, and in a 10-session Northern Italian Regional Cuisine course. Each class features tasting of at least four wines. All classes are limited to 15 students.

Concentrated classes for out-of-town students can be arranged, and Mario will assist with travel arrangements if requested.

Brochure available   Fees: moderate

Chinese Cooking School of the International Gourmet Center
323 Park Avenue
Baltimore, Maryland 21201
301/752-5501

Nutrition and Chinese cooking go hand in hand in the classes of Katherine M. Chin, a registered dietitian who teaches at the International Gourmet Center, Baltimore.

As owner/director of the school, Katherine says her philosophy is "to provide the student with the principles of nutrition and their application to the art of Chinese cooking."

Katherine has a B.S. in dietetics from the University of Maryland and interned at Johns Hopkins Hospital, Baltimore. She has been in business for nine years.

Katherine says she emphasizes maintaining a well-balanced nutritious diet, knowledge of caloric values of foods, and the economical and energy conservation aspects of food preparation. She includes instruction on sodium-restricted cooking and maintaining the nutrients of foods as they are prepared.

Her classes are a combination of lecture/demonstration and participation. The maximum number of students in each class is 16. She offers concentrated classes for the convenience of out-of-town students and will help with travel and hotel accommodations.

The International Gourmet Center is a business that sells Oriental food and equipment.

Class schedule available   Fees: moderate

Culinary Arts
5701 Newbury Street
Baltimore, Maryland 21209
301/542-6100

At Culinary Arts, Baltimore, directors Bonnie Rapoport and Anne Barry have put together a tantalizing array of specialty and series classes taught by well trained professionals.

Both Bonnie and Anne hold the grande diplome of the Cordon Bleu, London. Together, they team-teach several of the school's classes. They are also restaurant consultants in Detroit, Washington, and Baltimore, and are writing their first cookbook.

Staff teachers include Germaine Sharretts, who holds the advanced degree from La Varenne, Paris, and is director of Les Deux Gourmettes, another cooking school in Baltimore, and Lisa Lystad, a graduate of the Cordon Bleu, London.

Culinary Arts has played host to many celebrity cooks including John Clancy and Jacques Pepin. Local people teach ethnic specialties.

A focal point of the school is its many one-session clinics on a variety of subjects including game cooking, carving, and the foods of Mexico and the Mediterranean. The school also offers several series classes that present the cuisines of France, Greece, North Africa, and New Orleans. With the exception of the participation series for men and children, all classes are lecture/demonstration. Maximum class size is 30 students.

Brochure available   Fees: high

Les Deux Gourmettes
2015 Skyline Road
Baltimore, Maryland 21210
301/828-6586

"We feel that through our travels we have enjoyed some of the best food the world has to offer, and we strive to give our students not just recipes and cooking tips, but a whole 'gourmet' attitude toward food, its history and its pleasures," writes Pamela B. Meier, a teacher at Les Deux Gourmettes, Baltimore.

Director of Les Deux Gourmettes is Germaine A. Sharretts, who was born in Morocco of an Italian father and a French mother. She earned the advanced diploma from La Varenne and has taught for many years.

Pamela Meier studied under Mrs. Sharretts before becoming her associate. Pamela says she is a "widely traveled self-taught cook specializing in French cooking."

Because of other commitments the school has discontinued its daytime classes but continues to offer its evening practical (participation) classes, which are limited to 15 students.

No brochure available   Fees: moderate

The Junior Chef's Kitchen
3607 Barberry Court
Baltimore, Maryland 21208
301/486-2814

Only the young may learn at The Junior Chef's Kitchen in Baltimore. Here on weekday afternoons Ann M. Pumpian teaches cooking to children ages 10 to 14. The class repertoire includes an international menu, bread baking, and gift baking. Each class has a maximum of six students. The classes are basically lecture/demonstration, but participation is encouraged.

Ann is a home economist with 12 years' teaching experience in public schools. She has taken classes with Madeleine Kamman, Marcella Hazan, Giuliano Bugialli, and at the London Cordon Bleu.

Ann's philosophy, and her reason for teaching children, is stated in an old proverb: "Give a man a fish and you feed him for a day. Teach a man to fish and you feed him for life."

Brochure available   Fees: low

L'Academie De Cuisine
5021 Wilson Lane
Bethesda, Maryland 20014
301/986-9490

L'Academie De Cuisine, Bethesda, has chef-level courses and mini classes, lab-style participation classes and demonstration classes in a tiered theater-like classroom, classes that cost enough to consider a payment schedule and inexpensive classes.

Donald Miller and Francois Dionet are partners in this three-year-old school, which is approved by the Maryland State Department of Education. Francois, the director, is a graduate of a hotel school in Lausanne, Switzerland, and served in restaurants in Europe.

"We take the purist approach, but teach classical cooking with modern interpretations," Don says. "We don't encourage short cuts. Even in our one-session class on French fries, the students learn to select a potato, choose the best oil, what temperature to use, how to blanch, and how to double fry.''

The school's courses run the culinary gamut, but one of its most distinctive classes is Professional Techniques of French Cooking, which spans 25 weeks. The Practique which runs for 28 weeks, is a practical workshop associated with the Professional course. Students can take any one of the seven four-week sessions as they are given, and do not need to take them in sequence.

The school regularly has visiting celebrity cooks. It has hosted Diana Kennedy, Paula Wolfert, Florence Lin, Jack Lirio, Madhur Jaffrey, Giuliano Bugialli, and John Clancy.

The school has sponsored study trips to Europe and has concentrated classes for the convenience of out-of-town students. It will also assist with travel accommodations.

About the philosophy of the school, Don says, ''We are concerned with teaching the planning, purchasing, preparation, and presentation of food. Our objective is to familiarize the students with the theories, techniques, and tastes involved in creating dishes they will be able to reproduce in their own homes.''

Brochure available   Fees: low-moderate

WHAT'S COOKING

1776 East Jefferson
Rockville, Maryland 20852
301/881-2430

There's great diversity at What's Cooking! in Rockville, both in the classes and in the teaching staff. Phylis Frucht, the school's owner, studied with Grace Chu in New York and taught breadbaking and Chinese cooking. She has published Chinese and Jewish cookbooks. The director of the school, Suzanne Tonken, is a librarian who turned to cooking after studying with Phylis. Both Phylis and Suzanne teach at the school, along with 10 other instructors who have widely diverse backgrounds. ''Some have studied cooking here and abroad while others have developed their expertise themselves, often as an outgrowth of their own ethnic backgrounds,'' Suzanne says.

Cuisines taught at the school include French, Greek, and Spanish. A host of specialty classes is also offered. Classes are lecture/demonstration and are limited to 20 students.

''By offering a wide variety of classes, we hope to enhance our students' repertoires and increase their exposure to many different cuisines,'' adds Suzanne.

Brochure available   Fees: low

Contempra Cooking Center
Monmouth Mall
Eatontown, New Jersey 07724
201/542-3031

A cooking theatre that seats 75 persons, closed circuit television, and two teaching kitchens are the special features of the brand-new Contempra Cooking Center, Eatontown.

Miriam Brickman, director of curriculum for the school, attended classes at the Cordon Bleu in Paris, is a chef for Restaurant Associates, took classes with Giuliano Bugialli, and is on the faculty of the New School for Social Research, New York City. Carl Jerome, an instructor at the school, was an assistant to James Beard and is the author of *The Complete Chicken.*

The school plans to have many guest instructors. "We hope to present the best of instruction, with the most creditable staff of instructors and guest instructors, to the people in this area," Miriam says.

The class repertoire includes the fundamentals of French cooking and various ethnic cuisines. Participation classes are limited to 16 persons; lecture/demonstration classes are limited to 75.

The Contempra Cooking Center is associated with a cookware shop.

Brochure available   Fees:low-moderate

Carole's Capers
5 Lexington Avenue
Emerson, New Jersey 07630
201/967-9545

"Most of my recipes are original and emphasize French techniques," says Carole Walter, owner/director of Carole's Capers in Emerson.

At her in-home school, students are given assignments, but can feel free to season and substitute according to their own tastes. "Cooking is personal," Carole says. "Food should reflect the taste of the individual who prepares it as long as the proper techniques are followed." The only exception Carole notes is in baking classes where she feels recipes must be followed more accurately.

Courses taught at Carole's Capers include French and international cuisines, standard and advanced baking, party foods, and other specialized classes including food processor cooking.

Carole, who was an art major, has been teaching for 10 years. She has studied privately with a French chef in France and under Birte Rohweder in Copenhagen, Denmark. She worked for short periods at Taillevent in Paris and at D'Angelterre Hotel, Copenhagen. She has assisted Jacques Pepin, Giuliano Bugialli, and Paula Wolfert, and recently studied with Lydie Marshall.

Carole's school has both lecture/demonstration and participation classes. Lecture/demonstration classes are limited to 18 students; participation classes are limited to 10.

Carole is also on the staff of Cooktique, Tenafly, New Jersey.

Brochure available   Fees: high

Ann Mariotti Cooking School

70-37 Ingram Street
Forest Hills, New Jersey 11375
212/263-5540

Ann Mariotti feels that cooking and eating are two of the greatest joys in life. "Cooking should appeal to all of the senses," she says. "It should appeal to the eye by looking good, to the nose by smelling good, and to the ear through the praises from guests."

At her in-home school, Ann Mariotti Cooking School, Ann built a special kitchen for her classes. Here she teaches Italian, Sicilian, French, Greek, and Mediterranean cooking in a combination of lecture/demonstration and participation classes that are limited to six persons.

Ann has bachelor's and master's degrees in education and was an assistant to Dione Lucas in New York City for almost two years. She has been teaching for 10 years.

No brochure available   Fees: moderate

Sue Lyon's Essencial Cooking School

43 Saddle Ranch Lane
Hillsdale, New Jersey 07642
201/664-8775

"I named my school to reflect my emphasis on the essence of food," says Sue Lyon, owner/director of Sue Lyon's Essencial Cooking School in Hillsdale.

Sue considers herself to be a self-taught cook with an inquiring mind and a good palate. She lived in France for two years and has returned six times to study and travel. During one tour of three-star restaurants, she relates, one of the Troisgros brothers said, "She asked some of the best questions I've ever been asked about cooking." He then presented Sue with a complimentary certificate.

In her participation classes, which are limited to five students, Sue teaches with "a great emphasis on hand techniques, liaison sauces, and the appreciation of fine ingredients." Much time is spent, she says, on "appreciating the subtle differences in the produce that is available to the American cook." She teaches a class for beginners on preparing elegant dinners, another called Cook Today and Share Tonight, a class on nouvelle cuisine, and one on Indian specialties.

Sue's inquiring mind led her to develop and then market the Tin Lizzie, a kit for retinning copper cookware. With this kit, a do-it-yourselfer can re-tin a pot in about five minutes. The kit is available through Sue Lyon's Au Cuisine, at the above address.

No brochure available   Fees: low

Kitchen Caboodle

Mountainville
Route #2
Lebanon, New Jersey 08833
201/832-7218
201/832-7445

The authenticity of ethnic cuisines and the integrity of food itself are emphasized at the Kitchen Caboodle, Mountainville.

The school, which is directed by Elizabeth Wroth, teaches regional American cooking, the cuisines of Szechwan and Hunan, and French cooking in its full participation classes, which are limited to seven persons. Specialty classes offered include hors d'oeuvres, soups, breads, and pastry. The school's only demonstration class is in food processor cooking.

Elizabeth has taught for two years at Kitchen Caboodle. Her background includes "numerous cooking classes in New York and New Jersey." Susan de Groff, an instructor at the school, was apprenticed to Elizabeth Chu in San Francisco and has taught in California and Pottersville, New Jersey.

The school is associated with a cookware shop and catering business.

Brochure available   Fees: low

Epicure School of Fine Cooking

200 Franklin Avenue
Midland Park, New Jersey 07432
201/445-2776

"We believe in teaching techniques, urging creativity, and not teaching recipes," say Tullio and Gretchen Cominetto, who own and direct the Epicure School of Fine Cooking, Midland Park.

Tullio, one of the principal instructors at the school, took the advanced concentrated course for chefs at the Culinary Institute of America and has been an instructor at a local vocational high school. Other teachers include Gretchen Cominetto and Eileen Krasnow.

All classes at the school are participation and are usually limited to eight students each. The current schedule lists six different courses including beginning and advanced gourmet cooking, bread baking, classical Italian cooking, and pre-teen cooking.

In addition to teaching techniques, the school's teachers "include nutrition, buying knowledge, kitchen safety, and efficiency," says Tullio. "Our programs are carefully planned with definite goals, and are not 'coffee klatsch' sessions," he adds.

Brochure available   Fees: low

Emilie Taylor's Meat School

189 Kaywin Road
Paramus, New Jersey 07652
201/265-4145

Few, if any, schools have specialized to the extent of Emilie Taylor's Meat School in Paramus. Here Emilie Taylor, the school's owner/director, teaches almost everything you'll ever want to know about meat, from buying it to cutting and cooking it.

Emilie's professional credentials stem from more than 25 years of practical experience, beginning at the age of 16 when she learned the butchering trade from her father, who owned a food market. She began teaching during the American consumer boycott of meat. During the boycott she traveled around New Jersey, explaining how meat is merchandised and how consumers could purchase it for less. Before opening her school—something she had always dreamed of doing—she taught privately as well as in three adult education schools. She is the primary teacher at her school, but is assisted by two other teachers.

Emilie's classes are a combination of lecture/demonstration and full participation. Most are limited to six or eight students. Several classes are available for out-of-town students; the school will provide help with hotel and travel arrangements.

Emilie's philosophy is most interesting: "In today's world, life can be a constant choice-making struggle or an interesting experience. Since eating is something none of us can eliminate, I have chosen to turn it into an exciting, economical, time saving, nutritional, and rewarding experience not only for myself but for others.

"Once the perplexity of meat purchasing is eliminated, your mind can be opened to see the remarkable possibilities of each cut of meat. By learning my creative meat-cutting techniques, you can utilize each cut to its fullest advantage and enrich your meal planning more than you ever thought possible."

Brochure available   Fees: moderate

East/West Cooking School

137 Sibbald Drive
Park Ridge, New Jersey 07656
201/391-7068

Evening classes that focus on French and Chinese cooking are the specialty of Judy Nelson, owner/director of East/West Cooking School, Park Ridge.

Judy says she has "more than 20 years' experience cooking, testing, and experimenting." She studied at the China Institute with Florence Lin and Dorothy Lee as well as with Madame Grace Chu in New York City.

At her in-home school Judy teaches an introductory course in French cooking and basic and advanced Chinese cooking. The classes in French cuisine are lecture/demonstration with some participation. Chinese cooking classes are full participation. All classes are limited to six students.

"Basically, my philosophy is that *anyone* can learn to cook given the willingness, good quality fresh ingredients, good instruction, and good recipes," Judy says.

The East/West Cooking School has concentrated classes for out-of-town students.

Brochure available   Fees: low-moderate

433 Cedar Lane
Teaneck, New Jersey 07666
201/836-0833

"The Look & Cook cooking studio intends to present classic cooking techniques combined with contemporary concerns for nutrition and economy," says Bunny Dell, owner/director of this school in Teaneck. "We hope to de-mystify cooking and make the kitchen comfortable and friendly. We encourage exploring cuisines and have introduced courses in Indonesian, Russian, Spanish, and Japanese cooking," she adds.

Bunny, a former junior high school art teacher, has taken classes with many famous cooking teachers in New York City including James Beard, Marcella Hazan, Florence Lin, Grace Chu, Lydie P. Marshall, Madhur Jaffrey, Diana Kennedy, and Andrea Dodi. She has also studied with Simone Beck in France and attended classes at La Varenne.

Bunny taught independently for six years as The Happy Cooker before opening the Look & Cook cooking studio last year. Look & Cook is associated with a gourmet cookware shop.

Brochure available   Fees: moderate

Cooktique
9 Railroad Avenue
Tenafly, New Jersey 07670
201/568-7990

In-depth participation workshops are a special feature of Cooktique in Tenafly. The school has French, Northern Italian, and Chinese cooking workshops as well as an advanced baking series, children's classes, and one-day sessions on baking, bread, puff pastry, vegetables, fish, and other topics.

Silvia Lehrer, director, attended classes at the Cordon Bleu, London, for two summers and has had three series of classes in Florence with Giuliano Bugialli. She also studied with Marcella Hazan and Lydie Marshall. She "participated and observed" in three-star restaurants in the French countryside. Silvia, who has been teaching for eight years, also writes a weekly food column for a local newspaper.

Her staff includes Carole Walter, who has studied in France and Denmark. Carole has taken classes with Richard Olney and Julie Dannenbaum and is the author of *Your First Loaf.* Arlene Battifarano, another instructor, is a professional caterer who trained with Silvia and with Lydie Marshall. The school has also hosted Jacques Pepin, Giuliano Bugialli, and Paula Wolfert.

Most classes at Cooktique are participation and are limited to eight students. Occasional lecture/demonstration classes are limited to 18.

"My personal philosophy is to have students not use recipes as a crutch, but to be able to use common sense in executing techniques," Silvia says.

Brochure available   Fees: moderate-high

Italian Kitchen

309 Newtown Road
Wyckoff, New Jersey 07481
201/447-0696

Small, full participation classes held in a restaurant kitchen await students of the Italian Kitchen cooking school, which is owned and directed by Rose Geloso. The school's instructor, known professionally as Mr. John, is a self-taught cook who is also chef and buyer for a seafood restaurant and retail fresh fish store.

Class size at the Italian Kitchen is limited to four students. Half of the classes focus on Italian cooking and the rest are specialty classes devoted to breads, fish, vegetables, and other food groups. The school's philosophy is that "Cooking is an art that can be mastered by observing, performing, and practicing."

The Italian Kitchen is associated with a business that caters Italian dinners.

Brochure forthcoming   Fees: high

515 N. Latches Lane
Merion, Pennsylvania 19066
215/667-3898
215/544-8394

The Potpourri School of Cooking does, indeed, offer a melange of classes. They range from three-session series, one on easy gourmet cooking for busy people and another on entertaining at home, to one-session classes on specialty topics such as breads, chocolate, pasta, and cakes.

Charlotte Kursman and Bernice Sisson, partners in the three-year-old school, have studied and attended classes with many important food professionals including Julie Dannenbaum, Marcella Hazan, Georges Perrier, and Jacques Pepin. In addition, Charlotte studied privately with Dione Lucas in New York and with James Beard, Simone Beck, and other notables. Bernice attended classes at the Cordon Bleu in London, and studied cuisine minceur and advanced baking at the Culinary Institute of America. Both Charlotte and Bernice have worked with Chef Jean Morel at his country inn, Hostellerie Bressane, Hillside, New York.

The repertoire of classes at The Potpourri School of Cooking changes with the seasons. Classes are lecture/demonstration and have a maximum of 20 students. The class sessions are held in the kitchen of L'Epicure, a cookware store in Haverford, Pennsylvania.

Brochure available   Fees: high

Julie Dannenbaum's Creative Cooking, Inc.

2044 Rittenhouse Square
Philadelphia, Pennsylvania 19103
215/546-0442

Julie Dannenbaum directs cooking schools for all seasons and reasons. In the fall, winter, or spring, you can choose her original school, Julie Dannenbaum's Creative Cooking, Inc., in Philadelphia, where Julie teaches a wide variety of classes suited to many needs and situations.

One class, Improvisation, teaches how to create meals on the spur of the moment. In a Curry Buffet class, Julie demonstrates a complete meal of curry dishes. Another class, Potatoes, is said to be "the best opportunity you'll ever have to learn everything there is to know about the potato."

During the winter Julie also directs the Greenbrier Cooking School, White Sulphur Springs, West Virginia. And during the summer you'll find her directing the Gritti Palace Hotel Cooking School in Venice, Italy.

Julie studied for two years with Dione Lucas, worked with Dione for two years, and received Dione's Cordon Bleu certificate. She is the author of *Julie Dannenbaum's Creative Cooking School Cookbook* and *Menus for all Occasions.* She has written food articles for *House and Garden, House Beautiful,* and *Redbook.* Julie also taught at the James Beard Cooking School in New York City and was a consultant for the *Cook's Catalog*, a resource book and catalog for the cooking industry.

Julie's Philadelphia school is 15 years old. Her staff includes assistant Sandy Ainsworth and two teaching assistants, Corky Connor and Frank Kelly. Most classes are lecture/demonstration.

"My philosophy of teaching is that above all students should have fun cooking. I do not intimidate my students and I do not believe in participation classes unless every student is preparing the same thing. Otherwise it's a 'cop-out' for the teacher," Julie says.

A popular course at the Philadelphia school is a one-week "crash" course designed for out-of-town students. It is described as "everything you've ever wanted to know about cooking."

Brochure available   Fees: high

International Cuisine, Inc.

Chestnut Hill Hotel
8229 Germantown Avenue
Philadelphia, Pennsylvania 19118
215/247-2100

Not only does Master Chef Tell Erhardt, co-owner of International Cuisine, Inc., Philadelphia, have a cooking school, but he is also a nationally known television personality and owner of a restaurant.

In fact, his classes are presented in the spacious and professionally equipped kitchen of his restaurant in the Chestnut Hill Hotel. And he appears on a television program, Evening, shown in 15 cities.

Tell earned the title Master Chef in West Germany, where he was the youngest man ever to receive that degree.

Hermie Kranzdorf, Chef Tell's co-owner, is also the pastry chef at the restaurant. She has studied with many food notables including James Beard, Jacques Pepin, Richard Olney, Michel Fitousi, Georges Perrier, Julie Dannenbaum, and Giuliano Bugialli. She attended classes at La Varenne, Paris.

The class schedule at International Cuisine is produced for a year at a time and includes seasonal series classes and many one- and two-session specialty classes. International cuisine is taught in most of the series classes, and the foods of Germany, Italy, and the Far East are presented during the specialty sessions. All classes at International Cuisine are demonstration and are limited to 25 students.

Chef Tell says, "We're the only professional male-female team in the city. Our methods and short-cuts help to simplify and clarify home preparations. We stress technique and feel that by watching someone do things properly you can learn the most."

Brochure available   Fees: high

Station Square
Pittsburg, Pennsylvania 15219
412/261-9196

The Classic Cook, Ltd., may well win the prize for specialty classes! In addition to the several series it regularly offers, the school had single sessions on 32 different topics during a recent two-month period.

George Smith, the school's owner/director, has an extensive background in food. He has studied with James Beard, Julie Dannenbaum, John Clancy, Mahdur Jaffrey, and Barbara Kafka. He is a regional director for the American Wine Society, writes a weekly food column, and is at work on his first cookbook.

The Classic Cook's staff includes Jane Citron, who has studied with Julie Dannenbaum and Chef Ferdinand Metz; Robert Kao, who owns and operates a restaurant; Joanna Lange, a home economist with 14 years' teaching experience; and E. Margaret Pennell, a graduate of The Central Institute, Leicester, England, who has British hotel and catering service qualifications.

Most classes at the two-year-old school are participation and are limited to 18 students. The school offers special concentrated classes for out-of-town students.

Brochure available   Fees: low

428 Woodland Road
Sewickley, Pennsylvania 15143
412/741-3207
412/741-3112

A class in food garnishing called "Don't Buy Parsley" gives us an idea of the sense of humor Marlene Parrish brings to her cooking classes in Sewickley.

At her in-home school, Marlene Parrish Teaches Cooking, Marlene does indeed teach cooking—and more. "I view cooking as a sensual experience, one that uses all the senses," she says. Marlene includes a "taste seminar" as part of each series class. She describes this taste seminar as "pure taste identification in a controlled setting."

By and large her classes focus on specialty cooking. The schedule includes classes on fish, junior cooking, parties, and dinners. She has both lecture and participation classes. Lecture classes have a maximum of 10 students; participation classes are limited to six. All of Marlene's classes emphasize theory, principles, and techniques.

Marlene, a home economist, was assistant food editor of *McCall's* magazine under Helen McCully and did research in dietetics at the University of Pittsburgh. She has studied with James Beard, Paula Peck, and Marcella Hazan, and has taken classes at the Cordon Bleu, London. She is the author-publisher of *I'd Rather Play (Tennis, Golf, Ski) than Cook* (Garlic Press, MPM Productions).

Brochure available   Fees: moderate-high

Madame Colonna's School of Cooking

102 North Oak Street
Falls Church, Virginia 22046
703/534-7787

A native Parisian and a graduate of the Cordon Bleu, Paris, Madame Marie Therese Colonna founded her in-home cooking school almost 20 years ago. At her school, students "do everything," since all her classes are full participation and limited to eight persons.

"I teach my pupils confidence in the kitchen," says Madame Colonna. "This makes their cooking enjoyable and the results a pleasure for themselves, their families, and their guests."

Madame Colonna's travels have taken her across the European continent. She has gathered many recipes along the way, and her classes feature selections from classic French to peasant Russian cuisines.

There are three semesters each year at Madame Colonna's school, with both day and evening classes offered. Special concentrated sessions are available for out-of-town students.

Brochure available   Fees: moderate

The Greenbrier Cooking School
White Sulphur Springs, West Virginia 24986
800/624-6070
304/536-1110

An internationally known cooking teacher and one of the finest resorts in the United States combine to make The Greenbrier Cooking School an extraordinary experience. Julie Dannenbaum, who has her own school in Pennsylvania, directs 13 week-long sessions at The Greenbrier from November to March. Students are guests at the 200-year-old Greenbrier resort hotel, which is located on 6,500 acres of West Virginia woodlands.

Classes at the school are demonstration only, and are designed for out-of-town students. They begin on Monday morning and end on Friday at noon. "Do ahead" recipes, "quick to make" meals, and low-calorie dishes are just some of the lessons taught during the morning in the informal atmosphere of the beautifully equipped food preparation area. Afternoon classes are demonstrations by the award-winning staff of the hotel. They even impart the secrets of the Greenbrier methods of table setting and napkin folding.

The hotel offers a special rate for students who wish "to come early or stay late" and enjoy the Greenbrier facilities for a weekend.

Brochure available   Fees: high

New York-New England

Cook's Corner

115 Mason Street
Greenwich, Connecticut 06830
302/869-2653

The Cook's Corner, Greenwich, can boast of a teaching staff that includes the well known Malvina Kinard and Florence Lin. Until last year the Cook's Corner was associated with Cook's Corner schools in other locations, but it is now independent, according to Nancy B. Mott, owner/director.

Nancy has taught cooking for 12 years. She studied at the Cordon Bleu and La Varenne, Paris, and has taken classes with James Beard, Giuliano Bugialli in Florence, and with Malvina Kinard.

Malvina, founder of the Cook's Corner, is still actively teaching. She studied with James Beard, Simone Beck, and in Denmark and the Middle East. Florence Lin, Director of Cooking, the China Institute, has taught and lectured all over the United States. She is the author of three Chinese cookbooks and was consultant to the Time-Life Chinese cookbook. Mead Brownell, another teacher, studied at La Varenne, Paris, with John Clancy, and at The Culinary Institute of America. The school also hosts guest lecturers in specialized fields.

Baking and pastry classes at Cook's Corner are total participation for six to seven persons. Other classes are lecture/demonstration with a maximum of 15 students. Most classes are single sessions, but the school offers some series classes in classic French, Italian, and Chinese cooking. A children's cooking series is also offered.

Brochure available   Fees: high

Polly Fritch's Cooking Classes

969 North Street
Greenwich, Connecticut 06830
203/661-7742

"The 'whys' of cooking are very important," says Polly Fritch, owner/director of Polly Fritch's Cooking Classes, Greenwich.

At her in-home school Polly teaches lecture/demonstration classes that focus on international cooking and do-ahead seasonal cooking. She also offers a class in wine and cheese. All classes are limited to 10 students.

Polly has been teaching for 10 years. She says she learned from her parents, who were "excellent cooks." Polly was an assistant to Rita Leinwand, food editor of *Bon Appetit*. She has attended classes at La Varenne and the Cordon Bleu, Paris.

Brochure available   Fees: high

Cuisinier

934A Boston Post Road
Guilford, Connecticut 06437
203/453-6127

There are no "beginners" or "advanced" students at Cuisinier cooking school, Guilford. "We believe that with our good instruction a student should be able to learn anything we teach, from the simplest to the most complicated dishes," says Gloria Zimmerman, owner/director of the school.

Gloria, who taught at her home for 12 years, now holds her classes at the Kitchen Kupboard, a cookware shop. She attended classes at the China Institute and with John Clancy, and has worked at major department stores on the East Coast. She assisted Grace Chu in a national demonstration tour. Gloria is co-author, with Bach Ngo, of *The Classic Cuisine of Vietnam*, which will be published in French by Libre Expression and in English by Barron's.

Class offerings at Cuisinier focus on Chinese and Vietnamese cooking, but also include Italian family cooking and specialty classes such as soups, crepes, and souffles. Most classes are participation and are limited to 20 students.

Ed Giobbi, Jacques Pepin, Mme. Jeanne Pepin from Lyon, and Bach Ngo are some of the celebrity cooks who have taught at the school.

Brochure available   Fees: moderate

SILO COOKING SCHOOL
Upland Road
New Milford, Connecticut 06776
203/355-0300

The Silo Cooking School has the freshest possible vegetables and herbs for its classes—they come directly from the gardens just a few steps from the school's teaching kitchen at Hunt Hill Farm, New Milford.

The owner of this school is Ruth Henderson, an owner/partner of two New York restaurants and a director of the New York Restaurant Association. Ann Rowan, the school's director, attended the Cordon Bleu, Paris, and is a food writer.

The Silo Cooking School draws upon several food professionals as teachers. "We have only professional instructors, well qualified to teach their specialties," says Ann Rowan. "The Silo Cooking School maintains a high quality of instruction in cooking techniques and experience."

Classes at the school, which are offered Wednesday through Sunday each week, are both lecture/demonstration and participation. Demonstration classes are limited to 25 students; participation classes are limited to 10. The school emphasizes "country and casual entertaining" in the presentation of its prepared dishes.

The Silo Cooking School is part of a complex that includes a kitchen equipment store and a gallery of handicrafts, many of which are made by Connecticut artisans.

Brochure available   Fees: moderate-high

The Constance Quan Cooking School

39 Lockwood Drive
Old Greenwich, Connecticut 06870
203/637-9302

Award-winning Constance Quan says, "Using versatile recipes as a tool, I teach students the basics of fine food, be it classic or modern, simple or elaborate."

At her school, The Constance Quan Cooking School, Old Greenwich, the enjoyment and satisfaction of cooking are based on an understanding of and appreciation for fundamental principles and techniques, "knowing 'how and why.' I guide the students to recognize these fundamentals in different contexts, giving them familiarity with a full range of foods," she says.

Constance learned her "hows and whys" through in-depth study. She has earned the Diplome de Langue Francaise from the French ministry of education and the certificate of advanced study from the Cordon Bleu, Paris, and has taken advanced work at La Varenne and the Culinary Institute of America. She was awarded the Westchester Chef's Award and the first prize in Cuisine and Classical Pastry by the Societe Culinaire Philanthropique. She has done food research and development for major food corporations.

French cuisine is the focus of her school. Classes are lecture/demonstration and are limited to six students. She will arrange concentrated classes for out-of-town students and will help with travel accommodations.

Brochure available   Fees: high

Joanne Hush Cooking School

1254 Post Road
Westport, Connecticut 06880
203/227-4151

"I teach all of the basic cutting and cooking techniques from the various regions of China," says Joanne Hush, owner/director of Joanne Hush Cooking School in Westport.

Joanne studied at the China Institute and with various restaurant chefs in New York City. She has had her own school for six years and has taught in many other New York cooking schools. She has also demonstrated cooking at many large department stores in New York City. Joanne is co-author, along with Peter Wong, of *The Chinese Menu Cookbook,* published by Holt, Rinehart and Winston.

Joanne's classes include Beginning and Advanced Chinese Cooking, Dim Sum, and Mongolian Hot Pot Cookery. Classes are full participation and are limited to eight students.

Brochure available   Fees: moderate

Cook's Corner

11 Sherwood Square
Westport, Connecticut 06880
203/227-9554

"Anyone can learn to cook better, but to truly learn one must learn from highly qualified people, those who have done the hard work of study," says Stan Levy, owner/director of Cook's Corner, Westport.

Instructors at Cook's Corner include Robert MacKerroll, a graduate of the Cordon Bleu, Paris; Florence Lin from China, who heads the cooking program at the China Institute in New York City; and Marg Walter, a graduate of the D.C.C. Institute, Dieppe, France, and of the Gastronomisches Institute, Vienna, Austria.

Five different levels of French cooking are offered at the school. The cooking of four regions of China, Viennese cuisine, and baking are also taught.

Classes at Cook's Corner are lecture/demonstration with a maximum of 20 students. The school offers concentrated classes for out-of-town students, and will assist with travel arrangements.

Cook's Corner is associated with a cookware shop and catering service.

Brochure available   Fees: high

Gateway Shopping Center
Wilton, Connecticut 06897
203/762-7575

In 1975 Craig Claiborne, the noted food writer, called The Culinary Arts in Wilton one of the best cooking school/cookware shop/food specialty store combinations he had seen.

This three-faceted business is under the direction of Cecile Rivel, who says that when she moved to Wilton from New York City and found herself unable to locate food supplies and equipment as easily as she had in Manhattan, she decided to open her shop and school. She assumed others had the same frustrations and yearnings and she was right. Her business has flourished.

Cecile comes from a background of fine food. Her father was founder and owner of Murray's Sturgeon Shop on Broadway in New York City and her mother was a noted Eastern European cook. Cecile studied for two extended sessions at the Cordon Bleu, Paris.

Classes at The Culinary Arts focus on international cuisine. Cecile teaches most of the French cooking classes. Other cuisines are taught by "people of that nationality so that the recipes are authentic rather than Americanized, and these recipes are usually family heirlooms." All classes are lecture/demonstration and are limited to 26 students.

Brochure available   Fees: high

Suzanne Taylor's Cooking Classes

Meadow Rue
East Blue Hill, Maine 04629
207/374-9948

In a house nestled on the shore of the Atlantic, Suzanne Taylor's Cooking Classes at East Blue Hill feature small full participation classes in a lovely setting.

Suzanne Taylor, owner/director, studied at the Cordon Bleu, London, and is a graduate of Villa Brillantmont, Lausanne, Switzerland. She also studied with Dione Lucas and Maurice Moore-Betty in New York City. Suzanne is the author of a cookbook, *Young and Hungry,* and has written articles for *House and Garden* magazine.

Suzanne's classes feature French cuisine, although some Scandinavian and Chinese dishes are also taught. The classes are organized in six-week series. However, a three-day "crash course" is offered in August. A guest house is available to visitors and out-of-town students, at an additional fee.

No brochure available   Fees: moderate

La Cuisine Cooking Classes

92 Charles Street
Boston, Massachusetts 02114
617/227-7340

In a private home in the gracious Beacon Hill section of downtown Boston, La Cuisine offers individual attention for its students in participation and demonstration classes.

Owner/director Terence Janericco, a food professional for 28 years, has worked in hotels, restaurants, and private residences, and in catering in New York and New England. He was food editor of *Bostonian* magazine, and has been featured in articles in *Better Homes and Gardens,* the *Boston Globe,* the *Herald American,* and on Boston television programs.

Terence feels that his students should write out the recipes used in his classes "so that they receive a greater knowledge of the recipe and can ask more intelligent questions about its development." Because he has an extensive personal library and seldom prepares the same dish twice, Terence is "always able to give different and interesting recipes." He believes that cooking "must be made fun, relaxing, and informal so as to encourage creativity and improvisation."

Most of La Cuisine's courses are in series of six classes, three hours in length. Some single sessions that cover a particular area of cooking, such as soups, breads, or winter foods, are also offered. Basic techniques are stressed at this school, and the subject matter of the class offerings varies from baking classes to advanced gourmet cooking and Italian, French Provincial and Chinese cuisines. Concentrated classes are available during the summer months and European cooking tours are offered periodically by the school.

Brochure available   Fees: high

Creative Cuisine

2020 Massachusetts Avenue
Cambridge, Massachusetts 02140
617/354-3836

A repertoire of 25 challenging and interesting classes is taught at Creative Cuisine, Cambridge, by a highly qualified professional staff.

Included in the school's offerings are several series courses that feature Italian, provincial French, Mexican, Middle Eastern, Oriental, Pacific, and Southeast Asia cuisines. The school also offers an intriguing selection of specialty classes including some that focus on diets, some that are geared to junior cooks, a class entitled Dinner at Your Fingertips, which is designed for the cook with limited time, and many others.

The school has two separate kitchens, one for demonstration and one called the "practice kitchen." Demonstration classes are limited to 24 and participation classes are limited to 10 students.

As for professional qualifications, Roberta Avallone, the president and founder of Creative Cuisine, has a broad food background that includes extensive travel and study in Italy as well as in Eastern and Western Europe, the Middle East, the Orient, Africa, and South America. She has taught French, Italian, and European cuisines to professional chefs and restaurateurs in the Boston area. She is a member of the American Culinary Federation, the Academy of Chefs, and Les Amis d'Escoffier Society, and is certified by the National Institute of the Foodservice Industry.

The school has several other well-trained instructors. Roberta Gran, a home economist, has studied with Chef Claus at Frankfurterhof in Hochheim, Germany, with Madame Denise Schorr, and at La Varenne in Paris. She taught and catered for several years before becoming associated with Creative Cuisine. Susan Logozzo, a home economist, holds a teaching certificate from Creative Cuisine and is a graduate chef of Modern Gourmet. Bonita H. Markison has lived in France, was an intelligence officer for the U.S. Air Force, has traveled extensively in Europe, Asia, and Africa, has a teaching certificate from Creative Cuisine and a chef's diploma from Modern Gourmet, and is a member of the American Culinary Federation. Jean Wallick has a teaching certificate from Creative Cuisine and a diploma from Modern Gourmet. Miriam Talanian has "strong inherent talents in Eastern European cookery," and Florence Setsuk Mochizuki Martini is a Japanese-Hawaiian who learned Oriental cuisine while growing up in Hawaii.

Creative Cuisine is associated with DeGustibus, a catering service.

Brochure available   Fees: high-moderate

Mill and Speen Streets
Natick, Massachusetts 01760
617/653-8010

Do-ahead preparation is the theme of all courses at The Every Day Gourmet in Natick. Sheila Elion, owner/director, is the author of *The Every Day Gourmet*, the textbook for her classes. Sheila has studied in the United States, France, Denmark, and Japan.

The school's basic program is a revolving selection of 17 different courses. Six of the classes provide instruction in French cooking; the remaining classes focus on the cuisines of China, Japan, Italy and the Mediterranean, and on specialty topics such as desserts, baking, and buffets.

A special feature of The Every Day Gourmet is a wine series of nine classes, six sessions per class. It is taught by Dr. Herbert Elion, Chevalier du Tastevin (from the Clos de Vougeot), a wine industry consultant who studied at the University of Bordeaux in France and the University of California at Davis. The series consists of nine levels of wine appreciation, from a survey to advanced oenology for wine tasters.

The school is associated with a cookware shop and catering service.

Brochure available   Fees: moderate

Denise Schorr

50 Hartford Street
Natick, Massachusetts 01760
617/653-5188

Madame Denise Schorr began teaching French cooking in New England 26 years ago, and she's still at it. A Parisian by birth, Madame Schorr studied at the Cordon Bleu, Paris, and worked with P.J. Franchiolo, a great pastry chef.

"My approach to cooking is one that considers it an art, taking specific ingredients and blending them together to achieve a desired result. I try to teach my students to prepare food as pleasing to the eye as it is to the taste buds. Even the most simple dish must be attractive as well as palatable," says Madame Schorr.

All of Madame Schorr's classes concentrate on the cuisine of France. They are taught by lecture and demonstration, with students taking notes instead of being given printed recipes. The classes are limited to 15 students, and are held from October to June with summer classes available upon request.

"My desire has been to educate rather than to develop a commercial enterprise," says Madame Schorr. "Many who have come to my classes for spectator participation have become enthusiastic and almost addicted to the art of fine cuisine. Seeing such a transformation in them has been my greatest reward."

Brochure available   Fees: moderate

Jeanne Tahnk's Gourmet Kitchen, Inc.

910 Main Street
Winchester, Massachusetts 01890
617/729-8027

Jeanne Tahnk, a native of Taiwan, brings a wealth of cooking study to her school, Jeanne Tahnk's Gourmet Kitchen, in Winchester. She holds diplomas from several cooking schools in Taiwan that teach all types of Chinese cuisines, including the foods of Szechwan, Peking, and Canton. Jeanne also studied in Japan for six months.

In addition to Jeanne's classes in Oriental cookery, classes in French, Italian, and Mexican cuisines and specialty classes are taught by other well-trained instructors.

Classes at the school are a combination of lecture/demonstration and participation, and are limited to 10 students. They are held in two "brand new" classrooms that feature the latest in kitchen equipment.

No brochure available   Fees: low-moderate

Cooking With Mady
20 Bramble Brook Road
Ardsley, New York 10502
914/693-2698

"I believe in small informal classes with students participating fully," says Mady Brown, owner/director of Cooking with Mady, a school which has just moved from Manhattan to Ardsley in Westchester County.

Mady, who says she is self-taught, has done private catering, recipe testing, and magazine food articles, and is currently writing her first cookbook. She has taught cooking for four years.

Mady's classes focus on basic skills and gourmet cooking and include French, Middle-European, American, and Chinese cuisines. They are taught in a series and are a combination of lecture/demonstration and full participation.

"Most important to me is taking the mystery and intimidation out of cooking and leaving in the fun and relaxation," Mady says. She will arrange classes for out-of-town students by request.

Brochure available   Fees: moderate

Par Avion Pantry
361 Delaware Avenue
Buffalo, New York 14202
716/853-2900

The Par Avion Pantry in Buffalo is a cooking school that is part of a mini-conglomerate of five shops, all under the umbrella of Par Avion, Inc.

The school offers classes in several international cuisines including French (classic and nouvelle), Spanish, Italian, and Chinese. The lessons are arranged in series but students may take a single session if they wish. A combination of lecture/demonstration and limited participation is used. Demonstration classes are limited to 25 persons, while the participation classes are limited to 12.

Par Avion's owner is Mrs. Franz T. Stone, and the cooking school's director is Mrs. Thomas D. Stone. The school's primary instructor is Victoria Alfiero, who taught cooking in Wisconsin and in her home in Hamburg, N.Y. In addition, the school has "several other local people teaching special classes."

Class schedule available   Fees: low

The 1770 House Cooking School

143 Main Street
East Hampton, Long Island, New York 11937
516/324-1770

A charming 18th-Century inn is home for The 1770 House Cooking School, East Hampton, which is owned by Sidney and Miriam Perle. Classes are held in the inn's restaurant kitchen.

Miriam, who directs the school, was a founder of Les Chefettes Cooking School, Great Neck, and taught there from 1967 to 1977. She has a certificate from the Cordon Bleu, Paris, has studied in Florence with Giuliano Bugialli, and had a chef's refresher course at the Culinary Institute of America. She is chef for The 1770 House Restaurant, which serves 80 persons nightly in two seatings.

Course titles at the school include Great Dinner Parties, Ethnic Cooking, Baking, and Hors D'oeuvres. Participation classes are for six students; lecture/demonstration classes are limited to 12.

Miriam says, "Our aim is to remove the mystique from haute cuisine by demonstrating the proper timing and preparation of dishes and how to be a relaxed host or hostess serving the finest and most imaginative cuisine in an unharried ambiance."

The inn has six guest rooms with antique furnishings, wide-planked floors, and a home-like atmosphere. It is featured in *Classic Country Inns of America,* Volume 2, published by Knapp Press. In the seven-page story about the inn are many full color photographs of this historic and intimate house in what has been called "the most beautiful village in America."

Brochure available   Fees: moderate

Les Chefettes Cooking School, Inc.

123 Middle Neck Road
Great Neck, New York 11021
516/466-4022

At Les Chefettes Cooking School in Great Neck, Long Island, co-owners Rhoda Kafer and Sue Steger offer a potpourri of interesting classes including a series that features easy do-ahead party recipes. The school also has an ethnic cookery series focusing on Chinese, Jewish, Southern, and Mediterranean specialties. The two partners say their recipes are culled from studies in New York with Libby Hillman as well as from study and travel in Paris, London, Vienna, and the United States.

Classes at Les Chefettes are both lecture/demonstration and participation. Demonstration classes are limited to 20; participation classes are limited to six students. In addition to Rhoda and Sue, teachers at the school often include guest chefs from the area.

Les Chefettes Cooking School is associated with a catering service of the same name.

Brochure available   Fees: high

Continental Cooking

34 Parkway West
Mount Vernon, New York 10552
914/664-8482

Small, full participation classes in the cooking of France, Northern Italy, and China are the specialty of Carol Spitznas' in-home school, Continental Cooking, Mount Vernon.

Carol says her interest in fine food goes back a long way. "My grandmother came from Prague and with her came the traditions of fine baking and savory stews. The emphasis in my classes," she says, "is on French and Northern Italian cooking—which I have spent years mastering." Carol studied Viennese pastry with Lilly Joss Reich, author of *The Viennese Pastry Cookbook,* Italian cooking with Marcella Hazan, and Chinese Cooking at the China Institute in New York City.

Each of Carol's classes has a maximum of six students. After completing her basics class, students may take an advanced class in French or Northern Italian cooking. She also teaches a yearly class in fine baking and pastry.

Brochure available   Fees: moderate

Libby Hillman's Cooking School

17 Lawrence Street
New Hyde Park, New York 11040
516/437-6155

Even after 25 years of teaching cooking, Libby Hillman is still at it and so popular that her classes in New Hyde Park are always filled six months in advance!

Libby writes, "My school is personally conducted by me. Classes are small (eight to 10 students) and are arranged by appointment. I teach only mornings, Monday through Thursday, from September through May. Classes are conducted in a series of five lessons. Each lesson is three hours long with demonstration and some participation.

"My first connection with teaching started 25 years ago with the Great Neck Public Schools, where I developed the cooking program. Presently I am coordinator for that program. I engage the teachers for a wide variety of classes. Although I don't teach there regularly, I do a lecture series once a year and conduct one of my pet classes, the Teacher Training Seminar. Sometimes I can recruit teachers from this group, but mostly it has been rewarding because so many of my trainees are out in the field with their own businesses."

In addition to being a teacher, Libby is the author of *Lessons in Gourmet Cooking, The Menu Cookbook for Entertaining,* and *New Lessons in Gourmet Cooking,* all hard cover books published by Hearthside Press.

Libby did not start out to be a professional cook. Her real love was music, and she graduated with a B.S. in education from the Juilliard School of Music in New York City. "I started cooking in the normal way—I was married and cooking was a part of my wifely duties."

In 1947 Libby saw Dione Lucas on television, and, as Libby puts it, "it was a 'happening' in my head—that one could teach people to cook!" She started in a rather typical way with demonstrations for benefits. As her reputation grew so did her classes, but she continued to study and learn informally all of the time.

Libby says she does not have a brochure or advertise because "after 25 years of teaching my students are people who have read my books or been recommended."

For information on Libby's concentrated classes, see Vermont: Libby Hillman's Cooking School.

No brochure available   Fees: moderate

Alice M. Perlmutter Cooking School
67 Interlaken Avenue
New Rochelle, New York 10801
914/235-4528

Alice M. Perlmutter brings an eclectic educational and professional background to her classes in New Rochelle. She lived in France for 11 years and says she learned a lot about cooking from a French maid. She has studied with a number of private chefs, taken classes at the Cordon Bleu, Paris, and attended the Pratt Institute in Philadelphia.

Included in her teaching repertoire are classes in elementary and advanced French cooking, baking fundamentals and advanced baking, beginning, advanced, and advanced-advanced Chinese cuisine, as well as Italian cooking. Her classes are limited to eight persons and are "almost individual instruction."

At Alice Perlmutter's school the emphasis is on "eating qualitatively." Once the basic fundamentals are established, she maintains, "the rest is fun, and finesse, and magic. It's simple to do if you care. People who take the trouble to come to a class are special. They want to learn something, to give of themselves to others. Having a class of these people is a privilege," she says.

No brochure available   Fees: moderate

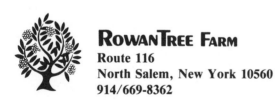

ROWANTREE FARM
Route 116
North Salem, New York 10560
914/669-8362

"We cook with fresh herbs and vegetables only, many of which we harvest just before class," says Ann Rowan, owner/director of Rowantree Farm Cooking School, North Salem.

Ann took advanced studies at the Cordon Bleu, Paris, and has worked in French restaurants in the United States. She teaches most of the classes at Rowantree, and says the school has no other permanent teachers but has from time to time brought in Chinese cooking instructors.

Her classes include basic and country French cooking as well as basics of seasonal cooking and regional American culinary classics. Classes are limited to eight persons and are a combination of lecture/demonstration and participation.

"Our cooking school follows the classic principles of good cooking," Ann says. "We use only fresh ingredients and pay careful attention to all ingredients in a dish. We also pay the same careful attention to the selection of good quality tools and kitchen equipment. We generally feel that 'less is more,' especially when we are cooking with only the best.''

In addition to her in-home school at Rowantree Farm, Ann is director of The Silo Cooking School, New Milford, Connecticut.

Brochure available   Fees: moderate

Andree's Mediterranean Cooking School
354 East 74th Street
New York, New York 10021
212/249-6619

Andree's Mediterranean Cooking School in New York City is part of a three-faceted business owned by the school's director and teacher, Andree Abramoff. A catering service, begun in 1971, preceded the cooking school, which opened four years later. In 1978 Andree's business grew to include a restaurant.

At the school Andree, who taught herself to cook ''with a lot of help from my mother and grandmother,'' teaches the foods of the Mediterranean and France as well as vegetarian cooking. Classes are limited to six students and are held in Andree's townhouse with its specially designed kitchen. For a nominal fee, students may invite guests to join them at the conclusion of a class to ''share the feast.''

''Cooking is fun,'' says Andree. ''Some of the myths about cooking should be eliminated. They only perpetuate a student's fear. And only fresh ingredients should go into the preparation of anything.'' Andree believes that ''There is a little bit of chef in every one of us.''

Brochure available   Fees: moderate

Annemarie's Cookingschool
164 Lexington Avenue
New York, New York 10016
212/685-5685

To most people in the world of food, the name Annemarie means only one person and one cooking school—Annemarie's Cookingschool in New York City. Its owner and director is Annemarie Huste, and the story of her career reads like a fairy tale come true.

Annemarie had a three-year cooking apprenticeship in four European countries before coming to the United States at the age of 19. Within two years she was chef and housekeeper to Billy Rose. Then came the Camelot years, when she served as chef to Mrs. John F. Kennedy. After two years in that position, she wrote her first best selling cookbook, *Annemarie's Personal Cookbook,* and won the prestigious RT French Tastemaker Award for it.

She opened her Cookingschool in 1970 and since then has taught hundreds in her specialized and intensive one-week Cooking Dynamics course. When she isn't teaching or directing her school, she's off lecturing and demonstrating, something she has done in every major city and in dozens of smaller communities all over the United States.

Annemarie has been featured in almost every major women's magazine and in *Time* and *Newsweek*, as well as in newspapers in New York and around the country.

Her Cooking Dynamics course focuses on the "whys" of cooking. Other classes include the basics of Chinese cookery taught by Dee Wang, a native of China who has translated most major Chinese cookbooks. A class in hors d'oeuvres is taught by Jos Herschdorfer, a native of Holland. Jos studied cooking in Belgium, France, and Italy and graduated from the Culinary Institute of America. A baking basics course is taught by Rena Smith. Also a graduate of the Culinary Institute of America, she became a protege of master baker Albert Kumin.

Of her philosophy Annemarie says, "We believe in teaching cooking in depth rather than just teaching recipes, but we are geared to today's lifestyle."

Brochure available   Fees: high

James A. Beard Cooking School
167 West 12th Street
New York, New York 10011
212/675-4984

James Beard has been unofficially crowned "the king of American cooking," and after more than 35 active years in the cooking school business he remains a vital and creative force in the profession. Not only does he continue his classes in New York, but he has classes in Oregon and California on a regular basis. And he's constantly creating, adding new classes to a repertoire that most cooking school teachers would consider quite sufficient, thank you. But not Mr. Beard!

Mr. Beard's (most call him Jim after the second day of classes) newest direction is toward the education of a discerning palate and is called, simply, a Taste Class. For five days students are totally involved in an intricate system of comparative tastings. If the subject is fish, they will taste raw fish, cured fish, smoked fish, salted fish, and anything else Mr. Beard and Barbara Kafka, his teaching assistant for the class, deem appropriate, interesting, and worthwhile.

Once the class tasted 13 different caviars; another time it was 20 variations of bleu (and blue) cheeses. Mr. Beard says the purpose for this new class is quite simple. "When students cook they need to know the taste of all the things in a dish. But they need to know them individually and intensely before they are combined."

Technique classes at the school represent a wide swath in the world of food, for there is little in that world that hasn't interested Mr. Beard. Just considering his cookbooks (he's written 20 at last count and another is coming), the prospective student knows there is a wealth of experience and information at the command of Mr. Beard.

All of his classes—New York, Oregon, and San Francisco—are full participation. Obviously Mr. Beard endorses this style of teaching. "Participation classes build confidence. I just don't feel that you can learn by watching. Most people want to do for themselves, but they are afraid. If you can break down the fear, that's the important thing." In his San Francisco class Mr. Beard is assisted by Marion Cunningham, who has her own school in the area. At his classes in Seaside, Oregon, he is assisted by Richard Nelson, who teaches in Portland. In New York City Richard Nimmo is an assistant and instructor who Mr. Beard says "is a natural cook who started as a secretary for me. I pushed him into teaching and he is very good."

If you've ever wanted to ask a great man for the secrets of his success, you might be surprised at James Beard's response. He has no miracle answers—only hard work and a love of what you want to do. He came from Oregon, where he developed a love of good food because good food was served to him. "I always liked to cook, but went into the theater and for many years was a performer. Today I am still a performer, but in a different form of entertainment."

His first venture into the food world was in New York City in the early 1930s, when he and a friend began making hors d'oeuvres in a very small catering service. After World War II he began teaching and has been at it ever since. Along the way, of course, he has made his way into American cooking with his books and into American hearts with his unabashed love of food and good eating.

Brochure available   Fees: high

Apartment 7B
60 West 76th Street
New York, New York 10023
212/362-2305

Blend a pharmaceutical chemist with a lover of food and you'll have created David Bernstein, owner/director of Do It the French Way, New York City.

"I apply scientific knowledge to cooking, mainly because I am aware of the chemical principles—the reasons why one thing works and another doesn't," David says. But his evening and Saturday classes are far from dull or purely academic.

"Knowing the 'why' is so important. I often do something the wrong way, just so students can see how it can be recovered. We also do lots of experiments in class. Cooking doesn't have to be static or rote," he says.

David offers five series of lecture/demonstration classes, each of which presents a variety of cooking experiences. He also offers a Cook-A-Thon, during which the students prepare a seven-course menu of their choosing and may invite a guest to the evening's dinner. His demonstration classes are limited to 10 and participation classes to six students.

David also offers a wine tasting evening and a beef class in which a professional butcher tells "everything you want to know about beef."

David says he has studied "informally" with Michael Field and Peg Kay, a graduate of the Cordon Bleu. In addition to teaching cooking, he is also a restaurant critic.

Brochure available   Fees: high

Helene Borey School of Creative Cooking

255 East 71st Street
New York, New York 10021
212/249-3883

"I want to bring out the abilities of each student," says Helene Borey. At her school, Helene Borey School of Creative Cooking, all classes are full participation and are limited to seven students.

In these small classes, Helene says, she can build her students' confidence and strengthen their skills. She also tries to "broaden their personal repertoires." All of her classes are based on Northern Italian or classical or regional French foods and have menus that change with the seasons.

Helene says she learned about cooking as a child and has been "privately tutored here and abroad in the culinary arts." She has traveled extensively in Northern Italy and France, and has had private tutoring at the Cordon Bleu in Paris.

Helene has been teaching for seven years and has been featured in many national magazines.

Brochure available   Fees: high

Miriam Brickman

175 West 13th Street
New York, New York 10011
212/929-5812

The techniques of French cuisine, taught on consecutive days in small participation classes, are the specialty of Miriam Brickman, New York City.

"I offer the foundations of good cooking and then encourage the students to develop their individual approaches to fine cuisine," Miriam says. At her in-home school classes are held for three or five straight days with a maximum of four students in each class.

Miriam is currently chef at a restaurant in Manhattan and is a member of the faculty, New School of Social Research, New York City. She has taken classes at the Cordon Bleu, Paris, and has studied in New York with Giuliano Bugialli. In addition to teaching her own classes, she is also director of curriculum for the Contempra Cooking Center in New Jersey.

Miriam has been teaching for nine years. She taught for seven years in Toledo, Ohio, before moving to New York.

If out-of-town students wish to attend her classes, Miriam says, she will help make hotel and transportation accommodations.

No brochure available   Fees: high

Giuliano Bugialli Cooking Classes

18 East 81st Street
New York, New York 10028
212/472-0760

The name of Giuliano Bugialli, owner/director of Giuliano Bugialli Cooking Classes, is almost a household word in the world of Italian cuisine. He is perhaps best known as the author of *The Fine Art of Italian Cooking,* (Time-Life Books) and as the teacher and co-director of a school in Italy, Cooking in Florence, that has become something of a mecca for those wanting to study Italian cuisine in Italy. For stateside learning Giuliano (most people call him by his first name) has organized classes in New York City where he offers three series composed of five lessons each.

Giuliano says, "The core of my teaching comes from a lifelong immersion in the classic Florentine culinary tradition. I have developed a refined and complex technique for making pasta, bread, pastries, forcemeats, as well as the more simple classic dishes. I stress authenticity and have studied Renaissance sources and manuscripts to return dishes to their classic purity."

Giuliano is known as a "non-authoritarian teacher with a relaxed teaching atmosphere," but feels that his main purpose is "to preserve and spread the long and great gastronomic tradition of Northern Italy, centered in Florence. I don't believe in compromises, short cuts, or modifications of classic dishes. The students can make those compromises on their own if they wish," he adds. "I stress technique, as I feel that the technique of Italian cooking is not widely known or understood. Finally, I like to place the food in its cultural background. Proper menu planning and presentation are a part of this."

Giuliano's New York demonstration classes are limited to 22; participation classes are limited to 14 students.

Brochure available   Fees: high

Cake Decorating

45 East 89th Street
New York, New York 10028
212/876-7403

Approximately half of the students who take classes at Cake Decorating, a specialized school in New York City, are food professionals, according to Reva Epstein, the school's owner.

Reva studied at Mrs. Mayo's School of Cake Decorating in Denver, at The Ballard School in New York City, and attended demonstrations at the Cordon Bleu.

Reva's classes are small—usually no more than three students at a time—and are a combination of lecture/demonstration and participation. They are offered during the day, in the evening, and on Saturday. She has concentrated classes for out-of-town students.

No brochure available   Fees: moderate

Madame Chu's Chinese Cooking Classes

370 Riverside Drive
New York, New York 10025
212/663-2182

Though many might want to crown her the "empress" of Chinese cooking in the United States, Madame Grace Chu would probably only agree that she was the first to teach Chinese cooking in America when she started 25 years ago. At 79 and still going strong, she looks back on a richly rewarding career of "wonderful experiences and wonderful students.

"I was it," she says of her pioneering years, which started when she was cooking "not so much for myself, but to please our friends. They liked my cooking and asked me to teach them and so I did."

Word got around to the China Institute and in 1954 she started the first cooking class there. "They loved it and so did I and it grew and grew." Madame Chu taught at the Institute from 1954 until 1968. During this time she wrote her first book, *The Pleasures of Chinese Cooking* (Simon and Schuster). The book came out in paperback in 1968; both hard cover and paperback versions still sell well. "It's a good book," Madame Chu says, "because it is clear and concise—the way I teach and the way I cook."

Madame Chu's second book, *Madame Chu's Chinese Cooking School,* was published in 1975 by Simon and Schuster. It also is available both in hard cover and in paperback.

When the classes at the China Institute became too popular and then too large, Madame Chu decided to teach in her home. "I just prefer the smaller classes," she says. "I really believe that students have to participate in everything to really learn well." Everything, that is, except doing the dishes. "I prefer to do my own dishes because we serve on real china plates from China and until very recently they would have been almost impossible and very expensive to replace."

Madame Chu's classes are limited to six persons and are held on a series basis every other week. "My students need time between lessons to absorb what they've been taught and to practice," she says. However, Madame Chu says she can be flexible and will be happy to arrange concentrated classes for out-of-town students.

In her classes Madame Chu teaches the basics of Chinese cooking common to all regions of China. Then students learn about all the different styles of Chinese cooking, region by region. At the same time they are learning to cook, Madame Chu shares with them the culture of each region. "Cooking is a reflection of the culture and is best understood not separately, but woven into the tapestry of a country."

Madame Chu says she learned to cook by herself, through trial and error. "When I grew up in Shanghai, we, of course, had servants. So when it came time for me to learn to cook, I had to do a lot of experimenting." And Madame Chu didn't plan to be a famous cooking teacher. She graduated from Wellesley College with a degree in physical education.

Madame Chu has taken a sabbatical leave in 1979. In 1980, when she resumes teaching, Madame Chu will not only offer her classes but will have a personally guided tour to her native land.

"I love to share and I love people. It is probably this more than anything else that makes me enjoy my work, and my students enjoy their classes," she says. "And even more I enjoy the opportunity to develop teachers, for in this way my work of spreading Chinese culture through its cuisine will go much farther than I could ever have taken it alone."

Brochure available   Fees: moderate-high

John Clancy's Kitchen Workshop

324 West 19th Street
New York, New York 10011
212/243-0958

The ovens most likely work overtime at John Clancy's Kitchen Workshop in New York City, where baking is the culinary *raison d'etre*. John Clancy, a nationally known teacher and author, can probably cook and teach anything, but he offers classes only in baking.

John's rationale for this choice is quite straightforward. "First, I like it, and second, students seem to get more out of a baking class than almost any other kind of food specialty.

"I am there to teach, not to perform," John says. In his classes he sets an informal and relaxed pace, which he feels builds confidence. "I start by putting everyone, myself included, on a first-name basis. And I try to communicate that cooking skill is something we are taught, not born with. Of course some people have more deft hands, and for them, learning comes faster. But if students can relax, they can learn even if they have less talented hands. In fact, once they begin to have confidence in their cooking, they can truly learn anything."

John started his culinary career 23 years ago with Rudolf Stanish, a New York caterer who became famous as the "omelet king." John later became associated with James Beard and eventually taught at Mr. Beard's school. He has also been a restaurant chef and a consultant to a food manufacturer.

John was the Executive Chef for the Time-Life *Foods of the World* book series and made 13 television programs, "Foods of the World with John Clancy," also for Time-Life.

His cookbooks include the *John Clancy Baking Book* (Popular Library), which is now available from Johnson Press, 49 Sheridan Avenue, Albany, New York; *Clancy's Oven Cookery* (Delacourte Press), which he co-authored with Frances Field; and *John Clancy's Fish Cookery* (Holt, Rinehart and Winston).

Classes at John's school are total participation and are limited to 12 students each. Concentrated classes for out-of-town students will be available in 1980.

Brochure available   Fees: high

Cooking with Class

226 East 54th Street
New York, New York 10022
212/355-5021

At Cooking with Class in New York City, owner/director Janeen Sarlin tries "to instill confidence and expertise in my students so they will be able to make dinners with the greatest of ease. I teach menus that use proper and classic techniques that are applicable to all foods, not just to what we make that day," she relates.

Janeen, a home economist, has studied with John Claude Suzdeck and Jacques Pepin, both former chefs to Charles De Gaulle, and with Karen Lee in New York City. She notes that she was first taught by her French grandmother, who was "a fine baker and cook," and by her mother, also a home economist.

Classes at Janeen's in-home school focus on French and Continental cuisines, but several specialty classes are offered as well. She limits class size to eight students and teaches primarily through demonstration with some participation "depending on student desire and the kind of food being taught."

Brochure available   Fees: high

A La Bonne Cocotte

23 Eighth Avenue
New York, New York 10014
212/675-7736

At A La Bonne Cocotte in New York, owner/director Lydie Marshall offers a continually changing series of classes in French cooking that she says are "too varied to describe."

Lydie, who was born and raised in Paris, teaches all of her classes in her home. "They are full participation. The students do all of the cooking and I supervise," she says. Her classes are limited to 10 students.

Lydie, a former professor of French, holds a grande diplome from L'Ecole des Trois Gourmandes in Paris, the school that was formed by Julia Child, Simone Beck, and Louisette Bertholle.

The professional reputation of A La Bonne Cocotte, as well as word of mouth advertising from students, has made it unnecessary for the seven-year-old school to publish a brochure. The school does not, as yet, offer classes for out-of-town students.

No brochure available   Fees: high

17 East 70th Street
New York, New York 10021
212/861-0453

In the heart of Manhattan's upper east side, the Epicurean Gallery, Ltd., offers full participation classes in French and Italian cooking as well as an in-depth class in baking, the specialty of one of the school's owners, Gilda Latzky.

Gilda is also the director of the school. Her professional background includes specialty courses at the Culinary Institute of America and classes at the Cordon Bleu, Paris. She has also visited kitchens and three-star restaurants in France and Italy. Her partner, Gerda Handler, studied at a hotel school in Switzerland. Gerda's newest class is Slimming French Cuisine.

The participation classes at the Epicurean Gallery are six weeks long and are limited to eight students. The school also regularly offers classes for teen-age cooks.

The Epicurean Gallery is "geared to make average cooks more comfortable in the kitchen and to familiarize them with techniques."

Brochure available   Fees: moderate

The Natural Gourmet Cookery School
365 West End Avenue
Apartment 1103
New York, New York 10024
212/580-7121

At The Natural Gourmet Cookery School in New York City, students can "learn to cook delicious and health-supportive dishes" under the direction of Annemarie Colbin, the owner/director of the two-year-old school.

Annemarie has been studying and practicing vegetarian-macrobiotic cooking since 1964. She has taught for the past five years at The New School for Social Research in New York City and at the New York East-West Center for Macrobiotics, of which she is one of the founders. She has lectured widely both in the United States and abroad.

Cooking at The Natural Gourmet Cookery School is "95 per cent vegetarian," says Annemarie. "We do not use artificially processed, canned, or frozen foodstuffs...sugar, honey, or artificial sweeteners; we avoid white flour and white rice as well as dairy products and meat." Still, the school offers such classes as The International Gourmet and Sugarless Holiday Baking, as well as a complete basic series on natural cooking and seminars directed toward "a sensible theory of nutrition."

Classes are limited to 16 persons and are primarily lecture/demonstration. Instead of receiving printed recipes, students take notes.

Brochure available   Fees: moderate

Le Cordon Bleu-New York
155 West 68th Street
New York, New York 10023
212/873-2434

There is only one Le Cordon Bleu in Paris, and only one official United States affiliate, located in New York City. Richard Grausman, the official representative of Le Cordon Bleu and director of the New York school, is not only a grande diplome graduate of the Paris school but was considered to be at the top of his class. He has been a chef-professor for Le Cordon Bleu since 1969 and says he has taught over 5,000 persons throughout the United States during the past 10 years.

Classes at Le Cordon Bleu-New York are lecture/demonstration, with a few participation classes open to students who have attended past classes and are enrolled in a current series. Participation classes are limited to six students; demonstration classes are limited to 30.

The school's philosophy is "to give the finest instruction possible in the techniques and principles of French cooking and pastry." The classes focus on classical and modern French cooking.

The school does not handle any travel or lodging arrangements for out-of-town students. It will arrange special concentrated classes, "but," warns Richard Grausman, "they are expensive."

Brochure available   Fees: high

The Marcella Hazan School of Classic Italian Cooking

155 East 76th Street
New York City, New York 10021
212/861-2825

Mere words can't begin to describe the classes offered at The Marcella Hazan School of Classic Italian Cooking. During the winter months in New York and from spring through fall in the school's specially designed teaching kitchen in Bologna, Italy, people from all walks of life come not just to study cooking, but to surround themselves with the food and culture of Italy.

James Beard, a recognized leader in the world of fine food, wrote about Marcella's classes in Bologna, "To take a week or two with Marcella in Italy is a sensually exciting experience of almost encyclopedic quality...a total experience in food." And the New York classes are much in demand—so much, in fact, that a wait of one to two years is usually required for a place in class.

Although Marcella has been teaching for 10 years, it was her first book, *The Classic Italian Cookbook,* published in 1973, which brought her universal praise. The book is credited with helping to bring fine Italian cooking to the position of high prestige and popularity it now enjoys. A second book, *More Classic Italian Cooking,* was an instant best seller that received the acclaim of the food press and attention in national publications such as *People, Time,* and *Newsweek.* Craig Claiborne wrote, "Marcella Hazan is a national treasure both in this country and in Italy. No one has done more to spread the gospel of fine Italian cookery in America."

Marcella is a scientist and teacher by profession. But as a native of Emilia-Romagna, Italy's foremost gastronomic region, she has always had a serious interest in good food. She became a cooking teacher, she relates, more from happenstance than by plan. Several years ago she took some time off from her profession as a biochemist to do "a little of everything...ikebana, yoga, flower arranging, and Chinese cooking." When other students in the cooking class asked her what she cooked at home she answered, "Regular food," meaning, of course, regular Italian food. From there it was a quick step to her first cooking class, a group of six students from the Chinese cooking school who wondered "what regular Italian cooking might be."

Now in her 11th year of regular classes in New York, Marcella offers a series of five consecutive weekly lessons. In Italy, the classes are concentrated sessions of one or two weeks. There the emphasis is on total immersion in the gastronomic culture of the country, both in and out of the kitchen.

Marcella Hazan does not provide printed recipes to students in her classes. "Students are permitted to take notes, record, video-tape, or photograph as they please," she says. "The emphasis, however, is on developing freedom from rigid measurements and inflexible procedures, on learning how to cook rather than how to read."

Brochure available   Fees: high

Madhur Jaffrey's Cooking Classes

Apt. 14N
101 West 12th Street
New York, New York 10011
212/924-6287

Madhur Jaffrey is one of the country's most famous Indian cooks. She is also an actress, author and artist.

Her cooking career began 20 years ago in Delhi and her first book, *An Invitation to Indian Cooking* (Knopf), brought India's cuisine and Madhur to the food world's attention. After her book was published, she taught at James Beard's school for three years. Madhur has been teaching at home for three years.

Only four students at a time are in Madhur's classes. She explains, "Students learn by doing, so my classes are small, well supervised, and involve total participation." Although her culinary career continues to blossom—she is working on another book—Madhur still remains an actress. Her latest film was with James Mason.

Madhur's writing has appeared in almost all major magazines. Her artistic endeavors include illustrations for her own cookbook and for *Shakti*, a book for Knopf on cosmic energy that won an award from the American Institute of Graphic Arts in 1974.

Brochure available   Fees: high

Mexican Cooking Classes

333 East 69th Street
New York, New York 10021
212/628-1778

After 20 years of research, three cookbooks and uncounted public demonstrations, magazine and newspaper articles, it is little wonder that Diana Kennedy is considered the foremost authority on the cuisines of Mexico.

In New York City, Mrs. Kennedy teaches cooking classes around her travel schedule and writing commitments. Her classes are lecture/demonstration with some participation and are limited to 15 students.

Mrs. Kennedy currently calls both New York City and Mexico City home. She resides in Mexico about half of the year, and she is planning to open a school of Mexican cooking in Mexico City within a short time.

Mrs. Kennedy's introduction to Mexican cuisines happened more by accident than by plan. It began when she moved to Mexico to marry Paul Kennedy, a Latin-American correspondent with the *New York Times*. During the 10 years they lived in Mexico, Mrs. Kennedy began the research that culminated in her first book, *The Cuisines of Mexico* (Harper and Row), which she says was inspired and encouraged by Craig Claiborne, food editor of the *New York Times*.

Since then she has written two more books, *The Tortilla Cookbook* and *Recipes from the Regional Cooks of Mexico* (both by Harper and Row).She is planning more books devoted to the foods of Mexico, but, as she says, "always with consideration for foods available in the United States."

Mrs. Kennedy is also planning to help organize culinary study trips to Mexico. In New York City she has special concentrated classes for the convenience of out-of-town students.

No brochure available   Fees: High

Lilah Kan's Chinese Cooking Classes

884 West End Avenue
New York, New York 10025
212/749-0550

In the full participation sessions at Lilah Kan's Chinese Cooking Classes in New York City, Lilah Kan stresses the use of the cleaver and restaurant frying pans instead of a wok. She explains, "The wok is cumbersome and unless it has a wooden handle, you have to use pot holders to empty food from it. The restaurant frying pan is light and has a long handle which does not get hot during stir-frying."

Lilah should know about restaurant equipment. She brings to her classes a rich background in restaurant work. She had her own restaurant, The Chinese Kitchen in Provincetown, Massachusetts, and has cooked French and continental cuisine in many New York City restaurants including PS 77, Soho Charcuterie and Restaurant, Imus, La Fronde, and Willie's Jazz Club as well as in Alice's Restaurant in Stockbridge, Massachusetts. She is the author of *Chinese Casserole Cookery* (Workman Publishing Company).

Lilah has a maximum of six students in her classes, which she says are taught in an "informal and relaxed atmosphere with much practical advice."

The classes focus on the various techniques of Chinese cooking. Particular attention is paid to "familiarization with Chinese condiments and sauces and the idea that Chinese cooking is nothing but variations on several themes.

"I urge the students to experiment and adjust according to their own tastes. I don't use MSG or food coloring," Lilah adds.

No brochure available   Fees: moderate

Peter Kump Cooking School

333 East 69th Street
New York, New York 10021
212/628-1778

Techniques, techniques, and more techniques of French cuisine are the focal point of courses at the Peter Kump Cooking School in New York City. Here Peter Kump, the owner/director, offers four in-depth, full participation courses in French cooking. Each course consists of five weekly classes lasting about four hours. "My primary interest is in teaching people 'why' and 'how.' Many times we literally have a chicken in every pot. If we are doing a roast chicken, everyone has a chicken to truss, to stuff, to roast. They truly learn by doing in my classes," Peter says.

Peter went to school in French-speaking Switzerland, and originally trained under Simone "Simca" Beck. He continues to work with Simca every summer in Europe. Peter also studied with James Beard, Diana Kennedy, and Marcella Hazan, all noted cookbook authors and leaders in the world of fine food.

Three of Peter's four classes relate directly to the school's primary goal: "To teach you how to cook so you will understand the fundamental techniques." Toward this end Peter limits his classes to seven participating students so that "each student has the opportunity to do every step of every recipe under supervision."

The school's classes are held on the east side of Manhattan, but inquiries should be directed to the above address. Plans are being made for concentrated classes for out-of-town students.

Brochure available   Fees: moderate

Karen Lee Cooking Classes

142 West End Avenue
New York, New York 10023
212/787-2227

Practical, adaptable, and flexible techniques mark the New York City cooking classes of Karen Lee, author of *Chinese Cooking for the American Kitchen* (Atheneum).

In my classes I *teach* cooking, not merely demonstrate it,'' Karen says. She offers full participation classes in three levels of Chinese cooking and a specialty class in Dim Sum cookery. Classes at her in-home school are limited to eight students.

"My primary concern is that students master the necessary basic techniques—stir-frying, steaming, and handling the cleaver. This background gives them the courage and confidence when the course is over to be able to open any Chinese cookbook and try a totally unfamiliar recipe."

Karen, a protege of Madame Grace Chu, studied with Madame Chu for three years and then was her assistant. Karen has been teaching on her own for seven years.

Although she is a disciple of Madame Chu, Karen has developed her own style. She adapts Chinese cooking to the American kitchen so that cooks who do not have easy access to Oriental food markets can still prepare her recipes. "If he or she has the Chinese staples, which can last for a year, and can make fresh vegetable substitutions, a cook in any part of the country can prepare a Chinese dinner simply by going to the local supermarket," Karen says.

Karen offers special concentrated classes, usually in May, for the convenience of out-of-town students.

Brochure available   Fees: moderate

Virginia Lee Chinese Cooking Classes

12 Mott Street
New York, New York 10013
212/689-8723

Virginia Lee, author of *The Chinese Cookbook* (Lippincot), was launched into a culinary career by a newspaper article. "In 1971 Craig Claiborne of the *New York Times* wrote about what a fabulous cook I was and suggested I start a cooking school. And so I did." Virginia started her school the next year and has been busy since then. She offers eight different series of classes on a weekly basis and with these covers all regions of Chinese cooking. Her classes are lecture/demonstration and are limited to 10 students.

"I was born in Shanghai, but was educated in Peking and have traveled all over China. I learned to cook from our family cooks." Virginia says that she could "stay in the kitchen all day...just testing and trying new ways. Once I go into the kitchen, I don't want to come out. I'm a 'new' New Yorker. I came to visit in 1960 and to live here in 1967 and through my cooking I've made many, many new friends."

Concentrated classes are available from Virginia by special arrangement.

Brochure available   Fees: high

Marique School of French Cooking

170 East 83rd Street
New York, New York 10028
212/879-4229

A love of haute cuisine and haute couture converge at Marique School of French Cooking, New York City, which is also the source of the practical Marique bakeware and molds, manufactured in Belgium and sold throughout the United States.

All of this was brought about by Isabelle Marique, who started her professional career in the fashion world. She says she brings "class and style" to cooking through her experiences in high fashion and through her family's background, "which goes back centuries and is a part of the Belgian 'Mercantile Noblesse.' "

During her haute couture career Isabelle began taking cooking classes. She attended the Magec Cooking School in Belgium and took classes at the Cordon Bleu, Paris. Eight years ago she started her school in Manhattan. She is now co-authoring a cookbook with a former chef of the Cordon Bleu, Paris, who is now at La Varenne.

The school offers classes in classic French cuisine as well as a specialty class, Stay Thin and Healthy. These full participation classes are limited to 10 students each. The classes emphasize menus that can be prepared ahead of time.

Brochure available   Fees: high

The Perla Meyers International Kitchen School

19 East 88th Street
New York, New York 10028
212/289-0556

A dedication to fresh and seasonal foods and blue-ribbon culinary credentials are the hallmark of Perla Meyers, owner/director and teacher of The Perla Meyers International Kitchen School. Perla's book, *The Seasonal Kitchen,* brought her public acclaim. In her school each class features a four course meal with emphasis on seasonal fruits and vegetables.

Perla's culinary training is characterized by both quality and quantity. She is a graduate of Ecole Hotelerrie, Lausanne, Switzerland, and has the grande diplome of the Cordon Bleu, Paris, as well as the grande diplome of the Hotel Sacher, Vienna, Austria. She was an apprentice at Grand Vefour in Paris, Fauchon Bakeries and Confection in Paris, and at Giannino's in Milan, Italy. She worked in the restaurants of Paul Bocuse and the Troisgros brothers, and at Moulin de Mougins in France, at Al Porto in Milan, and Camilo's in Florence, Italy.

All classes at Perla's school are basically demonstration, with two students assisting. Students' full participation is required for learning certain techniques such as crepe making and omelets. Each course consists of four weekly two-and-a-half-hour class sessions.

The philosophy behind the International Kitchen is that with the right knowledge of techniques everyone can become a great cook. The techniques taught are of the fine three-star restaurants, adapted for the American kitchen.

During the summer Perla takes her cooking school to Connecticut for cooking workshops.

Classes are limited to 12 students for the Connecticut workshops and 10 students in New York City.

Brochure available   Fees: high

Moore-Betty School of Fine Cooking
162 East 92nd Street
New York, New York 10028
212/860-4922

In the world of fine cuisine, Maurice Moore-Betty is well respected, and with good reason. In almost 15 years of teaching at his school, Moore-Betty School of Fine Cooking, Maurice, who trained under Monsieur Avignon at the Ritz Hotel in London, has probably inspired hundreds of students toward serious vocations in food.

"Style and chic is simplicity," is Maurice's philosophy for the school. All of his classes are full participation and are limited to eight students. The classes focus on French methods and principles, and include menus "that can, in part, be prepared ahead of time."

No brochure available   Fees: high

Anna Muffoletto's Cordon Bleu of New York, Ltd.
332 East 84th Street
New York, New York 10028
212/628-0264

A comprehensive curriculum of basic and advanced participation courses is but one of the many attractions of Anna Muffoletto's Cordon Bleu of New York, Ltd.

In addition, the school's 24-page catalog includes such intriguing offerings as a Great Chef's Seminar, Cook-A-Language (students learn to speak French or Italian as they cook these cuisines), market tours of New York City, Culinary Caravans to Faraway Places, Young People's Cooking (for ages eight through 17), and much more.

The school was started by Anna Muffoletto, a home economist who was a graduate of the Cordon Bleu, Paris; attended L'Alliance Francaise, Paris, and Dante Allighieri, Rome; and studied with William Mornay, Paris, and Madame Grace Chu, New York City. Since Ms. Muffoletto's death in 1978 the school is being continued by her sister, Lee Coleman.

The school's staff includes Nicola Zanghi, chef of Zanghi's Restaurant, Glen Cove, Long Island. Nicola has his own television show and has been a collaborator on many cookbooks. Carol Brock, food reporter for the *New York Daily News,* teaches Italian cooking. She is a home economist and has taught graduate classes in food demonstration and food photography at New York University. Carol is an honorary fellow of the Culinary Institute of America and received the Escoffier Medal for founding Les Dames d'Escoffier.

Jack Freedman, instructor for the basic skills course, is the banquet chef of the Waldorf-Astoria and is a graduate of the Culinary Institute of America. French cooking is taught by Catherine Alexandrou. A native of France, she is a chef, restaurant consultant, and private caterer. Barbara Jaff teaches baking at the school. She is president of her own baking company, A Taste of Class, and has been a caterer.

All classes at the school feature full participation and are limited to 12 students. Although concentrated classes are not part of the established program, the school will make special arrangements for out-of-town students upon request.

Brochure available   Fees: high

Murray Hill School of Cooking
125 East 36th Street
New York, New York 10016
212/684-4299

The Murray Hill School of Cooking, New York City, is located in a former residence of President Franklin D. Roosevelt. The school features a limited number of in-depth full participation classes under the direction of Fanny Farkas.

Fanny, who also owns the school, is a native of Sweden with an extensive professional background. She studied with Elisabeth Emery in Stockholm and took nutrition and diet cookery at Croydon Domestic Arts Institute, Croydon, England. She learned food preparation and service from Pan American Airways and was an instructor at the Domestic Arts Institute, Grenada, West Indies. She was a member of the faculty of the culinary arts program at The New School in New York City, a restaurant consultant and part owner of Pan Handlers Catering Service. Fanny attended classes at La Varenne, worked in several European restaurants, and studied with Paula Wolfert in New York City.

The Murray Hill School of Cooking offers a series of classes that features international techniques and principles of cooking and baking. The classes are limited to six students.

Fanny says her goal is "to take the mystique out of cooking by familiarizing students with fundamental techniques, terminology, and equipment."

No brochure available   Fees: moderate

School of Contemporary Cooking
75 East End Avenue
New York, New York 10028
212/794-2041

"Thoroughly Modern Millie" could well be a nickname for Sherri Zitron, owner/director of the School of Contemporary Cooking, New York City.

Not only does she attempt to "modernize classic techniques so people can do them today," but she offers a totally flexible curriculum in which students essentially chart their own programs. And in her morning classes students cook enough to enable them to take home dinner for two.

"I have no restrictions on what I will teach. If they want lobster, we'll do lobster. They have full freedom. My only criteria are that they will learn from what we do in class and that it has to be technique-focused, not just another recipe."

Her classes emphasize classic French cuisine. Sherri says they are "taught in such a way that students learn how to get organized in order to make something and to use modern machines such as the food processor to enable them to make their cooking fit today's lifestyle."

Sherri's career has evolved over a period of time, beginning with several years of study with Maurice Moore-Betty. She became his assistant and then taught with him. She also studied at the Cipriani Hotel in Venice, has done catering, and is currently at work on a cookbook based on her cooking school.

Classes at Sherri's in-home school are lecture/demonstration with some participation. "I don't demand participation," she says. "It makes some people uncomfortable. But with a class of six or eight persons, participation is certainly possible, if they want it."

Although she has no classes for out-of-town students, Sherri says, "I'm very flexible. There's almost always room for one more." She will accommodate visitors as space allows.

No brochure available   Fees: high

Margaret Spader's Chinese Cooking School
235 East 50th Street
New York, New York 10022
212/755-2661

Evening full participation classes in beginning Chinese cooking are the feature of Margaret Spader's Chinese Cooking School in New York City.

Margaret Spader, the owner/director, is a home economist who has studied at the China Institute and has taken special lessons from Madame Grace Chu, Florence Lin, and Dorothy Lee. She has traveled to the Orient several times and recently made a three-week tour of the People's Republic of China.

Margaret limits class size at her in-home cooking school to five students. One class session is a field trip to Chinatown.

"I believe Chinese food preparation is more suited, nutritionally, to sedentary Americans than our own cuisine. It's more economical, too," she says.

Her objective is, she continues, "to turn out students who are judicious food shoppers, more nutrition conscious and less inhibited in the kitchen."

Class schedule available   Fees: moderate

Michele Urvater

200 West 86th Street, #16K
New York, New York 10024
212/595-0768

It's the only cooking school in New York City that teaches a comprehensive curriculum based on methods of professional hotel schools," says Michele Urvater of her in-home school. She offers a comprehensive skills course of 12 weeks in which each session focuses on a different aspect of cooking—fish, meat, poultry, or eggs, for example. These are full participation classes limited to seven persons. In addition to recipes, students receive 10 to 15 pages of printed text on each session's subject.

Michele trained at New York City Community College and at La Bonne Cocotte in New York City. She was a chef at Ruskay's Restaurant in New York, and is currently the chef for an executive dining room. She studied three-star restaurants in France and observed in the kitchens of the Troisgros brothers in Roanne. She is co-author, with David Lieder-man, of *The New Cuisine in America,* which will be available late in 1979.

Brochure available   Fees: high

Jerome Walman

400 East 59th Street
New York, New York 10022
212/832-6659

Jerome Walman has been teaching cooking and doing private culinary tutoring at home in New York City for 15 years. His philosophy is "true, not artificial principles—that is, elegant food, not pretentious; healthy but tasty, gourmet but not fattening food; rules, not just recipes."

Jerome teaches gourmet, ethnic, nouvelle, diet, health, the "new American"—all types of cooking styles. Most of his classes are lecture/demonstration with some participation. Classes are limited to 10 students.

Jerome's culinary background includes work with "professional teachers and restaurateurs throughout the world." He says he also received training in Paris, Hong Kong, Rome, and the Middle East.

A special feature of his school is "private one-to-one [lessons] or specially constructed small groups." He stresses "sensory enhancement of food and appreciation of wine."

No brochure available   Fees: high

The Helen Worth Cooking School

106 East 31st Street
New York, New York 10016
212/532-2185

If you are knowledgeable about cooking but haven't heard of The Helen Worth Cooking School, it may be only because owner/director Helen Worth has been too busy teaching and writing award-winning cookbooks to publicize her work or her school. So read on, here is a veteran teacher worth knowing about.

Helen Worth began her culinary work in 1940 in Cleveland, Ohio. In 1948 she began teaching in New York, and is recognized as having the oldest—and some say the most prestigious—cooking school in the city. Harriet Van Horne has called it "the Radcliffe of cooking schools."

Helen Worth offers three types of lessons, two of which are private and custom-tailored to the individual student. Gael Greene, in *New York* magazine, likened a lesson with Helen Worth to a performance. "The kitchen was set up like a stage set—with a chair and a clipboard for the audience of one," she wrote. Mrs. Worth leads, demonstrates, teaches by doing—but will not see anyone who has not first digested her textbook, *Cooking Without Recipes.*

In addition to the private lessons, Mrs. Worth offers one group class for eight "fellow connoisseurs to prepare a complete menu, featuring a variety of dramatic specialties."

Besides *Cooking Without Recipes,* which she considers a classic, Helen Worth has published several award-winning, best selling cookbooks. They include *Hostess Without Help, Damnyankee in a Southern Kitchen* (written after three years of research), *The Down-on-the-Farm Cookbook,* and *Shrimp Cookery,* one of the first specialty cookbooks ever written. She is also the inventor of Brown-Quick, a seasoned soy sauce precooking aid that enhances flavor and intensifies tastes while helping to seal in meat juices.

Helen Worth has been a magazine and newspaper food editor, a Distinguished Visiting Professor at California State University, a member of the Continuing Education Department at Columbia University, and a member of the Lecture Bureau of the American Society of Journalists and Authors. In addition, she serves as a food consultant to major corporations and food and drink associations.

Of her teaching philosophy, Helen Worth writes, "I teach principles, relationships, and adaptations. I have developed and pioneered the reasons-behind-the-recipes method, which gives students complete understanding of all the important cooking techniques."

Brochure available   Fees: high high

Southern States

The Cooking School

2916 Linden Avenue
Birmingham, Alabama 35209
205/871-8785

Cooking with a light-hearted touch is the guiding thought of Lenore L. Picard and Isabelle L. Sterne, partners of The Cooking School, Birmingham.

"For us cooking is fun and we would like everyone to enjoy it as we do," says Lenore, who studied with Malvina Kinard. Isabelle learned Japanese cooking from Benedictine nuns in Tokyo, Chinese cooking in the Philippines, and did some study in Germany. Both have taken short courses from Marcella Hazan in Bologna, Julie Dannenbaum at The Greenbrier, West Virginia, and with a local chef.

"When we began in 1974, we did not presume to be experts, nor do we now. We said to prospective students, 'We will teach you what we know.' "

Classes at The Cooking School are demonstration only and are limited to 14 persons. Lenore and Isabelle teach at Kitchen Things, their cookware store.

No brochure available   Fees: low

The Kitchen Shoppe

2841 Cahaba Road
Birmingham, Alabama 35223
205/879-5277

"Good cooking with the right utensils can be made interesting and easy," says Sam Franks of the Kitchen Shoppe, Birmingham.

Sam, the school's owner/director, has had five years' experience owning and assisting cooking in three gourmet shops. His staff includes Elberta Reid and Catherine Cabannis, "self-taught perfectionists;" Thonk Maving, a native of Saigon who had training in European-style cooking schools; Dominique McCalla, a native of Paris; and Zoe Cassimus, of Greek descent, whose father had a restaurant. Zoe spent her childhood summers in Greece.

Most classes at The Kitchen Shoppe focus on Oriental and French cooking, but some specialty classes are offered also. All classes are lecture/demonstration and are limited to 20 students. Classes meet once a week for six weeks.

Brochure available   Fees: low

Cooking School at Lawrens

809 Madison
Huntsville, Alabama 35801
205/539-3812

"Don't be intimidated by recipes," says Jean Sparks, director of the Cooking School at Lawrens, Huntsville. "I tell my students to make the recipes work for them. Any recipe can be tackled, no matter how complicated it may seem," Jean continues. She also feels that anything she does in class, her students can do as well or better in their homes.

At her school Jean teaches Italian cooking, three levels of French cooking, and several specialty classes including party foods, holiday menus, and men's cooking classes. Her classes are lecture/demonstration and are limited to 16 students, except for the men's class, which is limited to 12 and features some participation.

Jean has studied in Italy with Marcella Hazan and Julie Dannenbaum. She studied for a month each with Jacques Pepin and Nathalie Dupree and has taken "a great many classes from teachers in the San Francisco area."

The school is associated with a gourmet cookware and giftware shop.

No brochure available   Fees: high

L'Ecole de Cuisine

10807 Crestdale Lane
Little Rock, Arkansas 72212
501/224-0542

There are two categories of classes at L'Ecole de Cuisine in Little Rock. Technique classes, which teach the preparation of one type of food such as breads, soups, or crepes, are usually offered in single sessions of three hours. Menu classes, in which several kinds of food are prepared, are offered in series of three or four sessions. All classes are a mixture of lecture/demonstration and participation, and are taught in the home of owner/director Sally Flanzer.

Sally's background includes a "crash course of fundamentals" with Madame Liane Kuony at The Postillon School of Culinary Arts in Fond du Lac, Wisconsin, and study with Terry Ladwig in Milwaukee. Sally is the author of *The Ideals Festive Party Cookbook,* now in its second printing.

In her classes, which are limited to 10 students, Sally emphasizes "building skills and confidence for the home cook/entertainer, as well as constructing menus."

L'Ecole de Cuisine's summer schedule is condensed to allow out-of-town students to attend a week of morning classes and to have afternoons free for shopping and sightseeing.

Brochure available   Fees: low

115 South Victory
Little Rock, Arkansas 72201
501/372-2319

Marilyn Myers, owner/director of Marilyn Myers' Kitchen, Little Rock, is a do-it-yourselfer par excellence.

Her school, an 80-year-old Victorian home, is proof of what one person can do—with enough talent and determination. Marilyn personally renovated the home to make it a school with a large working and teaching kitchen. This project included the excavation of two truck loads of mud from under the house, which she did by hand, shovelful by shovelful. She also tore down walls, worked on the foundation masonry, and tackled other tasks that might frighten even the most confident home remodeler.

To prepare herself for teaching, Marilyn received a diploma from L'Academie de Cuisine in Washington, D.C. She has studied in depth with Giuliano Bugialli and Florence Lin.

Marilyn's class schedule includes a variety of courses for many different interests. They range from one-day demonstration classes, offered on Saturday, that focus on a particular food or technique, to a six-week French cooking course and a fundamental techniques course that consists of four six-week segments.

The Saturday classes are lecture/demonstration and have a maximum of 10 students. Weekday classes are participation and are limited to eight students.

"We emphasize basic techniques and fresh and seasonal foods," Marilyn says.

Brochure available   Fees: Moderate-high

Ralph Varketta's Cooking School

428 South West 11th Street
Hallandale, Florida 33009
305/458-4946

"In a world filled with gadgets and gimmicks, we still retain the 'aroma' of yesteryear's kitchen," says Chef Ralph Varketta, owner of Ralph Varketta's Cooking School.

In-depth classes in continental cuisine are the hallmark of this 10-year-old school. There are three participation courses of six, 12 and 25 sessions that provide 25 to 100 hours of instruction. These classes are limited to six students. In addition, a special crash gourmet cooking course designed for out-of-town students meets twice a day for six days and features the preparation of 12 seven-course continental dinners. The crash course is lecture/demonstration and is limited to 25 persons. It is offered during the fourth week of every month.

Chef Varketta began his career as a kitchen porter on a Great Lakes vessel. During World War II he was a ship's cook in the U.S. Navy. After the war he earned a B.B.A. from Dyke and Spencerian College, Cleveland. He was a chef-steward for the Rocky Point Inn, Inlet, New York. The other instructor at the school is Chef Max Gewirtz, a chef of 10 years' experience.

Brochure available   Fees: high

**7251 Southwest 57th Court
S. Miami, Fla. 33143
305/667-5957**

"We teach cooking theory and philosophy, not recipes," say Bobbi Garber and Carole Kotkin, partners in Bobbi & Carole's Cooking School, Inc., in Miami.

Both Bobbi and Carole have attended classes at the Culinary Institute of America as well as short courses at La Varenne in Paris.

In addition to the owners, the school has 15 other instructors. "All of our teachers are well trained in various ethnic cuisines or in the specialties they teach," according to the owners. The school has also been host to guest teachers including Joyce Chen and Jacques Pepin.

Some notable classes offered during a current season were a wine appreciation series, classes on cooking for a healthy heart, easy cuisine, and natural foods for teenagers. The classes are lecture/demonstration and have a maximum of 25 students.

The school has sponsored a cooking trip to France. The owners say that out-of-town students would be able to join any of the classes at the school. Help with travel accommodations will be provided.

Brochure available   Fees: moderate

The Stock Pot
**7020 Central Avenue
St. Petersburg, Florida 33707
813/381-2179**

Classical cuisine brews daily at The Stock Pot, St. Petersburg. "I guess I'm really a purist and want to hang onto the tried and true classic cuisines," says Maryalice LaForest, the school's director and only teacher.

"My students can do what they want when they go home, but here at school they follow authentic recipes for classical cuisine. I use the same recipes again and again because they have stood the tests of both time and tastebuds," she adds.

Maryalice herself was literally steeped in classical cooking while living for 11 years in France and Italy. She studied at the Cordon Bleu, Paris, for six months and earned the advanced certificate from La Varenne in Paris. She took two series of classes with Giuliano Bugialli in Florence, Italy, and studied privately with Mary Bond, a grande diplome graduate of the Cordon Bleu, Paris. Maryalice is fluent in both Italian and French.

Most classes at the school are total participation. The basic classes are limited to nine or 10 students each. Other participation classes are limited to eight students. Demonstration classes are limited to 18 persons. Although The Stock Pot does not have organized classes for out-of-town students, it will accommodate them in on-going classes.

The school has sponsored cook-study trips to Europe and is associated with a cookware shop.

Brochure available   Fees: low

Betty Griffith Cooking School

2317 Clare Drive
Tallahassee, Florida 32308
904/893-4889

Five levels of French cooking make up a large part of the class repertoire at the Betty Griffith Cooking School, Tallahassee. Other classes include breadmaking, food processor cooking, flambe cooking, children's cooking, and hors d'oeuvres.

Betty Griffith, owner/director, took advanced classes at La Varenne, attended the teachers' course at Rich's in Atlanta, and studied at Lucy Waverman's Cooking School in Toronto, Canada. Betty has been teaching for four years.

The classes at Betty's in-home school are full participation and are limited to eight persons. Most are given on a weekly basis, but sometimes she offers week-long classes that would be convenient for visitors. She also teaches at a local cookware store, Culinary Shop.

No brochure available   Fees: low

Kathy Hendricks' The Compleat Cook

230 The Prado
Atlanta, Georgia 30309
404/892-2417

Decidedly different classes and a well-trained staff are the hallmarks of Kathy Hendrick's Atlanta school, The Compleat Cook. In addition to in-depth series on classical cooking techniques, students can enroll in a class called Domestic Arts, which covers everything from brunches to bed linens. A series of Continental dinner parties is also offered, in which students learn to prepare a dinner for eight for under $10. In addition, the school offers specialty classes on Southern cookery, summer foods, and Christmas gifts.

Kathy Hendricks was educated at Sweet Briar College and the University of Paris. She took a year of private lessons from Madame Verley in Paris, and continued her culinary studies with Malvina Kinard while managing Mrs. Kinard's Cook's Corner in Atlanta. Kathy has also taken classes with Florence Lin, Giuliano Bugialli, and Simone Beck.

In addition to Kathy, instructors at the school include George Beattie, one of Georgia's most famous living artists, who teaches bread baking; Tina Sawyers Patterson, German-born and a former manager of restaurants and hotels, who teaches German cuisine; Malvina Kinard, who owned and directed several cooking schools/cookware shops; and Mark Rosenstein, a chef who has studied in the United States and Europe.

Classes at The Compleat Cook are both lecture/demonstration and participation, and have a maximum of eight students.

The school has concentrated classes for out-of-town students and will provide help with travel and lodging arrangements. The Compleat Cook also sponsors a cooking-study trip to Europe.

In addition to being associated with a catering business, The Compleat Cook carries table and cookware, including glassware from Biot, France, and Italian and French pottery.

Brochure available   Fees: moderate

The Cooking School

Rich's
45 Broad Street
Atlanta, Georgia 30303
404/586-4727

Rich's Department Store is said to be synonymous "with the best of Atlanta," and The Cooking School, which is directed by Nathalie Dupree, surely appears to live up to that reputation. The school offers not only a complete repertoire of classes, but many extras as well.

Every month there is a new schedule of classes at Rich's, and each class sounds more appealing than the last. Some are one-session demonstrations, many are full-day participation workshops, and some are week-long, "all day, every day" sessions with full participation classes in the morning followed by lectures or demonstrations in the afternoon. Rich's even offers a How to Teach course, a one-week series "designed to guide people who would like to teach cooking."

The number of people in each class varies. Demonstrations in Rich's auditorium are said to be for "an almost unlimited number." Regular demonstration classes are limited to 20; participation classes are limited to 18 students.

Rich's cooking school director, Nathalie Dupree, earned the Advanced Certificate from the Cordon Bleu in London. She owned and operated a restaurant in Majorca, Spain, and another restaurant in Social Circle, Georgia. In addition she has attended classes at La Varenne and Chateau du Domiane in France, and at Villa D'Este, Italy. She has also studied with James Beard, Dione Lucas, and Julie Dannenbaum.

Nathalie's six assistants are trained at Rich's by Nathalie and usually "have taken at least six weeks of lessons at Cordon Bleu."

In their classes, Nathalie says, "we try to give a background of theory to support creative cookery. We think there is a way to combine joy and discipline for greater cooking," she concludes.

Brochure available   Fees: moderate

Truffles Gourmet Cooking School

Andrews Square
56 East Andrews Drive N.W.
Atlanta, Georgia 30305
404/237-7005

You'd hardly expect a school with a name like Truffles to be ordinary, and this one certainly isn't! It offers a lively round-robin of specialty classes, some series classes on French cooking, and splendid cooking-study trips to Europe.

Chip Kinlaw, the school's owner, is in the process of opening a second cooking school in a gourmet shop, Truffles Too, which will be located in another section of Atlanta.

Director of the school is Doris Koplin, a home economist who has taken classes at the Cordon Bleu, London. Other teachers at the school include a fourth generation candy maker, a wine authority, and others who have specialized in certain phases of cooking.

Most classes at Truffles are lecture/demonstration with a minimum of 10 and a maximum of 20 students.

Brochure available   Fees: moderate

Ursula's Cooking School

1764 Cheshire Bridge Road N.E.
Atlanta, Georgia 30324
404/876-7463

There's a three-year waiting list for classes at Ursula's Cooking School in Atlanta. Ursula Knaeusel, owner/director, credits the success of her school to word-of-mouth advertising and student satisfaction.

Ursula has been teaching for 13 years. Her professional background includes college courses in hotel and restaurant work and home economics study in East Germany as well as a classical European-style apprenticeship.

Her classes focus on international cuisine and are demonstration only with a maximum of 30 students. She offers help with travel arrangements and has some special classes for out-of-town students.

Ursula does not provide her students with printed recipes. Instead, she dictates the recipes step-by-step as she teaches. Her school's philosophy is "to have everything easy and practical, with many shortcuts and money-saving, eye-appealing foods.

No brochure available   Fees: low

Diane Wilkinson's Cooking School

4365 Harris Trail
Atlanta, Georgia 30327
404/233-0366

More Taste than Time, Putting on the Ritz, and Chicken A to Z are but three of the unusual specialty classes at Diane Wilkinson's Cooking School in Atlanta.

Diane, a former stewardess for an international airline, was able to study cooking around the world. After retiring from flying she lived in Europe and studied at the Cordon Bleu, Paris. She regularly returns to France and Italy for additional studies with Marcella Hazan, Philippe Bezout, and at La Varenne.

Diane has been teaching for five years. Her series classes include Fundamental French Techniques, Seasonal Menus, Pastry, and Bread Baking. Subject matter determines whether a class is lecture/demonstration or participation. For lecture/demonstration classes the limit is 12 students; for participation classes the maximum is eight.

"I want students to know all the pleasures of preparing food and of dining well—not only for special occasions but for everyday," Diane says. "To achieve this, I've got to do two things. First, give the students the tools with which to work, the techniques and understanding of the ingredients. Students need to know the 'whys' and not simply 'how to.' They can't improvise successfully until they know these things. Second, I need to inspire them by exposing them to interesting preparations and by training their senses to be discerning," she concludes.

Brochure available   Fees: moderate

Fran Crisco Cooks at Home and Away
Route 1, Box 84
White, Georgia 30184
404/382-5659

Chinese food has long been one of Frances Neel's loves, so she studied it and now teaches Chinese cooking along with Southern cooking and Provencal cuisine through her school, Fran Crisco Cooks at Home and Away.

"Cooking should be fulfilling and fun," Frances says. She studied with Nathalie Dupree and then assisted in Nathalie's Chinese cooking classes. She has also taken classes with Madame Grace Chu and Jacques Pepin, and continues to study with Chef Ging Young Ching of Forbidden City, Atlanta.

In addition to the lecture/demonstration and participation classes taught at her home, Frances teaches at Upstairs at the Meeting Place, a restored restaurant in downtown Cartersville, Georgia.

Brochure available   Fees: low

The Baker's Rack
Plainview Village
9952 Linn Station Road
Louisville, Kentucky 40223
502/425-2900

Located in the former courtyard area of the old Heilmueller Bakery in Louisville, The Baker's Rack offers classes in bread baking, of course, and in desserts as well as in French, Oriental, and Northern Italian cooking.

Midge Maetschki and D. Leon Carver, owner/directors, have assembled an eight-member teaching team with impressive professional credentials and experience.

Flora Chin, from China, and Nicole Thomas, from France, teach their specialties at the school. Vincenzo Gabrielle, Stan Petarsky, and Chef Harry Colgin are professionally involved in local restaurants. Julie Berman had formal training in Sheffield, England. Louis Cease, whose family has had three generations of chefs, is a grand diploma graduate of La Varenne, Paris. Valerie Rogers is the author of *Up to My Elbows,* a manual on breadbaking.

At this school the only participation class is breadbaking. All others are lecture/demonstration with a maximum of 20 students.

The school has published a cookbook, *The Baker's Rack Recipe Collection,* with recipes from its classes as well as from friends, family, and customers.

The Baker's Rack has sponsored a cooking trip to France and is associated with a cookware store.

Brochure available   Fees: moderate

Louisiana Cooking School

8742 West Fairway Drive
Baton Rouge, Louisiana 70809
504/927-2369

In the land of jambalaya and crawfish pie, it's just natural that the Louisiana Cooking School would offer specialty classes in preparing crawfish, oysters, and other seasonal and regional favorites. Sue Brown and Betty Ramsey, partners in the school, say these specialty classes reflect a new dimension of their school.

"We've gone from courses in Louisiana, French, and Italian cooking to more one-time classes on seasonal items," they relate. However, the school still offers classes in basic cooking in series that run for three to four weeks.

Both Sue and Betty bring a broad range of experiences to their school. Sue learned Cajun and Creole cooking at home. She followed this with classes from Julie Dannenbaum, James Beard, John Clancy, Michael James, and Jacques Pepin. In addition she has taken classes at the Cordon Bleu, London, and at Le Notre in France. She was a consultant for the Crawdaddy restaurant, New York City, as well as for Louisiana restaurants. Sue had a television show for two years and before opening her school, taught from her home.

Betty is a native of Paris. She studied at La Varenne, the Cordon Bleu, and Le Notre in France and at the Cordon Bleu, London. She is the author of a cookbook.

Almost all of the classes at the Louisiana Cooking School are lecture/demonstration and are limited to 20 students. The school offers concentrated classes for out-of-town studnets and will assist with travel arrangements.

Both Sue and Betty say, "Techniques are more important than recipes. Our knowledge stems from a lifelong love and study of good food. We hope to instill in our students this same excitement of doing things well and with confidence and love—and having fun in the kitchen. Everyone has to eat and most have to cook, so why not enjoy?"

Brochure available   Fees: moderate

Lee Barnes Cooking School

7808 Maple Street
New Orleans, Louisiana 70118
504/866-0246

Lee Barnes, owner/director of Lee Barnes Cooking School, New Orleans, went from one form of art to another. She received a bachelor's degree in art, with a focus on printmaking, but decided shortly thereafter that her real love was cooking.

"I started by teaching children in my apartment. Then word spread and I taught adults at home, then at community facilities."

When her classes continued to be popular, Lee decided to "take the plunge." She opened her school and shop in 1975.

One of the recognized specialties at her school is Creole cooking, which is taught by local people.

"We aren't too esoteric," Lee says about her classes. "We teach good basic cooking of many cuisines, and the classes change monthly."

Lee's professional background includes three months of study at the Cordon Bleu,

Paris, as well as study with many of the celebrity cooks who have visited her school including Jacques Pepin, Jack Lirio, Michael James, and Billy Cross.

Other instructors at the school include Beth Hughes, who specializes in baking, and Joe Middleton, who teaches Chinese cooking.

The school cooperates with tour groups coming to New Orleans and offers concentrated classes for the convenience of visiting students. The school will also assist with travel accommodations.

The Lee Barnes Cooking School offers both lecture/demonstration and participation classes. The lecture classes have a maximum of 15 students; participation classes are planned for 12 students.

Brochure available   Fees: low

Anne Byrd's Cookery

225 Florence Street
Greensboro, North Carolina 27401
919/275-7024

Anne Byrd's Cookery is a school designed for both seasoned cooks and beginners who love good food. Anne Byrd, the owner/director, emphasizes "the use of American foods properly prepared, well seasoned, appropriately sauced, and left as near to their natural state as possible."

Classes at the school are demonstration lessons of two to two-and-a-half hours, and run from one to four sessions. Anne teaches three four-session French cooking classes, a series on international cooking, and several seasonal and specialty classes with intriguing names such as Feasting Lightly and Grandmother's Turkey Dinner, a class that emphasizes the Southern way of doing things. Guest instructors have included Jack Lirio of San Francisco, Ric Chin of New York, Michel Stroot of the Golden Door in Escondido, California, and Beth Tartan, cookbook author.

Anne's professional background is highlighted by private study with names familiar in culinary circles: Irene Chalmer, Albert Stockli, and Michel Stroot. She studied at La Varenne in Paris and at the Cordon Bleu in London, and took a baking course at the Culinary Institute of America in Hyde Park, New York.

Anne Byrd's Cookery offers gourmet study trips abroad. The school also offers classes given on several consecutive days for the convenience of out-of-town students, and will make lodging accommodations if requested.

Brochure available   Fees: moderate

Le Pot de Chocolat
#17 Forest Lake Shopping Center
Columbia, South Carolina 29206
803/738-9585

"I would like to further the fine art of cooking and the respect for this art," says Marion B. Sullivan, director and co-owner of Le Pot de Chocolat, Columbia. "To me, this is similar to the efforts to keep alive all the cultural arts. Why give in to fast foods?" she asks.

Marion has taken short courses at the Cordon Bleu, London; La Varenne, Paris; and the Culinary Institute of America, Hyde Park, New York. She also studied with Helen Corbitt and Jacques Pepin in Atlanta.

Marion's co-owner is Mary H. Boyd. The school's staff includes Elizabeth Williams, who is "self-taught through traveling;" Gaither M. Scott, who studied at the Cordon Bleu, Paris; Iole Salomon, a native of Nationalist China; and Sue Langhorne, who studied under Dione Lucas.

Le Pot de Chocolat offers six different courses on the cuisines of France, Italy, and China, as well as a course for teens and another entitled Beautiful Basics.

The school is associated with a gourmet catering business and a retail gourmet food store.

Brochure available   Fees: moderate

608 Georgia Avenue
Chattanooga, Tennessee 37403
615/756-4222

"*The Thymes,* the newsletter with taste" is the brochure of the Happy Baker Cooking School in Chattanooga. It captures the flavor of the school, opened in 1977, and the enthusiasm of its owner/directors, Dwight and Happy Yates Baker.

Both Dwight and Happy (a childhood nickname that stuck) are self-taught cooks who have augmented their basic love of cooking with a variety of culinary study and experiences. Happy, an art history major at Vanderbilt University, was once a cook for a private family in Nantucket. She studied Oriental cooking with Florence Lin at the China Institute in New York City. Dwight's formal education was in environmental studies, but, says Happy, "he's a natural cook and his classes are the most popular." Dwight's specialty is outdoor cooking; at the Happy Baker he teaches in a charming outdoor patio area complete with grills and smokers.

The cuisines of France, Persia, Britain, Italy, and China are taught at the Happy Baker by well qualified instructors. The school's schedule is packed with in-depth classes that run for six weeks, as well as many specialty classes of shorter duration. The classes are a combination of lecture/demonstration and participation, and are limited to 10 or 15 students. Each session is four or five hours long.

"We think that cooking is the highest of the arts because it involves taste, touch, smell, sight, and creation. We encourage experimentation and we teach our students that the final product must appeal to the person preparing the dish, the meal—the creation. We encourage our students to realize the importance of cooking and we insist on long classes, making no exceptions even in the classes for four- to six-year-olds!''

The Happy Baker is located in an old area of Chattanooga, dating from 1880, that has been renovated over the past several years. Both the school and cookware shop of the same name are richly adorned with architectural antiques the Bakers have salvaged from near and far.

The school is planning a study tour in 1979 in cooperation with a local travel agency. Students from out of town can anticipate help with travel arrangements and lodging when attending the Happy Baker.

Brochure available   Fees: low

Cooking Under Glass
1111 Columbia Avenue
Franklin, Tennessee 37064
615/794-0927

Cooking Under Glass takes the honors for "most unusual atmosphere" because classes at this school are held in a greenhouse that is part of The Garden Room, Inc., a Franklin restaurant.

"We try not to take ourselves too seriously," says Larry W. Brown, owner/director of the school. But he adds that although the atmosphere in the classes is "very loose and informal, the instruction is top quality."

Larry's professional background is in credit and banking. He is owner and manager of The Garden Room and gives food lectures and demonstrations. He has assembled a teaching staff that includes Libby Hartman, a graduate of the Cordon Bleu, Paris, and assistant to Julie Dannenbaum; Mary Caldwell Clarke, caterer and party consultant from Los Angeles who has taught in the Nashville area; Betsy Hess, a travel agent who has studied cooking in various countries; Daisy King, owner/operator of Miss Daisy's Tearoom, a popular local restaurant; and Mary Cartwright, an expert grower and lecturer on herbs.

Classes at Cooking Under Glass reflect the staff's interests and expertise. Each session features a specialty and generally lasts from two to three hours. The repertoire includes cooking with herbs, brunches, emergency meals, luncheons, teas, and classes for men. All classes are lecture/demonstration.

Brochure available   Fees: low

Forty Carrots School of Creative Cookery

2087 Madison
Memphis, Tennessee 38104
901/726-1667

There's a bushel of professional expertise and experiences at Forty Carrots School of Creative Cookery, Memphis.

Mary Taylor, director, is a diploma graduate of Ecole des Trois Gourmandes, Paris. She apprenticed at L'Hotel de la Gare, Dijon, France, and at La Maison Cochet (pastry) in Paris. Before coming to Forty Carrots, she had a cooking school and catering business in Gainsville, Florida. Mary also has a degree in social psychology from the University of Florida.

Frances Averitt, owner of Forty Carrots, Memphis (there are three others in Little Rock and Jonesborrough, Arkansas, and Kalamazoo, Michigan) is a home economist with 20 years' experience.

John Grisanti teaches Italian cooking at the school. He owns a restaurant in Memphis and is considered very knowledgeable about wine. In the school's International Gourmet series, natives of other countries teach their ethnic specialties. Other classes at the school include a 12-week course in the techniques and skills of French cooking. Series classes are held once a week for four to eight weeks; special classes are single sessions. Lecture/demonstration classes are presented in a raised-seating amphitheater and have a maximum of 20 students. Some classes feature limited participation. The school has concentrated classes for out-of-town students.

Brochure available   Fees: low

John Simmons Cooking School

416 Grove Park Road
Memphis, Tennessee 38117
901/767-0428

"Good food served in a warm atmosphere is an occasion to remember," says Ruth Howse, director of the John Simmons Cooking School, Memphis.

The 11-year-old school regularly offers two classes, Beginning French Dishes and French Cooking for Company. Italian cooking and other topics are taught by visiting chefs. Classes are lecture/demonstration and have a maximum of 15 students.

"Our class schedule is quite flexible," Ruth says. "We have a men's class taught by a man who is a doctor by profession and a cook by avocation, and a Saturday morning class for teenagers."

Ruth, a home economist, has attended the Cordon Bleu and La Varenne in Paris. She took the Crash Course from Julie Dannenbaum and took classes with Jacques Pepin and Julia Child. Ruth is the author of *French Cooking Simplified with a Food Processor* (101 Productions), now in its second printing.

Brochure available   Fees: low

Culinary Classics

1145 Balbade Drive
Nashville, Tennessee 37215
615/297-3893

"The first in Nashville" is Culinary Classics cooking school, founded in 1963 in the home of Gloria Preston Olson, a teacher whose extensive travel and research augment her natural love of cooking. She is the author of a cookbook and restaurant guide, *Culinary Classics,* which was published in 1978 by Sherbourne Press.

A range of classes, from country and classical French cooking to foods of the Far East and Latin America, is offered at Culinary Classics. Classes are lecture/demonstration, and each session features the preparation of a full meal. Ethnic recipe names, historical information, and personal travel anecdotes add spice to each menu.

Gloria's classes are limited to 12 persons, and her students are invited to browse in her library of over 500 cookbooks. Students are also kept informed of gourmet and wine tours, which Culinary Classics promotes in the Nashville area through arrangements with several New York travel agents.

"I teach inspiration and confidence. I assure students that if they can read, they can cook," Gloria says. "I stress the reasons for differences in the cooking of various regions of a country, while at the same time explaining how many of the same dishes are found by different names throughout the world."

No brochure   Fees:low-moderate

Southwestern States

The House of Rice
3221 North Hayden Road
Scottsdale, Arizona 85251
602/947-6698

"We want to teach students cooking that can be used *all* the time, not just as something to do," says Kiyoko Johnson, owner of The House of Rice Cooking School, Scottsdale. Kiyoko is the daughter of Henry and Edna Matsubu, owners of The House of Rice Cooking School in Seattle.

Primary instructor at the school is Chau Yi Liaw, who learned to cook from her parents in Taiwan. She teaches three classes in Oriental cooking. They are participation classes and are limited to nine students.

The school is associated with an Oriental grocery and gift store.

No brochure available   Fees: low

C. Steele
7303 East Indian School Road
Scottsdale, Arizona 85251
602/947-4596

A cooking school, cookware shop, wines, coffees, gourmet foods, party planning, catering is the description offered by Carol Steele, owner/director of C. Steele's Kitchen, Scottsdale.

Carol's highly-trained staff teaches everything from slimming gourmet cooking to Asian, French, Provincial, German, and haute cuisine. Richard MacKenzie, whom she calls her resident chef, is a graduate of the New York Institute of Dietetics, the Culinary Institute of America, and the Cordon Bleu. With his mother he has catered parties for many luminaries. Another teacher, Sylvia Smith, also a graduate of the Culinary Institute of America, owned and operated two restaurants and a gourmet shop and has a catering

69

business. Peter Wimmer, from Cologne, Germany, has worked in several hotels and clubs. He also has a catering service.

Phyllis Weinstein, a home economist, graduated from the China Institute, studied with Madame Grace Chu, and was a caterer. Harris Golden has an associate of arts degree in culinary arts and a bachelor of science degree in hotel and restaurant management. He is executive chef at Elizabeth Arden's Maine Chance in Arizona.

Edward and Thelma Agopians team teach. Edward's avocation is food. He studied with master chefs at the Cordon Bleu and holds certificates in desserts and pastries from Ecole LeNotre. Thelma has studied at the Cordon Bleu, La Varenne, and Ecole LeNotre.

Classes at C. Steele's Kitchen are both lecture/demonstration and particpation and are limited to 15 students.

Brochure available   Fees: moderate

Lynne Kasper's Lid and Ladle Cooking School
2575 Youngfield Street
Golden, Colorado 80401
303/232-7288

Improvisation is the byword at Lynne Kasper's Lid and Ladle Cooking School, Golden. "Cooking is a pleasure and a never-ending source of challenge and creativity. We stress the reasons behind the recipes. This frees the students from the written word and encourages them to trust their instincts and training," says Lynne Kasper, the school's director.

Lynne says she has been carrying on a love affair with all things culinary since her childhood. She has traveled through the kitchens of the United States and Europe, learning about the cuisines of the world. She has studied with Chef Kenneth Steins of the London Savoy, with Marcella Hazan in Bologna, with Chef Jean Morel of L'Hostellerie Bressane, at La Varenne, and at The School of Restaurant and Hotel Management at New York Community College. She also studied improvisational cooking with James Beard.

Before coming to Colorado, Lynne was the gourmet consultant to Abraham and Straus department store in Brooklyn, New York, and taught for two years at Anna Muffoletto's Cordon Bleu of New York, Inc. She now writes for *Bon Appetit* magazine.

Classes at the Lid and Ladle include a five-part series, Foundations of Cooking, three levels of French cooking, regional Italian cooking, and a host of specialty classes. Lecture/demonstration classes are limited to 24 persons; participation classes are planned for eight students.

The instructors at the school are Mollie Ng, Sam Arnold, and many guests from the restaurant, catering and teaching fields. Mollie, who is a native of Canton, China, has a doctorate in biochemistry. She teaches Mandarin, Cantonese, Szechwan, and Peking cuisines. Sam is "one of the country's leading authorities on the foods of the early West and Southwest and has a thorough knowledge of the cuisines of Ceylon, China, and Asia," according to Lynne.

The school offers concentrated classes for the convenience of out-of-town students and will assist with travel arrangements.

Brochure available   Fees: moderate

Culinary Art
9321 Alhambra
Shawnee Mission, Kansas 66207
913/381-2122

"Cooking is mind over matter, with lots of love," says Bobbi Saper, owner/director of Culinary Art, Shawnee Mission. "I want the students to feel that they can accomplish great feats once they know the basics," she adds.

Classes at Bobbi's in-home school focus on menu components such as appetizers, desserts, crepes, and souffles. The school also offers classes in buffets and in cooking with the food processor and microwave.

Bobbi has taken classes with Nathalie Dupree and Jacques Pepin, and attended classes at the Cordon Bleu, London, and La Varenne, Paris. Both of her regular teachers have taken classes at the Cordon Bleu.

The Culinary Art school offers both lecture/demonstration classes and participation classes with a maximum of 12 students in each class. The school will help with travel accommodations for out-of-town students.

No brochure available   Fees: moderate

L'Epicure
School of Cooking
First Plaza Galeria
Albuquerque, New Mexico 87102
505/242-0430

From the foods of Azerbaijan in the U.S.S.R. to the Piedmont region of Italy, the bounty of the world's cuisines is offered through classes at L'Epicure School of Cooking in Albuquerque.

Rosa Rajkovic, the school's owner/director, brings a colorful combination of cultural, academic, and practical experiences to her school. Rosa's parents emigrated from Yugoslavia, and after sojourns in Italy, Austria, Germany, and England, they came to the United States and settled near Chicago. Rosa entered Indiana University, Bloomington, Indiana, to study opera, but after a year switched to Slavic languages and literature. She developed an interest in ethno-musicology, which led to what she calls her penchant for folk dancing. Then, she relates, "I began to be fascinated by the discovery that a country's cuisine is as distinctive an expression of its people as its folk dancing, art, and music are." It was, she says, almost by instinct that she began catering, first trying her recipes out on friends and acquaintances, then preparing parties for 200 persons.

In 1973 Rosa and some friends opened a restaurant in Bloomington. It flourished—they eventually employed 45 people—but she left the business when a change in her husband's career took them to Albuquerque. Shortly after arriving there she opened a delicatessen, patisserie, and wine and liquor store. She opened her cooking school two years ago.

Although Rosa is active in teaching many of the classes at the school, she employs other teachers who have solid professional credentials, including some who own their own food businesses. Most classes are lecture/demonstration with a maximum of 40 students. Participation classes are limited to 20. The school will provide help with arrangements for out-of-town students.

Brochure available   Fees: high

Creative Cookery

6509 North May Avenue
Oklahoma City, Oklahoma 73116
405/840-1719

"We believe students learn by doing," says Jacque Orenstein, owner/director of Creative Cookery, Oklahoma City. "They have a sense of accomplishment when they make a souffle, and it comes out beautifully. We also feel that they are more likely to do it themselves at home if they have done it at cooking school."

To this end the school is equipped with 17 ovens and an array of other equipment that make the school's full participation classes for 30 students possible. A limited number of demonstration classes, which focus on microwave cooking and the use of the food processor, are also offered.

Jacque has been in the restaurant business for 17 years, and has had restaurants in Oklahoma City, St. Louis, and Tucson. He was on television for almost eight years, and is the owner of another Creative Cookery school in Dallas. Reva Kaden, an instructor at the school, taught for eight years in Boston and has been the owner of a catering business. Other teachers at the school are drawn from the community and often include restaurant owners and chefs.

The school is associated with a gourmet cookware shop.

Brochure available   Fees: low

Colonial Cooking School

3948 East 31st Street
Tulsa, Oklahoma 74105
918/742-8730

"Back to basics" is the philosophy of the Colonial Cooking School, Tulsa.

Dolores Pfaff, owner/director, grew up in a small town in which most residents were of Italian heritage. She has taken classes at Anna Muffaletto's Cordon Bleu of New York, took a week of classes at the Culinary Institute, and has attended demonstrations by Jacques Pepin and Michael James.

Classes at Dolores' in-home school include sessions on basic skills, bread making, breakfasts, and Italian cooking. Demonstration classes are limited to 20, and participation classes are limited to six students. The school has concentrated classes for out-of-town students and will make arrangements for travel and hotel accommodations.

No brochure available   Fees: low-moderate

Mary Gubser's Cooking School
2499 East 49th Street
Tulsa, Oklahoma 74105
918/742-2200

Breads and soups are Mary Gubser's specialty, and her knowledge of both has made her in-home cooking school in Tulsa a popular place indeed. Although she has been teaching for eight years, Mary is still amazed by the demand for her classes. But with a homey atmosphere, coffee and tea ready for the students when they arrive, a chance to knead and work with bread dough, and a tasting luncheon at the end of each session, it's easy to see why Oklahomans flock to Mary's school. "I have a marvelous kitchen—with a clubroom attached—which is completely open except for a counter in the center. I limit my usual classes to 30 but can seat as many as 65 for special demonstrations," explains Mary.

Although she considers herself self-taught, Mary has taken lessons from Jacques Pepin and James Beard. As the result of her early years of teaching, she wrote *Mary's Bread Basket and Soup Kettle,* which she published herself but later sold to William Morrow and Company after offers from several publishers. The book was subsequently chosen as a Book-of-the-Month Club selection.

Mary's newest classes will be special weekend sessions designed for out-of-town students and business people. The school will make arrangements for hotel accommodations if needed. These classes will be a family affair; Mary's son and daughter-in-law will join her in conveying to the students Mary's philosophy. "Bread is so basic," she explains. "One is creating something from a live object, the yeast. It's exciting, rewarding, and a positive part of life."

Brochure available

Fees: moderate

Irene Wong's Great Asia Cooking School
803-B Robert E. Lee Road
Austin, Texas 78704
512/441-5986

Irene Wong has been a demonstrator, teacher, and author and is considered an authority on authentic Asian steam-cooking. Her book, *Great Asia Steambook,* was published in 1978.

As a demonstrator for Taylor and Ng, a San Francisco firm, Irene traveled the nation lecturing and teaching. In 1974, she started her own school, which she now calls Irene Wong's Great Asia Cooking School. Here she offers a variety of classes, all based on Oriental foods. She teaches steam-cooking the Asian way, of course, as well as basic and regional Chinese cooking, seafoods, and Oriental desserts. Her classes are both lecture/demonstration and participation and are limited to 15 students.

Irene was a protege of Rhoda Yee, with whom she "studied for years." Rhoda Yee is the author of *Chinese Village Cookbook* and *Dim Sum Cookbook.*

Irene says her philosophy is to "impart knowledge of the culture and histories of Asian nations as well as to train students in the skills of Oriental food preparation." Her students learn "imaginative meal planning, sensible shopping, flavorful cooking, inspired table settings, and effortless cleaning up."

No brochure available

Fees: moderate

2945 Walnut Hill Lane
Dallas, Texas 75229
214/358-4201

Everyone knows they do it big in Texas. But a cooking school that has three separate classrooms, 65 gas ranges, and an air-conditioned cooking theater that seats 104 persons—well, that begins to boggle the minds of those not native to the Lone Star State.

The founders of Creative Cookery, a new school and cookware shop in Dallas, have created a large and impressive setting for their classes. Jacque Orenstein, the school's director, is a veteran of 17 years as a restaurant owner in Oklahoma City, St. Louis, and Tucson and did a weekly television cooking show for nearly eight years. Jacque owns and directs another cooking school in Oklahoma City. His partner in Dallas is Sherman Markman.

Pierre Garbit, the school's head chef and instructor, is a classically trained French chef with more than 46 years' professional experience all over the world. Ramon Annen, the pastry chef, was trained in Switzerland. Besides the regular classes taught by the two chefs, ethnic courses and some specialty classes are taught by local restaurateurs and chefs. The school also features traveling celebrity cooking teachers.

Although Creative Cookery is just in its first year, it lists 25 different classes. They include some that focus on particular techniques and some that teach French, International Mexican, and Chinese cuisines, as well as vegetarian and macrobiotic cooking classes. There are several nutrition classes including a seminar on pre-natal nutrition taught by a nutrition consultant. Another class, entitled Filling Your Child's Sweet Tooth, features "yummy alternatives to the sugar-filled delights your little ones are hooked on." Classes at the school are taught by demonstration, lecture, or participation. The maximum number of students in participation classes is 24.

"The key words at this cooking school are participation and technique," says Jacque. "We believe that students learn by doing. When they try it here, at home they'll know they can do it. We always start with the basics," he adds.

Brochure available   Fees: moderate

Florence Simon

3669 Manderly Place
Fort Worth, Texas 76109
817/926-5566

"The most important thing I do is take the fear out of cooking," Florence Simon says of classes at her school, Florence Simon School of Gourmet Cooking, Fort Worth.

"Through tips, tricks, and cautions, my students learn not to be afraid. At the same time they learn the basic principles each step of the way," she continues.

Florence's professional credentials include classes with Michael Field in New York City, study at both the Paris and London Cordon Bleu and at La Varenne, with Simone Beck, and with Julie Dannenbaum. Florence is the author of the *Party Planning/Menu Cookbook*. She has been teaching and lecturing for 12 years.

Regular instructors at Florence's school are Diane Hightower and Joy Mohr, both former students. Ruth Tucker, a guest instructor, is a former head of the home economics department, Lone Star Gas Company.

The cooking classes at Florence's school are truly international. French, Italian, Greek, Spanish, Russian, Moroccan, and Chinese cooking are all a part of the repertoire. In addition, the school offers specialty classes in baking, pastries, and hors d'oeuvres. Classes are lecture/demonstration with limited participation and are limited to 14 students.

Brochure available   Fees: moderate

La Cuisine Culinary Arts Center

1114 Barkdull
Houston, Texas 77006
713/521-9900

"I teach confidence in the kitchen," says Mary Nell Reck, a home economist who is the owner/director of La Cuisine Culinary Arts Center, Houston. "With confidence, students can relax in the kitchen; they can have fun and learn at the same time."

Be it outdoor cooking, couscous, creole cooking, specialty classes, or in-depth series classes in basic or advanced Provincial French cooking, Italian, Greek, or Chinese cuisine, Mary Nell and her staff can teach it.

The school is also a frequent host to celebrity cooks including Diana Kennedy, Giuliano Bugialli, and Maurice Cazalis, a Maitre Cuisinier of France who is known for his restaurant, Henri IV, in Chartres, France.

In addition to her home economics background, Mary Nell has studied with James Beard and Jacques Pepin in New York City and has attended classes at La Varenne in Paris. She says she has learned, too, from visiting three-star restaurants in France and has "continued to learn from chefs" as well as from special classes with cooking notables. Her staff is composed primarily of people who have "self-developed" and then studied with various chefs.

Lecture/demonstration classes at La Cuisine are limited to 30 persons; participation classes are limited to 12. The school offers concentrated classes for out-of-town students and will assist with travel and lodging arrangements.

Mary Nell and her school arrange travel-study trips to Europe and are associated with a cookware shop and catering business.

Brochure available   Fees: moderate-high

The Cooking School

2520½ Westcreek
Houston, Texas 77027
713/626-8360

A jam-packed schedule of classes taught by experienced professionals is a sign of the excitement at The Cooking School (formerly Verlyn Campbell's Cooking School) in Houston. New owner Miriam Kalmans has a master's degree in home economics and is the author of *Cooking Collectibles,* a cookbook sponsored by the American Cancer Society that is now in its third printing. Other instructors at the school include Anthony Piazza, whose family has owned and operated a fish market for three generations; Monte Palmiter, a home economist; Jane Bauer and Jeannetta Davis, who have degrees in nutrition; and Beverly Lerner, who specializes in cooking classes for children and teenagers.

Classes at The Cooking School are primarily lecture/demonstration and are limited to 20 students. The school offers classes for out-of-town students and will make lodging arrangements with nearby hotels.

The Cooking School shares the second floor of a quaint building in the Galleria area of Houston with a cookware and antique shop called Good Things.

Brochure available   Fees: high

Midwestern States

Helen Baetz Cooking School
225 Bellingham Drive
Barrington, Illinois 60010
312/381-5931

At her in-home cooking school, says Helen Baetz, she tries "to bring to students the best tasting foods from the most concise recipes available."

Classes at the Helen Baetz Cooking School are limited to six students and are full participation. This allows the owner/director to "teach students the techniques and the uses of various kinds of equipment to speed them to a finished product." At the same time Helen tries to impart to her students excitement in cooking and a love of fine ingredients, good food, and excellent equipment.

Helen is "mostly self-taught." She lived and studied in Rome for six months, was assistant at a cooking school in Maryland, and studied under a Chinese caterer in Washington, D.C. The classes in French, Italian, and Chinese cuisines reflect her experiences.

The Helen Baetz Cooking School has been in existence for over five years. It began in West Chester, Pennsylvania, and after two years moved to its present location in Barrington.

Class schedule available   Fees: low

Cook's Mart, Ltd.
609 North LaSalle Street
Chicago, Illinois 60610
312/642-3526

Celebrity cooks, evening series classes, and Saturday afternoon specials—they're all part of the Cook's Mart, Ltd., Chicago.

Pat Bruno, the school's owner, draws from a seemingly unending pool of talent for his regular schedule. Many of his teachers are other local cooking school owners, restaurateurs, or respected home economists. His school at Cook's Mart on LaSalle (he has another cookware-only shop in Watertower Place) has also been host to Maurice Moore-Betty,

Diana Kennedy, Madeleine Kamman, Joyce Chen, and Giuliano Bugialli—all well known cooks.

Cuisines represented in the class schedule include the foods of Japan, France, Italy, China, Brazil, Morocco, and New Orleans. The school also has classes in Oriental specialties such as sushi and dim sum, in chocolate candy-making, and much more. All classes are lecture/demonstration.

Brochure available   Fees: high

Culinarion
113 East Oak Street
Chicago, Illinois 60611
312/266-7840

Located just off North Michigan Avenue near Lake Michigan, the Culinarion in Chicago is a school that has "always offered the advanced type of cooking—not for beginners."

Richard and Dorothy Irwin, the school's owners, do not have a permanent staff of teachers. "We hire local teachers as well as chefs from our better restaurants. All of our teachers have good schooling and experience."

Classes at the Culinarion are held in the evening. The cuisines of France, Northern Italy, and China are taught. Specialty classes on breads, food processor cooking, and puff pastry are also offered. All classes are lecture/demonstration and are limited to 20 students.

"We believe that if the students have recipes and watch someone cook a meal and are able to ask questions and take notes, they can do the same thing at home."

Brochure available   Fees: high

Jane Salzfass Freiman Cooking Classes
837 West Oakdale Avenue
Chicago, Illinois 60657
312/549-7526

Chicago-based Jane Freiman says that in her school there are "no chairs in the kitchen because there is no time to sit. Students are here to learn to taste, to season, and to refine."

Jane has studied extensively with James Beard and Richard Olney, and was Olney's teaching assistant. She has also studied with Marcella Hazan, Giuliano Bugialli, and Simone Beck.

Jane's classes are constantly changing. Most are offered in the evening in her special teaching kitchen. These full participation classes are limited to 10 students.

Jane feels that students should be given not only the "what" of a recipe but the "why" as well, so that the learned techniques can become part of their experience even after they have left the classroom.

No brochure available: write for details   Fees: high

**710 North Rush Street
Chicago, Illinois 60611
312/664-7800**

Alma Lach, owner/director of the Alma Lach Cooking School, has an impressive professional background and an impressive school for serious cooks in the heart of Chicago.

Alma holds the grande diplome de Cordon Bleu, Paris. She was food editor of the *Chicago Sun-Times* from 1957 to 1976, and is the author of several cookbooks including the excellent *Hows and Whys of French Cooking.* She has appeared regularly on radio and television programs as a nutrition and cooking expert. Alma has lived and studied in France, India, and the Far East.

In 1967, Alma began teaching on a regular basis in Chicago through classes sponsored by the Alliance Francaise. In 1977, she moved her cooking school to its present location in the new kitchens of an old Victorian mansion one block from the posh north end of Michigan Avenue, the most elegant area of downtown Chicago.

The Alma Lach Cooking School specializes in French and Chinese cooking. "I teach the basics of both cuisines and teach students how to apply and use the basics to create food," says this superb teacher. "I want my students to be creative cooks...and to stop copying others because this is when the fun of cooking begins."

In her weekly lecture/demonstration classes (each series is five weeks long), a complete French dinner or Chinese banquet is prepared and then served with appropriate wines for each course. In addition, participation classes—limited to five students—are available for "qualified persons."

Specialty classes at the school are taught by other qualified instructors. Elizabeth Baum, who teaches cake decorating, was trained in England. Ed Shannon, who teaches sugar work, trained at LeNorte School of Pastry in France. Other classes at the school include single sessions on the foods of India and the foods of Japan.

Brochure available   Fees: high

Monique's

**684 West Irving Park Road
Chicago, Illinois 60613
312/935-9019**

At Monique's in Chicago, owner/director Monique Jamet Hooker brings to her students a rich heritage of culinary experiences. She was born in Brittany, and as one of 10 children, she "learned about cooking at a very early age." Later, in Paris, she assisted in publishing a cookbook for children. During this time she traveled extensively in Europe, collecting recipes and studying cooking techniques. In 1966 Monique came to the United States to work with her older brother, a chef, in his restaurant and resort in New York state. She taught in New York City and has had many years of catering experience.

In 1973 Monique opened her school in Chicago's Old Town. In 1977 she moved to her present location in a personally designed, spacious French country kitchen just a block from North Lake Shore Drive.

Monique teaches with the motto "Do not get uptight about cooking. Enjoy it!" She offers an in-depth series in French cooking, a class for children age eight to 12, and a specialty class using the food processor in French cuisine. Classes are full participation and are limited to 10 students.

Brochure available   Fees: low

Oriental Food Market and Cooking School
7411 North Clark Street
Chicago, Illinois 60626
312/274-2826

Tucked into the back room of their Oriental food market is a spotless kitchen from which Pansy and Chu Yen Luke have developed a cooking school that ranks, according to *Chicago* magazine, as "one of the area's best."

Pansy and Chu Yen alternate as teachers for their classes, which are organized in series of six lessons each. Classes are lecture/demonstration and each session is followed by a full meal in which students can enjoy the results of the three recipes they have prepared.

Pansy and Chu Yen Luke are self-taught cooks. Pansy was an elementary school teacher and Chu Yen an electrical engineer. Both have worked in Chinese restaurants. Their cooking classes started eight years ago when customers in their newly opened Oriental food market wanted to know how to use various foods the Lukes were selling. When the lessons began, from 10 to 14 eager students crowded into the tiny back room of their store. Now the Lukes' classes are in a demonstration area that seats 25 persons, and they've expanded their selection of courses to include Chinese vegetarian cooking and Filipino, Korean, and Japanese cooking classes taught by guest instructors.

New classes at the Oriental Food Market and Cooking School begin every seven weeks. Concentrated classes are available for out-of-town students.

Brochure available   Fees: moderate

PersimmonTree
127 South Third Street
Geneva, Illinois 60134
312/232-6446

A lively potpourri of classes awaits students at the Persimmon Tree cooking school in Geneva, Illinois. The mixture includes such offerings as Moroccan couscous, taught by a Parisian, a three-hour class in which an Italian peasant dinner is prepared, and favorite pork dishes of a native Czechoslovakian, Vlasta Giese.

Owners Jane and Bill Briner and school director Lee Chalfant say that their goal is to develop an appreciation of fine cuisines and new trends in cooking. To accomplish this they have assembled a staff of 12 instructors, all of whom have comprehensive credentials and teaching experience.

The Persimmon Tree offers demonstration classes that are limited to 12 students. The school is associated with a cookware shop of the same name.

Brochure available   Fees: low

Abby Cooks & Cooks & Cooks

P.O. Box 118
Glencoe, Illinois 60022
312/835-1134

The food processor is king in the classes of Abby Mandel, owner/director of Abby Cooks & Cooks & Cooks, Glencoe. All of her classes focus on the use of the food processor and other modern equipment including the microwave and convection ovens.

At her in-home school, Abby teaches how to "maximize the time you spend at the pleasurable parts of cooking and minimize the uncreative drudgery parts." She teaches everything "from soup to nuts" but has a special fondness for French foods. She has studied and worked with French restaurant chefs, including Claude Deligne at Taillevent, Alain Chapel at La Mere Charles, Jean Delaveyne at le Camelia, and with Lionel Poilane, a leading baker in Paris.

Abby is a newspaper columnist and a contributor to *Bon Appetit* magazine. She is the author of *The Cuisinart Food Processor Cookbook,* now in its fourth printing.

All of Abby's classes are lecture/demonstration and are limited to 40 students. Special concentrated classes are available for the convenience of out-of-town students.

Brochure available   Fees: high

Microcookery Center, Inc.

413 Main Street
Glen Ellyn, Illinois 60137
312/858-2853

Professional and comprehensive instruction in microwave cooking is available at Microcookery Center, a school owned and directed by Mary Jo Bergland, home economist and author.

The use of the microwave, meat microcookery, and vegetable cooking are some of the basic classes offered. In addition, a three-session class in low-calorie cooking, microcookery for kids, and even food preservation with the microwave are some of the unique classes available at this school.

Most classes at Microcookery Center are lecture/demonstration with a maximum of 18 students. Participation workshops in microwave basics are limited to 12 students. All of the instructors are home economists.

Microcookery Center, Inc., is both a school and a shop that handles microwave accessories, cookbooks, and gourmet cookware. It does not sell microwave ovens, but offers advice to consumers on what to look for when purchasing an oven. Microcookery Center specializes "in the promotion of consumer understanding of microwave cooking through classes, seminars, programs, consulting, and the retail sale of microwave accessories and cookbooks."

Brochure available   Fees: moderate

222 Waukegan Road
Glenview, Illinois 60025
312/729-7687

The Complete Cook has classes to satisfy almost every culinary interest. From series taught by celebrity cooks with worldwide reputations to sessions on party planning, this cooking school has all bases covered.

Some classes are taught by co-owner and director Elaine Sherman, who trained under John Snowden of Dumas Pere L'Ecole de la Cuisine Francaise in Chicago. Elaine taught adult education cooking for 10 years before opening The Complete Cook.

Other classes are taught by Chicago area teachers whose expertise meets the standards of Elaine and her partner, Wilma Sugarman. In addition, the school draws an impressive list of guest teachers. Perla Meyers, Simone Beck, Jacques Pepin, Julie Dannenbaum, Maida Hatter, John Clancy, and Marcella Hazan have all taught at The Complete Cook.

Classes at The Complete Cook are lecture/demonstration only and are limited to 20 students. Each session lasts approximately two-and-a-half hours.

The school is connected with a gourmet cookware store of the same name, and free demonstrations of equipment, food, and supplies sold by the store are listed in The Complete Cook's brochure. The combination school and cookware shop outgrew its original space within two years; as a result The Complete Cook recently moved to new and larger facilities.

The Complete Cook will assist with hotel arrangements for out-of-town students attending classes taught by the special guest cooks.

Brochure available   Fees: moderate

Dumas Pere L'Ecole de la Cuisine Francaise
1129 North Depot Street
Glenview, Illinois 60025
312/729-4823

If you haven't heard about Dumas Pere l'Ecole de la Cuisine Francaise, there's a reason: Master Chef John Snowden, the school's owner/director, is an uncompromising professional who says he has "never tried to be a big (or well publicized) school—only a good school."

For 16 years he has devoted his time to teaching French cuisine in a thoroughly classical manner in Glenview, a suburb of Chicago. Here he holds two classes a day, four days a week. His basic Diploma Course is 40 weeks long and is broken into four 10-week quarters. Following the diploma course, students are eligible to take the graduate program.

His methods are based on the techniques of classical French cooking. The classes are total participation workshops that are limited to 15 students. The school's teaching kitchen is equipped with 15 ranges, and each student works individually under the personal supervision of Chef Snowden.

Snowden's career began when he was a boy and wanted to be an artist. "I got a job in a restaurant to pay for art lessons," he says, "but it was obvious after two hours there that I was not qualified. The restaurant owner then arranged for me to serve as an apprentice in

France. I expressed more interest than I felt because all I really wanted was to get away from home.'' However, he studied in France for six and a half years, then attended L'Ecole de l'Hotelerrie, a famous cooking school in Lausanne, Switzerland. He has had three restaurants in Chicago: The Drexel Club, Le Provencal, and Cafe la Cloche. Chef Snowden did not forget about art along the way; he received a bachelor of arts degree from the Art Institute of Chicago in 1946.

Snowden's students are often culinary professionals themselves. Out-of-town students sometimes make special arrangements to take the classes simultaneously.

On weekends, the school becomes a fixed-menu restaurant. Snowden serves one group of 20 persons each Friday and Saturday evening at 8 p.m.

Brochure available   Fees: moderate

Ruth's Kitchen
3206 Maple Lane
Hazel Crest, Illinois 60429
312/335-4758

For Ruth Ratowitz, owner/director of Ruth's Kitchen in Hazel Crest, cooking is a hobby that has blossomed into a busy schedule of classes in her home. Included in her offerings are a series of French dinners, Jewish, Chinese, and Italian Ethnic dinners, and several dessert and baking classes.

All of Ruth's classes are held in the evening and are a combination of lecture/demonstration and participation. Class size is limited to 10 students.

Brochure available   Fees: low

Shirley Waterloo Culinary Instruction
307 North Quincy
Hinsdale, Illinois 60521
312/323-3903

Interesting classes spark the repertoire of the in-home cooking school of Shirley Waterloo. One, The Contemporary Kitchen, features classic recipes prepared with a food processor and microwave oven. Another, Trends in French Cooking, focuses on nouvelle, minceur, and classic cuisines. Most classes are lecture/demonstration and are limited to 15 students.

Shirley Waterloo is the mother of eight children who started cooking "of necessity" and learned to love it. A food writer, she was formerly culinary editor for *The Doings,* Hinsdale, Illinois, and is now a contributing editor for *DuPage Magazine,* Villa Park, Illinois. She is on the teaching staff of a Chicago gourmet cookware shop.

Brochure available   Fees: moderate

What's Cooking

P.O. Box 323
Hinsdale, Illinois 60521
312/986-1595

What's Cooking, selected by *Chicago* magazine as one of the area's best cooking schools, has both lecture and participation classes in Chinese cookery. Ruth Law, owner/director, says, "In these classes students learn to easily and successfully prepare a Chinese meal or banquet with a lot of do-ahead dishes." Students are also taught how to use modern equipment, including the food processor and microwave oven, as well as to use the wok in a variety of ways.

Ruth started her in-home cooking school after several years as a demonstrator and representative for a wok manufacturer. She has studied with many chefs, including Dr. Shen, Bennie Moy, Mai Leung, and Rhoda Lee in Chicago. She has also worked in restaurant kitchens, and offers Chinese cooking classes with chef and restaurateur Doo Huan Lee in Chicago.

What's Cooking will arrange special classes and hotel and travel accommodations for out-of-town students.

Brochure available   Fees: moderate-high

Tin Pan Galley

P.O. Box 445
Lake Bluff, Illinois 60044
312/234-0346

"I want students to learn the basic skills and theories of cooking and then apply them in as many ways as possible," says Nancy Kirby, owner/director of Tin Pan Galley in Lake Bluff.

At her in-home school Nancy teaches three different series of classical foods classes each week. Almost all of her classes are full participation and are limited to eight students.

Nancy worked for six years for a general contractor, designing commercial kitchens, before launching her cooking school. She has taken a short course at the Cordon Bleu, London, and has studied in the Chicago area with Ben May, Jane Freiman, and John Clancy.

Brochure available   Fees: low

Continental Cookery

1144 South Elmhurst Road
Mt. Prospect, Illinois 60056
312/593-3020

"We want to provide students with the joy of cooking in general, not just gourmet," say Larry and Sue Bress, owners/partners of Continental Cookery, Mt. Prospect.

"At our school we try to encourage the pleasures and fulfillment of the total spectrum of food and wine."

The staff at the school includes Michael Bantel, a European-trained chef; Michael LaCroix, a Certified Executive Chef and graduate of the Culinary Institute of America; Nancy Abrams, a university and secondary-level educator who is on the advisory board of a food processor company; Carol Cerney, a home economist and former director of food quality at Henrici's restaurant, and Ann Hamrick, who has the "Second Kitchen," a catering business.

Continental Cookery offers a 16-week professional chef's series as well as courses in the cuisines of France, Germany, and Italy. They also have numerous specialty classes on food processor cooking and microwave cooking.

Their ellipse-shaped demonstration area seats 20. Participation classes are limited to 18 students.

The school sponsors cooking-study trips to other American cities as well as a "Cook's Tour" of Chicago. They also sponsor tours of ethnic restaurants followed by classes at the school in ethnic cuisines.

Brochure available   Fees: moderate

Napercurean House, Inc.

28 West Chicago Avenue
Naperville, Illinois 60540
312/357-4100

A restored 1860 house in Naperville, a western suburb of Chicago, is the home of Napercurean House, Inc., a cooking school and cookware shop. Here in a bright and modern kitchen Mary Ann Wright and Joan Ruble offer a full range of cooking classes.

Both partners in this six-year-old venture are home economists with impressive professional credentials. Other instructors at the school include Patricia Tung, who has taken advanced classes in cooking in Taiwan; Ruth Unik, who has taken classes at the Cordon Bleu in London; and Melinda Orzoff, who specializes in the techniques of candy making.

Napercurean House classes vary in length from single sessions in specialty subjects such as sauces, Chinese seafood, and Mongolian hot pot cookery to a six-week-class in the basics of Oriental cooking. All are lecture/demonstration with the exception of the Oriental cooking classes, which involve student participation. Enrollment is limited to 10 students.

The objective of Napercurean House, according to its owners, is "to encourage the enjoyment of culinary arts and to provide the environment and support for our students to increase their skills and self-esteem."

Brochure available   Fees: moderate

the proper pan cooking school

4620 North University
Metro Centre
Peoria, Illinois 61614
309/692-6382

An appetizing assortment of specialty classes taught by seven different instructors is offered at The Proper Pan, a cooking school which opened in Peoria in March 1978.

Included in the school's schedule are classes in natural foods and cooking for a crowd, a session on "sweets and savories" for tea time, and classes in Italian, Chinese, and Mexican cooking, to name just a few.

Cynthia Schmitt, the school's owner/director, is a former English teacher who says, "I developed a love of gourmet cooking with my husband, who owns a fine dining restaurant, Sea Merchant." Her staff includes Dottie Cannell, from England, caterer and owner of Tea Cozy tea shop; Joe De Fabbio and Steven and Val West-Rosenthal, who all have restaurant backgrounds; and Jan Pierce and Mary Garner, home economists who teach microwave and natural foods, respectively.

Most of the classes at The Proper Pan are lecture/demonstration and are limited to 20 students. Participation "depends on and varies with each teacher but there is ample room for this style of teaching," Cynthia says.

The school is associated with a cookware shop. It hopes to develop more extensive classes for out-of-town students.

Brochure available   Fees: low

Charie's Kitchen

2111 Beechwood
Wilmette, Illinois 60091
312/256-3979

"Good eats don't just happen" is the motto of Charie MacDonald, owner/director of Charie's Kitchen in Wilmette. "Glorious food can be produced with a minimum of effort if care and thought go into the planning of meals," says Charie. This "ongoing cooking" becomes "a way of life that benefits those around you."

Charie's Kitchen was started in 1974 and now features total participation classes with a maximum of six students. A special feature of this in-home cooking school is that students take home the food they prepare.

Says Charie MacDonald, "I'm basically self-taught. I've cooked from scratch since the age of nine and have been cooking creatively for the past 20 years. I was brought up in a family where food presentation and food preservation played an important role. My early teachers were family members who believed strongly in nutrition and good food."

Charie's Kitchen focuses on specialty classes, including a wide variety of bread-baking lessons, classes in pickling and preserving foods, Christmas baking, and preparation of desserts and sauces.

Class schedule available   Fees: moderate

CHEZ MIMI

621 Holt Avenue
Iowa City, Iowa 52240
319/351-4071

Most people do not remember giving much thought, as teenagers, to the preparation of food. Not so with Mimi F. Gormezano. While still a teen, she began studying with Dione Lucas. Today she is owner/director of her own cooking school, Chez Mimi, Iowa City.

Here she teaches in-depth courses in classic and country French cooking and in nouvelle cuisine as well as a number of specialty classes including one for teens, of course, and a class in cuisine minceur, a class in pasta, and even one on the French influence on Mexican cooking.

After college, Mimi furthered her culinary training with Simone Beck, Madeleine Kamman, and in classes at the Cordon Bleu, Paris. She says, too, "I have worked with numerous chefs in France, learning their techniques and styles, as well as with chefs in other parts of the world. I have also taught privately in California and Australia." She is currently at work on a cookbook, *Company is Coming.*

At Mimi's school all classes are lecture/demonstration with the exception of a full participation class for men which is preceded by a lecture so that there is "an understanding of how things are to be done." Mimi's classes are generally limited to 10 students.

"I stress techniques as well as the hows and whys of cooking. I believe if everything is fully explained there is no mystery. Therefore every stage of cooking is called to the students' attention as well as what happens if you add one ingredient rather than another. As students progress, this gives them the confidence to try more difficult things and to improvise more because they understand."

Chez Mimi has hosted celebrity cooks including Richard Olney, Giuliano Bugialli, and Paula Wolfert, and has concentrated classes for out-of-town students, sometimes coinciding with football weekends at the University of Iowa in Iowa City. Chez Mimi also sponsors cooking-study tours in the United States and France. The school is associated with a cookware shop.

Brochure available   Fees: high

Chef's Connection

9324 Thunder Hill Place
Fort Wayne, Indiana 46804
219/432-4221
219/745-0458

International cooking with emphases on French, Italian, and Oriental cuisines are the specialties of Margaret Miller and Patricia Keenan, partners in the Chef's Connection, Fort Wayne.

Margaret, who teaches the Oriental foods classes, says she has been studying informally for 20 years. "I began by 'hanging around' the Chinatowns in San Francisco, New York, and Chicago." She took Chinese cooking classes in San Jose and had Japanese cooking classes from Kimiko Suzano Jansen, who teaches on a San Francisco public television station. Margaret says she also learned by asking lots of questions in Oriental grocery stores.

Patricia's family background includes a home where the provincial way of cooking was an art and where she learned her mother's methods. Later she attended cooking classes in New York, San Francisco, and Chicago and trained with Chef Pierre Bilterer.

In addition to Oriental, Italian, and French cuisines, the school also teaches classes in Indonesian, Mediterranean, and food-processor cooking. The classes are limited to 14 students.

Brochure available   Fees: low

8702 Keystone Crossing
Indianapolis, Indiana 46240
317/844-8160

Cuisines of eight countries and many specialty classes make The Pan Handler in Indianapolis as active as a bee hive.

Katie Kruse and Dian Hutchison, owner/directors, started the school two years ago. Their primary teachers are Rita Jo Kuehnert and Margrith Strates. Rita Jo, a specialist in French cooking, studied for four years in Paris with Chef John Desmond. Margrith, who is Swiss, has "studied all over the world." Her husband is Greek, and her specialty is Chinese cooking. Four additional teachers round out the school's staff.

The Pan Handler's class schedule includes the cuisines of Switzerland, Italy, Greece, China, India, and Russia, as well as Creole and Mediterranean-style cooking. Classes are lecture/demonstration and are limited to 25 students.

Brochure available   Fees: low

Market Square
Lafayette, Indiana 47904
317/447-5255

The eight children of Joanne Force were inspiration for the name of her cooking school, The Eight Mice Cooking School, Lafayette.

"Once we had a boat, which we called 'The Eight Mates,' and somehow that evolved into Eight Mice when our school was formed," Joanne says.

The school is directed by Joan Bain and draws mainly from the community for its instructors. Because it is the location of Purdue University the community is able to provide people of diverse ethnic backgrounds "who are interested in and able to teach cooking."

Breads, souffles, tortes, pasta, Chinese foods, brunches, and soups are but a few of the many specialty classes taught at the school.

The Eight Mice Cooking School is associated with a cookware shop.

Brochure available   Fees:low

Microwave Kitchen Shop

3506 West Jackson
Muncie, Indiana 47304
317/282-7555

One of the first microwave cooking schools in the Midwest, The Microwave Kitchen Shop offers a wide variety of classes taught by well-qualified instructors. Owner/director Jacqueline Johnston is a home economist with advanced training in microwave education. Other instructors are home economists who have taught at the college level.

Now in its third year of operation, this school lists a changing repertoire of 20 different classes. Included are sessions on microwave cooking for the junior chef, instruction in converting recipes to microwave cooking, senior citizens' classes offered at a discount for persons over 60, low-calorie microwave cooking classes, and lessons on microwave cooking with a gourmet flair.

Most classes are of one session with the exception of the more detailed classes, which are two or three sessions in length. The classes are lecture/demonstration; each has a minimum enrollment of 10 and a maximum enrollment of 20 students. Hotel arrangements for out-of-town students will be handled by the school.

"We design classes that enable our students to make better use of their microwave ovens. At the same time, classes at our school will guide prospective owners in selecting a microwave oven that will fit their needs," Jacqueline says. The school is an integral part of a shop that carries microwave ovens, microwave accessories, cookbooks, and even some prepared foods designed for microwave cooking.

Brochure available   Fees: low

The Creative Cook

56 West Indiana
Valparaiso, Indiana 46383
219/464-3398

Hardly a day goes by, it seems, that something isn't cooking at The Creative Cook in Valparaiso. Although the school opened just recently—in the fall of 1978—co-owners Judith Dittmer and Carolyn Bone have put together quite an array of class offerings. They range from unusual topics such as ice sculpture to everyday, practical classes such as Butcher Block Talks, in which a local meat cutter teaches the tricks of his trade.

Judith and Carolyn are registered nurses with no professional culinary backgrounds. Their primary teachers include Russ Adams, a graduate of the Culinary Institute of America and chef at a local restaurant; Judith Nagy Goldinger, from Budapest, Hungary, who taught at L'Ecole de Cuisine under the direction of William Rice; Moxie Shaw, food editor and graduate of Dumas Pere L'Ecole de la Cuisine Francaise; and Fanny Wu, a native of China.

Only a few classes at The Creative Cook are participation; most are lecture/demonstration with a maximum of 16 students. A special feature is the school's one-hour demonstration class, Lunch 'n Learn, which provides a lesson and a light lunch for a nominal fee.

"Our accent is on techniques and realistic results within the realm of practicality and availability of materials. We have always a professional yet personal and caring atmosphere," say the owners.

The school is associated with a cookware shop of the same name.

Brochure available   Fees: low-moderate

Complete Cuisine, Ltd.

322 South Main Street
Ann Arbor, Michigan 48104
313/662-0046

With 10,000 square feet of space, it is unlikely that there is anything incomplete about Complete Cuisine, Ltd., Ann Arbor. Not only does Complete Cuisine have a well organized school, but it also has a bakery, restaurant, catering service, and a chic Viennese-style coffee house.

Co-principals of the venture are Alexandra (Sandi) Cooper and Janine Gontard Meadows. Sandi studied for six months at the Cordon Bleu, London, and at Westminster Polytechnic Institute, a London vocational school for restaurant and hotel training. She also took the advanced course at La Varenne, Paris. Janine was born in Bourg-en-Bresse, France. She learned to cook from her mother and was inspired by the world of cuisine she saw at her grandparents' family restaurant near Lyon, France.

Both Sandi and Janine feel that enthusiasm is an important element in their work. "Once a student becomes enthusiastic, he or she belongs to the world of good cooking and good food forever. Our basic goal is to de-mystify cooking—and we practically guarantee success. We are very non-recipe and technique oriented," Sandi says. "We're also very practical."

Classes offered at Complete Cuisine range from the foods of Japan, France, Italy, Mexico, Australia, and China to specialty classes on pastry, bread baking, cake decorating, and many other topics. The school's lecture/demonstration classes have a maximum of 40 students; participation classes are limited to 16. The school has special concentrated classes for out-of-town students and will assist with travel accommodations even to the point, says Sandi, of "putting them up at our houses. We've done it before."

Brochure available   Fees: low

Kitchen Mechanics

945 Robbins Road
Grand Haven, Michigan 49417
616/846-3630

"If a tool is not useful, don't have it," says Sandra Cole, manager of Kitchen Mechanics, Grand Haven.

French and Italian cooking are taught at this school, along with practical specialty classes such as bread baking and children's and men's cooking classes.

Penny Harvey, the school's owner/director, says she is basically self-taught but has taken classes with Julie Dannenbaum. Joyce Bradford, an instructor at the school, assisted Madeleine Kamman for a year and took classes with Giuliano Bugialli.

Kitchen Mechanics offers both lecture/demonstration and participation classes. There are 12 students in each demonstration class and eight students in each participation class. The school has concentrated classes for out-of-town students and will assist with accommodations. Kitchen Mechanics is associated with a cookware shop.

Brochure available   Fees: low

Le Petit Cordon Bleu School of International Cuisine

591 Fisher Road
Grosse Pointe, Michigan 48230
313/885-2124

Madame Charity de Vicq Suczek, owner/director of Le Petit Cordon Bleu in Grosse Pointe, brings an unusual combination of education and experience to her school.

Madame Suczek, who has a degree in nutrition, studied for two years at the Cordon Bleu in Paris, has been a chef, world traveler, and author, and, as she says, "above all, a peripatetic kitchen philosopher."

In addition to teaching how to prepare the great classic dishes and make even the simplest foods attractive and delicious, Madame Suczek is "concerned with the cultural role of food in family life and society. Food as a tradition enriches the lifestyle and reflects the quality of hospitality and mutual esteem between host and guest and between homemaker and family.

"Cooking is, after all, more than the preparation of food for survival. It is also a means of artistic expression, a demonstration of affection, a symbol of cultural achievement, and a ritual bond between people. That, too, is how I approach the subject," she concludes.

Madame Suczek has been teaching for 25 years. Participation classes at her in-home school run for four hours and are limited to 10 students. Madame Suczek also offers demonstration classes and classes for professional chefs.

Brochure available   Fees: moderate-high

beatrice ojakangas

1150 Emerson Road
Duluth, Minnesota 55803
218/721-3026

Duluth, Minnesota, might not be everyone's ideal cooking school location, but Beatrice Ojakangas' school proves the merits of an idyllic setting. Her school is located on 40 lovely acres, has its own cross country ski trails for winter sports lovers, and has nearby Lake Superior for summer recreation.

Bea is a home economist who has done graduate work in nutrition and education, traveled extensively in Europe, written three cookbooks (*The Finnish Cookbook, Fondue Menu Cookbook,* and *Gourmet Cooking for Two*), and written for major food magazines such as *Cuisine* and *Gourmet*. She was food editor for *Sunset Magazine* for three years.

Bea offers a broad range of classes with emphasis on "do-able" things, so that "people are able to apply what they've learned at home, immediately." Many one-day classes, as well as two- and four-session series, are offered. Bea also teaches classes with a group's needs in mind. At present, her classes are scheduled by special arrangement only.

Brochure available   Fees: vary

La Cuvette, Inc.

250 Paisley Lane
Golden Valley, Minnesota 55422
612/545-9554

"Planning, presentation, and improvisation—plus fun" is the philosophy of Lois Lee, owner of La Cuvette, a school in Golden Valley, a Minneapolis suburb.

Lois studied over a period of four years at the Antoinette Pope School in Chicago, with Dione Lucas in Boston, and more recently with Simone Beck in France. She has also spent some time at La Varenne and the Cordon Bleu, Paris, and at many schools here in the United States.

For many years Lois had a gourmet shop and one of the first cooking schools in the Twin Cities. She now concentrates her efforts only on her school. Her classes are lecture/demonstration and are limited to 10 students.

Brochure available   Fees: moderate

Judith Bell's Cooking Kitchen

3940 West 50th Street
Minneapolis, Minnesota 55424
612/926-7262

My cooking school, Judith Bell's Cooking Kitchen, Minneapolis, may sometimes seem like a three-ring circus. But behind this ambiance and fun, there is professional commitment to excellent teaching on various levels of French, Italian, Chinese, and American cuisines.

The teaching staff must not only have solid credentials and experience, but must also be able to speak to the needs of students and teach accordingly. We often feel we are teaching as much self-confidence as we are teaching solid classic cooking techniques. Without self-confidence it seems difficult for students to have the courage to venture beyond basic cooking, but with confidence and experience they can really enjoy cooking.

My culinary credentials rest on 16 years as a home economist. A home economics-journalism graduate, I was for seven years a staff writer about foods for metropolitan newspapers in Chicago and Minneapolis. My cooking school began in my home five years ago and moved to its present location three years later. I have studied cooking in France with Simone "Simca" Beck and attended classes with James Beard and Phillip Brown, at the Cordon Bleu, London, the Cordon Bleu, Paris, and at La Varenne.

Sharon Lane, my associate, attended Cordon Bleu, Paris, and has the advanced diploma from La Varenne. She lived in Milan, Italy, for four years and in Geneva, Switzerland, for two years. Between her European travels, Sharon had her own cooking school in Sudbury, Massachusetts.

Catherine Kunkle, an instructor at the school, has studied Oriental cooking for 16 years. She has taken intensive classes with Madame Grace Chu and Karen Lee. Diana Denecke, a home economist with 20 years' experience, specializes in herb cookery and teaches the cultivation and culinary uses of herbs.

Almost all classes at the school are total participation and are limited to eight students. When there are demonstration classes, they are limited to 15 students. In addition to the regular teaching staff, local chefs and visiting celebrity cooks also occasionally hold classes. We sponsor cooking-school study trips to France and Italy a well as local shopping trips to ethnic markets and cookware shops.

The school's home is within Mutschler Kitchens of Minneapolis, a kitchen design and remodeling business in which I serve as a kitchen designer.

Brochure available   Fees: moderate

Marvel Chong's Cantonese Cooking School

75 West Island Avenue
Minneapolis, Minnestoa 55401
612/379-2335

Marvel Chong has been teaching Chinese cooking at the International House of Foods in Minneapolis for 19 years. Both Marvel and her husband Stanley, who also teaches at the school, are graduate food technologists. They were pioneers in the freezing of Chinese foods.

Emphasis at their school is on Cantonese-style cooking, but classes are also given in Indonesian, Japanese, and Filipino cuisines.

The Chongs are importers of foods from 35 countries. They have been conducting "person-to-person programs of learning about other countries through the medium of a universal subject—food" for many years. They lead popular tours to the Orient.

Classes at Marvel Chong's school are limited participation and demonstration. The school can arrange classes for groups of up to 50 persons.

Brochure available   Fees: low

Elizabeth B. Germaine Cookery Demonstrations

2945 Torchwood Drive
New Brighton, Minnesota 55112
612/636-5750

To broaden her students' knowledge of the cuisines of the world and to prepare and serve meals a hostess is proud of are the aims of Elizabeth Germaine, who recently started cooking classes in her suburban Minnesota home.

A native of Australia, Elizabeth has a broad food background that includes diplomas in Italian and French cooking from the Cordon Bleu in London, study at Invergowrie Homecraft Hostel in Melbourne, managing a restaurant at a ski resort, and being a household manager at the Women's College of Sydney University, Australia. She was the cookery editor for the Paul Hamlyn Publishing Company in Australia, and is the author of four cookbooks including one especially for children.

Elizabeth's demonstrations last for two-and-a-half hours, after which the students dine on the results. Class size is limited to 12 students. In addition to her regular classes, Elizabeth also designs classes based on student requests.

No brochure available   Fees: moderate

Kitchen Klutter

113 West Argonne
Kirkwood, Missouri 63122
314/822-0666

"I guess we teach just about everything," says John Sutter, co-owner with Nanette

White of Kitchen Klutter, Kirkwood.

The "everything" John refers to includes French and Italian cuisines, candymaking, cake decorating, breads, and cooking for children ages five to seven and eight to 11. The school also offers a one-hour Lunch and Learn demonstration. Lecture classes at Kitchen Klutter are limited to 20, and participation classes are limited to 10 students.

Instructors at the school include home economists, executive chefs from the area, and visiting celebrity chefs.

"We want to give people the confidence to do good cooking—and to help them know good food," John says.

Kitchen Klutter does not offer concentrated classes, but will help with accommodations for visiting students. The school is associated with a cookware shop.

Brochure available   Fees: low

THE PAMPERED PANTRY
8139 Maryland Avenue
St. Louis, Missouri 63105
314/721-1617

Mix a full measure of professional instructors with a nice blend of classic and contemporary cooking classes and you have The Pampered Pantry, a six-year-old St. Louis cooking school.

Owner/director Marie Mosher feels "blessed" with the teaching talent she has been able to assemble at her school. Her staff includes Jean Pierre Auge, second chef to the Duke and Duchess of Windsor and now chef at a private residence; Andre Gotti, French-trained and now executive chef at a St. Louis country club; Tony Bommarito, co-owner of an award winning Italian restaurant; Carol Zieman, home economist; and Susan Katzman, cookbook author.

In addition to the regular staff, other chefs and cooking specialists come to demonstrate at the school. And on Saturdays, various instructors and local food specialists give free demonstrations.

The Pampered Pantry has sponsored cooking study trips to France and Italy. The school is associated with a cookware shop of the same name.

Brochure available   Fees: moderate-high

Everything Microwave
340 Northland Boulevard
Cincinnati, Ohio 45246
513/771-4935

All aspects of microwave cooking are covered in a basic series of six lecture/demonstration lessons at Everything Microwave. Other classes, including seasonal lessons for junior cooks, classes in international cuisines, and lessons for "waist watchers," are also offered.

Pauline Dunn, Everything Microwave's owner, is a home economist with several years' experience in microwave work. She says, "Our basic series is designed to teach microwave oven owners how to achieve the full potential of their ovens—and to teach the microwave's limitations as well."

The school is part of a retail shop which handles microwave ovens and accessories. Everything Microwave tests all of the accessories it sells, and those who purchase from the store may call "Micro Line" for answers to microwave cooking problems and questions.

Brochure available   Fees: low

HURRAH!
Kitchen Shop and Cooking School

8008 Hosbrook Road
Cincinnati, Ohio 45236
513/793-5575

A carefully measured balance of classical techniques and attention to various food groups (breads, desserts) and cooking problems (quantity or do-ahead cooking) is good reason for the enthusiasm at Hurrah! Cooking School in Cincinnati.

Jane Miller, the school's owner, is a home economist who has attended the Cordon Bleu and La Varenne in Paris. Carol Robinson, director of the school, holds a certificate from L'Academie Maxim, Paris. Other instructors at Hurrah! include Marilyn Harris, a home economist with a degree from the Cordon Bleu in London; Dora Ang, who has completed several cooking programs in the Orient; Melanie Barnard, a home economist; and William Matthews, who is self-taught.

As part of the "oldest and largest" kitchenware shop in Cincinnati, this school offers a flexible schedule of classes and occasionally features celebrity cooks and local chefs. Classes are lecture/demonstration with a maximum of 20 students. Oriental, Creole, French, Italian, and Mexican cuisines are represented at Hurrah!

Brochure available   Fees: moderate

La Belle Pomme
1412 Presidential Drive
Columbus, Ohio 43212
614/488-3898

The repertoire of classes at "La Belle Pomme, a school for creative cooking" is a bountiful blend of sessions on European cuisines and unusual specialty and seasonal classes.

Betty Rosbottom, owner/director, studied with a former instructor of London's Cordon Bleu, Jacques Pepin, and has attended classes at La Varenne in Paris. She speaks French fluently and has spent several summers living in France.

"At La Belle Pomme," Betty says, "we try to teach techniques of fine cooking emphasizing French cuisine, but also including European and Chinese techniques. At the same time we encourage culinary creativity in our students by teaching them to cook and create rather than just follow recipes. We also emphasize the attractive presentation of foods.''

Most classes at this school are limited to 10 or 12 persons. The prevailing format is lecture/demonstration, but there is limited participation in some classes. Teachers include the owner/director and her staff, local guest instructors, and celebrity guests who come to teach at La Belle Pomme. Arrangements for special classes for groups of out-of-town students will be made. The school also sponsors cooking tours to France.

La Belle Pomme is associated with a cookware shop, but it is, according to its director, "primarily a school."

Brochure available   Fees: moderate-high

A Matter of Taste
92 West Fifth Avenue
Columbus, Ohio 43201
619/299-1714
619/294-0452

In a handsome restored home near Victorian Village in Columbus, Ohio, Lisa Galat has created a European style cooking school in conjunction with an intimate restaurant and imported wine shop. All deserve the attention of serious cooks.

A Matter of Taste cooking school offers in-depth full participation classes that are limited to 12 students. The cuisines of France, Italy, Germany, Greece, Austria, Hungary, Spain, Morocco, Russia, and Switzerland are studied. Seasonal specialty classes are also offered. Most sessions run from three to four hours in length.

Lisa Galat, the owner/director and teacher of most of the classes at A Matter of Taste, has an impressive professional background. It includes 12 years living abroad, study in restaurants in Italy, France, and Germany, and classes at the Cordon Bleu and La Varenne in Paris. She has also studied privately with Camille Cadier in Paris and Princess Marie Blanche de Broglie in Normandy.

Every year this school sponsors a series of lessons by Camille Cadier, former assistant to Simone Beck and Julia Child, who now teaches cooking in Paris. If requested, the school will make hotel and travel arrangements for out-of-town students. A Matter of Taste also offers cooking tours to France twice each year.

The small, 38-seat restaurant connected with this school serves fixed menu dinners and a la carte luncheons. A different menu is featured each week.

Brochure available   Fees: moderate

zona spray
cooking
school

140 North Main Street
Hudson, Ohio 44236
216/653-9727

An unusual and systematic approach to cooking is apparent at the Zona Spray Cooking School in Hudson, Ohio. This approach reflects the philosophy of owner/director Zona Spray, who states: "Cooking is a logical body of knowledge simplified by 'methods.' All recipes can be categorized by method; once a method is mastered, every recipe that uses that particular method will be perfectly and easily executed. Therein lie the seed of creation and the basic premise of my school."

Students at the Zona Spray Cooking School can select from eight different categories of classes. Within each category there is a combination of lecture/demonstration sessions of two hours and participation lessons, which are from three to five hours long. Some unusual classes include a basic category called Kitchen Techniques, to which the students bring pots, pans, and main ingredients and take the finished product home. In other classes, for an additional fee, students may invite non-cooking guests to enjoy the meal they have prepared.

The Zona Spray Cooking School also offers classes in nutrition "for those who want to feed the family better but don't know where to start," cake decorating, and a chef's series taught by visiting professionals.

Zona Spray has studied intensively at La Varenne, Paris; at Dumas Pere L'Ecole de la Cuisine Francaise, Chicago; and at the Antoinette Pope Cooking School in Kent, Ohio. She has taught in Toronto and in Kent, Ohio, and is currently a visiting staff instructor at the Culinarian School of Cuisine in Toledo and at Brandeis University. Other permanent instructors at the school are home economists with extensive professional experience.

Brochure available

Fees: moderate

Iris Bailin Cooking School
18405 Van Aken Boulevard
Shaker Heights
Cleveland, Ohio 44122
216/921-5267

"I do not believe in teaching recipes; I teach techniques," says Iris Bailin, owner of Iris Bailin Cooking School in Shaker Heights. Iris says she strives to "impart an understanding of basic principles, regardless of the specific dishes involved."

At her in-home school Iris focuses on Chinese and regional Italian cooking. Classes are lecture/demonstration with limited participation and have a maximum of eight students.

Iris studied with Kathryn Moy in Washington, D.C., and with Marcella Hazan in Bologna, Italy. She has been a menu consultant to a catering firm and is a free-lance food writer for *Cleveland Magazine*.

No brochure available

Fees: moderate-high

La Cuisinique School of Cookery

20696 South Woodland Road
Shaker Heights, Ohio 44122
216/751-7026

"There's no such thing as a difficult recipe," says Shirley C. Fernberg, owner/director of La Cuisinique School of Cookery in Shaker Heights. "It is the mark of a good teacher to simplify the complex and explain the flourishes," she adds.

Shirley, a home economist, knows about teaching. She has a secondary teaching certificate and a master's degree in counseling. She is also a registered and licensed occupational therapist, has a degree in marketing and management, and has done doctoral work in organizational behavior and changes.

Shirley has taken graduate nutrition courses and has a certificate from the Cordon Bleu, Paris. She has taken several courses with Madame Grace Chu, New York City, and with other teachers, including Theresa Cheng. She has attended classes at the Culinary Institute of America. Shirley writes and edits *Phancy Fixins*, a food-related newsletter, and is known also as "Phancy, the Gourmet Clown."

At present, Shirley says, she has classes "by request only." Her repertoire is extensive and includes French, Chinese, Italian, Greek, Spanish, Mexican, Jewish, Japanese, Scandinavian, and other ethnic cuisines.

No brochure available   Fees: high

Jill Heavenrich Cooking School

2443 North Wahl Avenue
Milwaukee, Wisconsin 53211
414/961-0213

"My philosophy is to take the fear out of cooking and put the joy into it," says Jill Heavenrich, owner/director of the Jill Heavenrich Cooking School in Milwaukee.

Jill studied for three years with Madam Kuony in Fond du Lac, Wisconsin, and has attended classes with Marcella Hazan in Bologna, Italy, and with Jacques Pepin and Alma Lach in Chicago.

Classes at Jill's school focus on Franco-Italian cuisine but include some specialty offerings as well. Participation classes are limited to eight persons; lecture/demonstration classes are limited to 20.

"I teach techniques and organization that enable people to cook seasonally and cook ahead. I try to expand their horizons on every aspect of food—buying, tasting, using fresh ingredients, smelling, touching, enjoying," she says.

No brochure available   Fees: high

Wholistic Nutrition Center

3902 North Mayfair Road
Milwaukee, Wisconsin 53222
414/463-1707

Preparation of natural foods is the focus of the Wholistic Nutrition Center, which is owned and directed by Karen Walker and James Ehmke. Karen has a master's degree in nutritional sciences, is a registered dietitian, and was formerly a nutrition instructor at the University of Wisconsin, Milwaukee. James is a certified nutrition consultant and a graduate of Dr. William Donald Kelley's nutritional academy. Roger Ullenberg, who was co-owner and head chef of Au Naturel, a natural foods restaurant, joins Karen and James in teaching at the Wholistic Nutrition Center.

The school offers one six-week-long lecture/demonstration course, The Art of Natural Food Cookery and the Science of Nutrition. Each class is limited to 15 students. The staff also provides individual nutrition evaluations and counseling.

Brochure available   Fees: moderate

Western States

The Lillian Haines School of Culinary Arts
P.O. Box 5248
Beverly Hills, California 90210
213/271-9173

"Good food, well prepared and beautifully served—something for everybody," is the guiding philosophy of The Lillian Haines School of Culinary Arts in Beverly Hills.

Lillian Haines, the owner/director, is a Certified Executive Chef, a member of the American Academy of Chefs, and since 1957 has been the owner and chef of Haines Catering, a firm established in 1930. She was trained both in the United States and in France and holds a lifetime teaching certificate from the state of California. All other instructors at the school are also professional chefs.

The school offers a variety of classes during the day and evening and on weekends. Cook-ins are held Friday through Sunday evenings, and there are week-long workshops as well. Both are especially suitable for out-of-town students. The workshops are limited to six students, the participation classes to 10 students, and the demonstrations to a maximum of 20 students.

With advance notice the school will help with travel arrangements.

Brochure available   Fees: high

Microwave Cooking Center
17728 Marcello Place
Encino, California 91316
213/987-1701

Now in its twelfth year of business, the Microwave Cooking Center has probably been teaching microwave cooking longer than almost any other school.

Thelma Pressman, owner/director, has an extensive professional background with appliance manufacturers. She was supervisor of the test kitchen at Waste King Corp., was on the staff at Amana when the first countertop Amana microwave oven was introduced, and has been very active in consumer education for microwave cooking.

The Microwave Cooking Center offers a full range of classes including basic, advanced, and international diet series as well as a class for children. The school also has workshops and training sessions for professionals. All regular classes are lecture/demonstration with a maximum of 25 students.

Thelma has developed and marketed a line of microwave "Cook and Serve" ware and will soon publish a microwave cookbook. In January of 1979 she was appointed Microwave Editor of *Bon Appetit* magazine.

"It is our intention," Thelma says, "to make every student an expert in the art of microwave cookery. We have done this successfully for 12 years."

Brochure available   Fees: high

Walbert & Co.
17200 Ventura Boulevard
Encino, California 91316
213/789-7508
213/990-5761

"Many of our classes are designed to give confidence to the novice cook," says Rosemary Walbert, owner/director of Walbert & Co., Encino. "We want to make our students feel confident enough to express themselves in different ways," she continues.

The school offers a variety of cuisines including French, Italian, Chinese, and Mexican, and specialty classes on brunches, souffles, microwave cooking, food processor cooking, and omelets.

Instructors at the school include Thelma Pressman, a nationally known expert on microwave cooking; Monique Truong Miller, a native of Saigon who has lived in France; Grayce Flanagan, a "self-taught specialist in cooking with the food processor;" and Evelyn Nelson, who has studied with Simone Beck and Camille Cadier in France. Ray Marshall, a restaurateur who received the 1978 Chef of the Year award from the National Restaurant Association, teaches Mexican cooking at the school. He is the founder and executive chef of the Los Arcos/Acapulco restaurants.

Most classes at Walbert & Co. are lecture/demonstration with a maximum of 20 students.

Brochure available   Fees: moderate

The Cupboard
Felicita Village
330 West Felicita Avenue
Escondido, California 92025
714/743-0421

A cooking school is an unusual birthday present, but The Cupboard in Escondido was a gift that Marian Seifert, owner/director, gave to herself for her 40th birthday. Marian notes that the idea and the desire for a cooking school had been brewing for more than 10 years.

Marian, who has a doctorate in administration, has taken cooking classes and interned at several restaurants during the past decade. Although she continues her professional administrative consulting work both in this country and abroad, she does teach some classes at her school.

"We teach no-nonsense cooking to provide our students with elegant and wholesome fare for family and friends, but in such a way that they aren't slaves to the kitchen," Marian says.

In addition to her interest in good food, Marian is concerned with health issues. "Many students have potential weight or health problems so we try to present good food that is also nutritionally balanced." By preference, not doctor's orders, she cooks without salt and encourages her students to do the same.

The Cupboard's staff includes Tillie Clements, Leslie Williams, Irving Erdos, and Ray Thelen. Tillie, who specializes in Oriental cuisine, studied with Alice Hart and interned in restaurants. Leslie is a graduate of Madeleine Kamman's school. She teaches breadmaking and provincial French cooking. Irving is a "self-taught master," according to Marian, who teaches "grand desserts" and pasta. Ray, an international baking consultant, has baking clinics at The Cupboard. The school has 10 other cooks "on call" for specialty classes.

The Cupboard has a few concentrated classes for visiting students. It is associated with a cookware shop.

Brochure available   Fees: low

The Kitchen Emporium Cooking School

240 Main Street
Los Altos, California 94022
415/941-1670

A professional staff of 12 highly trained instructors and a wine merchant offer a combination of 35 different classes and 11 wine tastings at The Kitchen Emporium Cooking School, Los Altos.

Arlene Brennan, director and co-owner with her husband, Mark Day, has a bachelor's degree in education, a master's degree in business administration, and the advanced diploma from La Varenne. She also attended classes at the Cordon Bleu, London. Arlene teaches most of the pastry and dessert classes and some specialty classes.

Her staff includes Chef de Cuisine Arturo Lionetti, who is classically trained; Jane Hammond, who took comprehensive training at the Cordon Bleu, London; Veronica de Rose, author of *Good News Brown Bread;* Marcia Rigel, who has bachelor's and master's degrees in home economics and a specialty in microwave cooking; and Executive Chef Lillian Haines, the first woman to be awarded the prestigious Executive Chef's Certificate and who is now the third generation of her family to head Beverly Hills' oldest and most famous catering company. In addition to the regular staff, guest instructors often come to the school to present their specialties.

The school offers a bounty of series classes focusing on the cuisines of France and Italy and many specialty classes on boning, garnishing, pastry, croissants, and hors d'oeuvres. Some of the school's more unusual classes include How to Cater Your Own Party and Low Cholesterol Cookery.

At The Kitchen Emporium classes are both lecture/demonstration and participation. In the participation classes the maximum number of students varies from eight to 12, depending on the subject.

The school is associated with a cookware shop of the same name.

Brochure available   Fees: moderate

THE VON WELANETZ
COOKING WORKSHOP

The Cookstore
8634 Sunset Boulevard
Los Angeles, California 90069
213/657-1555

A Parisian courtship that blossomed into marriage and then into dual careers in the food world is the happy story of Paul and Diana von Welanetz, who team-teach in their own school, The Von Welanetz Cooking Workshop, at a gourmet shop in Los Angeles.

It all began once upon a time when Diana was studying at the Cordon Bleu in Paris. She met Paul. They courted and married. At the time Paul was an architect, but because he liked to be with Diana, who liked to cook, he soon found that he, too, loved food.

After Cordon Bleu, Diana studied privately for five years with a chef in Los Angeles. She started teaching 10 years ago. In the meantime, Paul became more and more interested in cooking. It became apparent that although his training was in architecture, his natural vocation was food. In 1976 Paul and Diana wrote their first book, *The Pleasure of Your Company* (Atheneum). Since then they have written two more books, *With Love from Your Kitchen* and *The Art of Buffet Entertaining,* both published by Tarcher-St. Martin. The latter book is now in its second printing.

As in all good partnerships, the von Welanetz' each have a specialty. Diana says she began with a more serious interest in the taste of food; Paul, with his design training, was more interested in the aesthetics—how food looks. Now they have a merged philosophy that represents their combined interests: "Food that is beautiful, done ahead, free of hassles, tastes good—and shows flair."

Their classes run the gamut from Fabulous Fish and Seafood to Great Looking Cooking. Included in the ever-changing schedule of classes are ethnic and specialty classes for which Diana and Paul engage local professional teachers. Alice M. Hart, who holds the grande diplome of the Cordon Bleu, Paris, is a regular instructor.

Diana and Paul's lecture/demonstration classes are limited to 25 students; participation classes are for a maximum of eight. The school offers a five-day crash course for the convenience of out-of-town students. Lodging accommodations are made at the Continental Hyatt, Los Angeles. The school also sponsors cooking-related travel, including cruises and a trip to Hawaii.

Brochure available   Fees: moderate-high

The Gourmet School of Cooking
3915 Carnavon Way
Los Angeles, California 90027
213/666-5080

"Complicated dishes are just sets of easy steps put together." With this statement Judythe Roberts begins to make students feel at ease at her school, The Gourmet School of Cooking, Los Angeles. Judythe encourages her students to allow themselves to be creative, to learn to love food, and above all, to have fun in the kitchen.

At Judythe's in-home school she offers eight different series of classes based on her students' needs. She teaches "unique and unusual, but not taxing, recipes that will fit into their lifestyles." Her classes are participation and are limited to 12 students.

Judythe, who has been teaching for seven years, is a second-generation graduate of the Cordon Bleu, Paris. She traveled "all over the world," accompanying her husband, who was on a Fulbright scholarship. Judythe was an English major at Wellesley, and worked in the education departments of the St. Louis Museum and the Fogg Museum in Cambridge, Massachusetts.

The school has sponsored trips to France and has plans for cooking-study trips to Scandinavia and Italy, although Judythe feels that "there is as much or more to learn in America. The trips are great fun, but it's no longer necessary to go to Europe to learn cooking. We've come to the point, in this country, where classes and schools are available to suit any purpose."

Brochure available   Fees: low

568 San Fernando Road
Los Angeles, California 90065
213/225-2491 (ext. 299)

Public service, public relations, and product promotion are neatly teamed at Lawry's California Center. Here Lawry's Foods, Inc., has day and evening demonstration classes that often star actors and well known cooking teachers as well as the company's own staff of home economists.

The program is supervised by Vicki Vance and Elvie Wilkinson, both home economists who have had chef's training and work in catering.

Lawry's also has demonstration-dining classes where students watch a cooking demonstration and then stay on for lunch or dinner.

Brochure available   Fees: low

 **10988 West Pico Boulevard**
Los Angeles, California 90064
213/474-3113

"We're very pragmatic," says Shirley Cytron-Corden, owner of the Microwave Oven Workshop, Los Angeles. "We teach the students to meet their individual needs. The future teacher, the housewife, the professional, and the working person—each is taught how to use the appliance (microwave) so it will fit into his or her lifestyle."

The school offers a basic course and two specialty classes, low calorie cooking and ethnic cooking with the microwave. The classes are lecture/demonstration and are limited to 20 students.

Shirley has owned and operated a restaurant, a gourmet cooking school, and a cookware shop. She is an accredited teacher and has a theater and catering background. She has over 20 years' experience in the food world.

The Microwave Oven Workshop will arrange special classes for out-of-town students as time permits.

The school is associated with a shop that sells microwave ovens and microwave oven accessories.

Brochure available   Fees: moderate

317 Montclair Road
Los Gatos, California 95030
408/354-4677

At Mary Kathryn's Gourmet Kitchen in Los Gatos, the focus is on teaching "basic techniques of cooking with emphasis on the 'hows and whys' that make those techniques work correctly," says Mary Kathryn Genova, owner/director.

Mary Kathryn was a school teacher before she started her cooking school three years ago. She has studied with Rick O'Connell, Jack Lirio, Josephine Araldo, Jacques Pepin, Richard Grausman, and James Beard, all in San Francisco.

She also took a two-week course from Madame Kuony in Fond du Lac, Wisconsin, and has been a private cook for a family in California.

Mary Kathryn's class schedule includes a course in contemporary entertaining, which is designed to teach techniques with time-saving steps, and a French and International series as well as several specialty classes. Her classes are lecture/demonstration and are limited to 15 students.

In addition to teaching in her home, Mary Kathryn teaches identical classes in a cookware shop in Oakridge Mall, San Jose. The shop will provide care for the children of her students during class sessions.

Brochure available   Fees: moderate

inner gourmet

691 La Loma Road
Pasadena, California 91105
213/441-2075

Inner Gourmet Cooking Classes are taught in the turn-of-the-century Pasadena homes of Susan Kranwinkle and Peg Rahn. After each class session lunch is served in the garden.

Both Susan and Peg have taken classes at the Cordon Bleu and La Varenne in Paris and have studied privately with Simone Beck. The cooking twosome is often featured on a television show, AM Los Angeles, and on a CBS radio show, Meet the Cook.

The school's schedule lists an interesting mix of specialty and series classes including one entitled Chocolate Day, a barbecue class for men, a bread and sausage class, and another entitled Truffles and Flourishes. Classes are participation and are limited to 14 students each. In addition to the regular classes, the school has sponsored cooking demonstrations by such notables as Simone Beck, Diana Kennedy, Michael James, and Luciano Parolari, an Italian hotel chef. The school has also sponsored cooking-study trips to France.

Susan and Peg say, "We really try to teach confidence in the kitchen to make cooking and entertaining fun and easy without sacrificing good taste."

Brochure available   Fees: moderate

Charlotte Combe Cooking School
959 Woodside Road
Redwood City, California 94061
415/365-0548

With a certificate of apprenticeship from Jacques Pepin and a 13-year career in catering and teaching, Scottish-born Charlotte Combe started her cooking school in Redwood City two years ago.

"I have worked with Jacques for five years, often for two or three months at a time. He gave me the certificate, the only one he has ever given anyone," Charlotte says. She has also assisted Jack Lirio and Marcella Hazan.

About her school, Charlotte says, "We think good cooking is simple. We take the fear out of it. What we teach not only works, it works well. This gives the students encouragement and they keep coming back."

They may also come back for another reason—Jacques Pepin. This is the only school to which he comes for an extended period of time. "I guess it is more or less his home base," Charlotte says, and adds that his mother, Madame Jeanette Pepin, comes to the school to teach, too.

International cuisine with a special nod toward French food is the primary focus of classes at the school, although Charlotte also teaches the foods of Britain. Classes at the school are lecture/demonstration and are limited to 24 students each. Classes for out-of-town students are available by special arrangement.

Brochure available   Fees: high

William Glen

2651 El Paseo Lane
Sacramento, California 95821
916/483-2935

Spacious facilities, celebrity cooks, a staff of 11 instructors, and a challenging variety of classes make an interesting blend at the William Glen Cooking School in Sacramento. According to Mary Jane Drinkwater, director, the school has demonstration/lecture facilities to accommodate 50 persons, series classes for up to 24 students, and participation classes for a maximum of 12 to 15 students.

The teachers on the William Glen staff have a wide variety of professional experiences. Mary Jane, a certified teacher, has taken short courses at La Varenne and with Jacques Pepin and Marc Menot. David Berkley, a wine merchant, is a candidate for Master of Wine in England. Biba Caggiano trained in Bologna, Italy.

Jean-Luc Chassereau, who was apprenticed in France at the age of 14, worked at Cafe de la Paix and Maxim's in Paris, at Claridges in London, and at Le Trianon in San Francisco. Vincent Mandella has a degree in economics and worked in restaurants in France. Alice Medrich has a master's degree in business administration and studied privately at LeNotre. She has a shop called "Chocolat."

Paulette Soulier trained in France and is on the University of California (Davis) faculty. Man Tat Yan apprenticed in Chinese restaurants and has a master's degree in food technology. Gino Zepponi has a degree in chemical engineering, is co-owner of ZD Winery, Sonoma, and is director of operations for Domaine Chandon in the Napa Valley.

Diane Dexter has the grande diplome from the Cordon Bleu and is a chef at Berkley's Inn Seasons restaurant. Evie Lieb, the school's "happy cooker," is a self-taught specialist in bread baking. In addition, the school recently hosted celebrity cooks Jack Lirio, Paula Wolfert, Diana Kennedy, Marcella Hazan, and Maurice Moore-Betty.

Cuisines offered at the school include French, Italian, and Chinese. Specialty classes are also offered in pastry, wines, patés, and hors d'oeuvres. The school has special concentrated classes for visiting students. It is associated with a cookware shop.

Brochure available   Fees: moderate

antonia allegra griffin

6845 Condon Drive
San Diego, California 92122
714/452-9427

Although French and Italian cuisines are the focal point of the Antonia Allegra Griffin School of Cooking in San Diego, the school's repertoire includes classes in catering, charcuterie (sausage-making), pastries and desserts, as well as a class for senior citizens on cooking and eating well on a budget.

Antonia "Toni" Griffin, the school's owner/director, has had intensive culinary training in the United States and abroad. She studied with Madame Suzanne Bergeaud, French author and restaurateur; attended advanced classes at La Varenne, Paris; did pastry work at the Cordon Bleu, Paris; took classes at LeNotre's School of Pastry, Paris; and is a member of "Les Gourmettes," a food society in Paris. She lived near Paris for two years and is fluent in both French and Italian.

At her in-home school, Toni has lecture/demonstration classes that are limited to 15 persons. She also teaches at Tambo de Oro, a private restaurant-club, with Chef Rinse Jan deKoning and leads tours to San Francisco for gourmet food shopping.

No brochure available   Fees: moderate

Gibson Girl, The American School of International Cuisine
University Towne Center
4405 La Jolla Village Drive
San Diego, California 92122
714/455-6255

The Gibson Girl motto, "You know you can do it because you've done it," reflects the school's commitment to total participation classes. "We have complete cooking facilities for 24 students," says Karen Gibson, owner/director of the school. Karen's husband is a cousin of Charles Dana Gibson, the famous artist of the early years of this century whose avant-garde Gibson Girl is a celebrated part of American art.

Karen, who taught cooking in her home for nine years, has worked in the restaurant business for nine years and holds the elementary certificate from the Cordon Bleu, Paris. She attended classes at La Varenne and studied cake decorating at the Wilton School in Chicago. She is the author of *The Symphony Cookbook,* published by the American Symphony Orchestra League, and toured the country for two years doing promotion for the book.

Karen's staff includes Willy Hauser, executive chef at La Costa Spa; Andre Mena, chef of Arnaud's in New Orleans, who comes to Gibson Girl to teach each month; and Roger Jones, executive chef of Little America restaurants.

The school has three in-depth series classes in French cuisine for which it awards copper, silver, and gold certificates. The Gibson Girl also offers Oriental, Moroccan, Scandinavian, country French, and local American specialties. Another featured class is a weekly restaurant series taught by local chefs.

The Gibson Girl school offers concentrated classes for out-of-town students during the summer and in January, and will assist visiting students with travel accommodations. The school also sponsors travel-study trips to New Orleans.

Brochure available   Fees: low

THE PERFECT PAN
™

4040 Goldfinch Street
San Diego, California 92103
714/299-8442

Perfection is the implied goal of The Perfect Pan School of Gourmet Cooking in San Diego. The school's 22-page brochure is almost overwhelming. Be it basic or esoteric, taught by world-famous celebrity cooks, local ethnic specialists, or the Perfect Pan's own staff, almost everything can be found at this school.

A list of recent guest stars is dazzling: Anne Willan (director of La Varenne, Paris), John Clancy, Diana Kennedy, Marcella Hazan, Giuliano Bugialli, Biba Caggiano, Josephine Gatan, Jacques Pepin, Maurice Moore-Betty, Paula Wolfert, Katie Milhiser, and Princess Marie-Blanche de Broglie. Wow, and wow again!

The Perfect Pan holds classes in two locations, one in San Diego's Mission Hills and one in Del Mar. In addition to classes with the visiting teachers, the school offers many in-depth classes including a 17-week course, The Fundamentals of Good Cooking. Graduates of this course receive the school's Premier Diplome.

There are also specialty classes of diverse appeal: Feeding the Long Distance Runner, Vegetarian Gourmet Cooking, Preserving for Beginners, Wines of a King on the Budget of a Pauper, Goodies from a Russian Easter Feast, Gluttony without Tears (a dieter's class), and many more.

All of the cooking classes are under the guidance of Anne Otterson, director of the school. Anne's professional background began with a degree in physical chemistry. She received a Fulbright scholarship to Tubingen and Munich, Germany. She says she has "always loved to cook," so she chose a culinary career. She studied with James Beard, Julie Dannenbaum, Jacques Pepin, and has three specialty certificates from La Varenne. In addition she has had the opportunity to "learn on the job" as she assists all of the celebrity cooks the school has hosted during its three years in business.

There are too many regular instructors at The Perfect Pan to mention each individually. Suffice it to say that all are well trained professionals or outstanding local cooks with ethnic specialties.

The Perfect Pan's classes are primarily demonstration and are limited to 20 students. As for cooking-study tours, the school has offered "Ski and Cook" trips, provincial tours of France and Mexico, and local shopping tours including one to Tijuana.

According to George Munger, the school's owner, there will soon be a third Perfect Pan School, to be opened at an undisclosed location. Most classes at the Del Mar location are held during the day; classes at Mission Hills are held during the day, evening, and on Saturday.

Ann Otterson says, "George is our backbone and nurturer of creativity." She gives him credit for many of the innovative ideas incorporated into the school.

The Perfect Pan serves lunch by reservation only. Sometimes reservations must be made four to six weeks in advance. Not surprisingly, many feel it's well worth the wait.

Brochure available   Fees: moderate-high

Malvi Doshi's Cooking Classes

180 Blake Street
San Francisco, California 94118
415/387-3782

Malvi Doshi, who has two master's degrees in political science, is also a veteran of 20 years of teaching Indian cooking in New York, India, and Kenya. She now holds classes in her San Francisco home, limiting each to three to five students.

Malvi says she is self-taught. "I have been cooking since the age of nine when I started rolling paper-thin chapatis. I have just finished writing a cookbook," she adds.

No brochure available   Fees: low

1802 Bush Street
San Francisco, California 94109
415/922-4603

At the Judith Ets-Hokin Culinary Institute in San Francisco, the founder and staff seem to have thought of everything. Not only can a person choose from a comprehensive curriculum of courses in French, Italian, and Viennese cuisines and specialty classes of many kinds (including three separate children's classes), but the school has introduced two unusual programs as well. One, a professional apprenticeship program, is a two-year course for students who intend to make cooking their career. The other is a complete correspondence course—"for those too busy or too far away to attend classes."

Judith Ets-Hokin, the owner/director of the school, has studied with Paul Mayer and Paul Quiaud in the United States, and has certificates from the Cordon Bleu in London and cooking schools in Dieppe, France, and Florence, Italy. She is the author of *San Francisco Dinner Party Cookbook,* published by Houghton Mifflin Company, and is currently preparing two new cookbooks for publication.

The school has a 10-member staff with impressive credentials and experience. One of the instructors founded her own cooking school in Vienna, Austria, in 1921; another has completed the London Cordon Bleu Intensive Advanced Course. Two student apprentices assist this large staff, which is trained in the "Judith Ets-Hokin philosophy and techniques." The school occasionally has prominent local restaurant chefs as guest instructors.

Classes at the Judith Ets-Hokin Culinary Institute are either lecture/demonstration or participation, when the subject—such as pastry or bread making—lends itself to this style of teaching. Demonstration classes are limited to 25, while participation classes are limited to 10 students.

"Our goal is to give the aspiring cook an opportunity to learn the methods and basic skills necessary to create interesting and exciting meals," says Judith Ets-Hokin. "No matter what the cuisine, we always conform to the highest standards of fine cookery. We use the freshest, best-quality ingredients available. We always use careful, thoughtful food preparation techniques and encourage the students to develop their creative abilities in preparing dishes that reflect their own personalities."

A week-long traveler's package—in which students can take up to nine classes at the Institute—is offered throughout the year except for the month of August. Out-of-town students can anticipate help in making hotel and travel arrangements.

The school is associated with a cookware store that handles food items, and also operates a catering service.

Brochure available   Fees: moderate

Maybelle Iribe

1913 Grant Avenue
San Francisco, California 94133
415/421-4164

After 20 years as a resident of Paris and the Loire, Provence, and Champagne areas of France, Maybelle Iribe brings a wealth of experience to her in-home cooking school in San Francisco.

Maybelle's professional training has been "from the great French chefs, male and female, that I have been privileged to know." She is a lecturer and author of cookbooks, including *Pates for Kings and Commoners, The San Francisco Cookbook,* and a new book about the cooking of New Orleans, which will be produced by a German publishing company.

"I have small, informal, attentive groups—not for beginners," Maybelle says. The classes are a combination of lecture/demonstration and participation and are limited to eight students.

Emphasis on "simplicity, the finest ingredients, the treasures of French country cuisine and French charcuterie" is the philosophy of the school.

No brochure available   Fees: high

The Great Chefs of France at the Robert Mondavi Winery

1496 Dolores Street
San Francisco, California 94110
415/648-0909

Michel Guerard is quoted in *House and Garden* magazine as saying, "There is no other cooking school with such style; it's like an elegant house party." The school that evoked such praise is none other than The Great Chefs of France at the Robert Mondavi Winery.

Michael James and Billy Cross, directors of the school, say their primary purpose is "to provide an intimate experience with some of the great food talent of the world." "And," Michael continues, "to bring people close to the source of the art in a way that is not possible even in France. When the chefs are in their kitchens, they are inaccessible. Here students can be in a small group right with the chef and truly learn."

To fulfill this purpose, over the past four years the school has brought to the Napa

Valley such notables as Guerard, Jean Troisgros, Roger Verge, Gaston LeNotre, and Simone Beck.

To call this a school is perhaps too narrow a definition. It is, in reality, a carefully orchestrated live-in experience that provides intense immersion in the world of fine food, a prime concern of the school's directors and the Robert Mondavi people. "The school is an attempt to preserve and record a quality of life that is vanishing from the world, even in France," Michael says. "Beautiful food, beautiful service—they're both almost endangered species."

The school is the direct result of the Robert Mondavi Winery's concern for the potential plight of fine food, and the winery's endowment more than matches the students' tuition. Even so, fees are high.

"But the high cost of attending this school," Michael says, "is an unfortunate by-product of the cost of quality, not an attempt by anyone to make it into anything snobbish. In fact, part of the rationale for establishing the school was to remove the mystique and false snobbery that exist not only toward food, but toward wine as well."

The secondary reason for founding the school was to bring the world's attention to the many fine wines produced in the Napa Valley. "I suppose we could have done this on a mass scale and that would have been less expensive, but everyone rejected that in favor of the opportunity for chefs and students to have close contact in an intimate and wonderful setting," Michael says.

Classes at the school are held for two, three, or five consecutive days. They are semi-participatory and are limited to 14 students.

In addition to the courses taught by visiting chefs, Michael teaches classes based on French cuisine. These are lecture/demonstrations and are limited to 30 students.

Michael is the protege of Simone "Simca" Beck, with whom he has worked and studied for seven years. He worked also at Fauchon's in Paris, in the kitchens at Jamin, and for LeNotre.

Billy's background includes professional theater training. He has been a drama instructor and has had a catering business.

Brochure available   Fees: high-high

2235 Greenwich Street
San Francisco, California 94123
415/931-4152

Cooking at La Grande Bouffe in San Francisco is both eclectic and versatile. Regular instructors come from varied backgrounds and teach dishes of many countries including Greece, Mexico, China, Japan, Morocco, India, and France. In addition, the school offers a host of specialty classes including a session on gifts from the kitchen, a crust workshop (pastry), and instruction in sauces and patés.

The owner and main instructor at La Grande Bouffe is Donna Nordin, who trained at the Cordon Bleu, Paris. She has demonstrated cooking in department stores, advertising agencies, and on television. She speaks French fluently, and is married to a native of Paris, Alain Efron, who occasionally teaches at the school.

Special events at La Grande Bouffe include seminars held by several prestigious master chefs from France. Other guest chefs are often those who have their own schools or restaurants. Most classes at the school are demonstration and are limited to 12 persons. Participation classes are limited to six persons.

"La Grande Bouffe is a creative cooking school designed to please gourmets and gourmands alike. There are no prerequisites," says Donna Nordin. "If you are willing, we will make you able. My intention is to provide students first with incentive for cooking, then excellent techniques, then use of the freshest ingredients in order to turn out well rounded and well presented meals."

La Grande Bouffe is associated with a cookware store of the same name. The school arranges cooking tours to France. A concentrated series of classes is available for out-of-town students, and help with hotel and travel arrangements can be provided by the school.

Brochure available   Fees: moderate-high

The Jack Lirio Cooking School

757 Monterey Boulevard
San Francisco, California 94127
415/587-8908

At the well established Jack Lirio Cooking School in San Francisco, students are presented with a tantalizing selection of classes throughout the year and a sumptuous concentration of classes in the summer.

Jack Lirio, the school's owner/director and only teacher, has a dazzling professional background and is recognized as one of the foremost cooking teachers in the United States. He studied intensively at the Cordon Bleu in Paris and later specialized at L'Ecole de Cuisine Gaston LeNotre near Versailles. He then pursued his interest in pastry by working as an apprentice in fine pastry shops in France. Jack's pastry course in San Francisco is 40 sessions long and includes almost every French and international pastry known, plus many of Jack's personal inventions. This class is considered by many to be the finest of its kind in the United States.

In 1973, Jack became interested in Chinese cooking. He studied the Mandarin dialect for two-and-a-half years, after which he lived in Taipei with a Chinese family, studying and cooking at Wei Chuan School and at Pei Mei's Cooking School. When he returned to San Francisco he began teaching Chinese cooking at his school.

In the program for regular classes the cuisine is "basically French but with international dishes now and then." These demonstration classes are limited and last for three hours.

Summer classes are full participation and are limited to five students. During these week-long classes, students are at the school from 10 until five every day. Before they come to the school, the students select from a list of more than 100 dishes those they would most like to prepare. When they are at the school, the students prepare more than 60 recipes. A highlight of the week's lessons is a gala buffet, which students prepare and to which they may each invite five or six guests. "These buffets," says Jack, "are spectacular."

The school will recommend a local travel agent to help with arrangements for out-of-town students.

Brochure available   Fees: high

Loni Kuhn's Cook's Tour
91 Commonwealth Avenue
San Francisco, California 94118
415/752-5265

"Everyone needs to eat, so cooking should be both fun and creative," says Loni Kuhn, a well known cook in San Francisco. Loni believes in "no ancient strictures—just in learning a few basics, then improvising intelligently."

Through her school, Loni Kuhn's Cook's Tour, she offers Italian, country French, Mexican, Middle Eastern, Moroccan, and Indian cuisines in full participation classes that are limited to eight students.

Loni's interest in cooking was initially pragmatic, but it had a touch of glamour. "I grew up with a mother who didn't like to cook and couldn't boil water. But we were blessed with a succession of wonderful cooks, Italian and Mexican women who taught me."

After growing up, Loni studied with native cooks all over America and Europe. She also studied for years with James Beard and Marcella Hazan. Currently Loni is food editor of *San Francisco* magazine and has done recipe and menu consulting for major manufacturers.

Loni teaches in her San Francisco home. She says that although she does not have special classes for out-of-town students, these can be easily arranged.

Brochure available   Fees: moderate

The Mandarin Salon de Cuisine
Ghirardelli Square
900 North Point
San Francisco, California 94109
415/673-8812

Madame Cecilia Chiang, founder and owner of the award-winning Mandarin Restaurants in San Francisco and Beverly Hills, is the author of a memoir-cookbook, *The Mandarin Way,* and the creator of an unusual cooking school, The Mandarin Salon de Cuisine.

Classes at this widely acclaimed school are available to groups only, with a maximum enrollment of 12 students. (Individuals wishing to attend a class are accommodated if space permits, but they must call or write the school in advance.) Neighborhood groups, members of fraternal orders, and delegates to conventions and meetings in San Francisco attend the school's Tuesday morning sessions, which are held at The Mandarin Restaurant in Ghirardelli Square.

The demonstration classes feature The Mandarin's chef, Tony Ming Chan, with Madame Chiang offering explanations of special techniques. Following the class, students enjoy a banquet luncheon.

"Our students learn quickly that chop suey is a dish invented by Americans," explains Madame Chiang. "Few have ever seen Beggar's Chicken baked in ceramic clay, duck smoked in tea leaves, or heard the history of these dishes. Each is unique and expressive of the artistic talent of old China."

The Mandarin's classes have been attended by Japanese, French, and Chinese chefs. Among those who have enrolled are Danny Kaye, James Beard, Jacques Pepin, and Marion Cunningham.

Brochure available   Fees: high

Tante Marie's Cooking School
271 Francisco Street
San Francisco, California 94133
415/771-8667

Tante Marie's Cooking School in San Francisco is growing, according to owner Mary Risley. "I've been giving small participation classes in my home for six years. This spring I am opening a separate school with two kitchens. We'll have a full-time teaching chef and guest instructors, too."

Courses at Tante Marie's Cooking School will vary in length from one week to nine months. The school will feature both lecture/demonstration and full participation classes. "We will emphasize the classical and simplified techniques of French cooking and will have guest speakers on a wide range of cooking-related topics," Mary says.

Before starting her cooking school Mary was an investment banker. She has studied cooking in San Francisco under Paul Mayer and has also taken short courses at the Cordon Bleu in London and at La Varenne in Paris. For several years Mary has done the cooking segments for The A.M. Show on an ABC-affiliated television station in San Francisco.

"Basically, we feel cooking is fun. You don't need fancy ingredients or gadgets, but a good basic knowledge of principles of cooking can help you become a good cook," concludes Mary as she expresses the philosophy of her school.

Brochure available   Fees: moderate-high

Paul Mayer Cooking School
740 Bay Street
San Francisco, California 94109
415/474-7221

Established in 1956, the Paul Mayer Cooking School may well be the oldest cooking school in San Francisco. His students "must be having a good time—they keep coming back," says Paul Mayer, owner/director. One group of students has been together for 11 years and has booked classes with Paul through 1981. They are not entirely unusual, however, since 75 per cent of his students return every year.

Paul and his assistant, A. David Stork, teach classes twice a day every week throughout the year. Paul then takes the summer off to "travel and collect recipes."

Students at the Paul Mayer Cooking School decide what they want to learn and Paul accommodates them. "The students have continual input. Each week we decide together what we will do the next week. There are too many recipes for me to choose for them," he says.

His students come "to learn—why else would they be here? But they also come to have a good time. And while we're having fun, they learn. I don't believe you have to be too rigid with people. I prefer to be flexible," Paul says.

Before his cooking career began, Paul planned to become a radio disk jockey. While he was in New York City preparing for his radio career, he took classes and received a diploma from Dione Lucas. "Cooking at that time was still a hobby. I guess I did have an eye to the future, but I wasn't sure if or how I could work into a career in food.

"Then Jim Beard came to my home for dinner and afterward encouraged me to pursue a career in food. Soon, I quit what I was doing and started teaching and catering on a small scale. And it just grew."

Paul left the New York area in 1956 and came to San Francisco to continue what he loves and knows, teaching cooking.

Classes at the Paul Mayer school are total participation and are limited to eight students. Although it does not have a set program of concentrated classes, the school will "try to accommodate visiting students."

No brochure available   Fees: moderate

Jean Brady Cooking School

680 Brooktree Road
Santa Monica, California 90402
213/454-4220

Jean Brady, owner/director of the Jean Brady Cooking School in Santa Monica, has cultivated a flair for food through her work as a technical consultant-food stylist to the Colombo television series, and as culinary consultant to The Pottery Barn Stores. She has been written about in major newspapers and national magazines. Her culinary studies include classes with Jacques Pepin, Julie Dannenbaum, and other notables.

At her school Jean offers a series of seven lessons, "mostly on French cuisine with a smattering of Italian, American, Greek, and Moroccan," in which she stresses "variation and creative license."

Classes are lecture/demonstration and are limited to 20 students. The school has sponsored study trips to France and New York.

No brochure available   Fees: moderate

1435 Main Street
Seal Beach, California 90740
213/430-2157

Impressive professional credentials and a spacious, well planned teaching kitchen are key elements of La Bonne Cuisine School of Culinary Arts in Seal Beach.

Margaret M. Dennis, the school's director, is both a home economist and a cooking professional. She has a degree in home economics from Queen Margaret College, Edinburgh, Scotland, with a specialty in classical French cooking. She also holds a diploma from the Cordon Bleu, London. In addition she has lived and traveled in several European countries, studying their cuisines, and has taught European and French cooking since 1961.

Guest instructors at the seven-year-old school are usually home economists or, for ethnic cooking classes, people with first-hand knowledge of the cuisine.

"We believe cooking is an art form," Margaret says. "At La Bonne Cuisine we stress good health through good nutrition and use only seasonal foods. Cooking is fun, whether for everyday or for entertaining," she concludes.

Most of the classes at La Bonne Cuisine are lecture/demonstration sessions that last for three hours and are limited to 15 persons. About half of the classes are in series continuing for four weeks; the rest are single sessions that focus on techniques.

Although the study of French cuisine, both classical and nouvelle, predominates at this school, there are also classes in European and Oriental cooking, low calorie foods, microwave cooking, and baking.

The school is not associated with a cookware store, but it does sell cookware to its students. It is affiliated with a wine store.

La Bonne Cuisine is willing to help with hotel and travel arrangements for out-of-town students.

Brochure available   Fees: high

Marlene Sorosky's
COOKING CENTER

18440 Burbank Boulevard
Tarzana, California 91356
213/345-4003

Marlene Sorosky's specialty is cooking for entertaining. In fact, she wrote a book about it: *Cooking for Entertaining* (HP Books), published in 1979. At her cooking school, Marlene Sorosky's Cooking Center, Tarzana, the focus is on advance preparation and complete meal planning so that every host and hostess can be guests at their own party.

"Cooking is a social experience," Marlene says. She encourages her students to feel that it can be both creative and fun. "My main emphasis is to help the student gain confidence not only in the theory and practice of cooking techniques, but in those aspects of cooking that make one feel more secure in the kitchen."

Classes at her school include creative menus for entertaining, pastry making, holiday gifts from the kitchen, low-calorie cooking, basic French techniques, breads, and fish cookery.

Marlene studied cooking for two years while she lived in France and has worked in restaurants and with chefs. She took a "crash course" with Madame Kuony in Wisconsin and has taken classes with Anne Willan, Jacques Pepin, Paula Wolfert, and John Clancy. She has assisted Julia Child in West Coast cooking demonstrations.

Classes at her school are mainly lecture/demonstration with a maximum of 24 students. Participation classes are limited to 10 students. The school sponsors cooking-study tours. It offers special concentrated classes for out-of-town students and will assist with travel accommodations.

The school is associated with a gourmet cookware shop.

Brochure available   Fees: moderate

Helen's Happy Thought

3338-B South Mooney Boulevard
Visalia, California 93277
209/733-4747

Midway between Los Angeles and San Francisco you'll find Visalia, the home of Helen's Happy Thought cooking school. "But look at the map before you start," advises Helen Harrell, owner/director of the three-year-old school.

At Helen's Happy Thought classes are primarily of one or two sessions, "because we've found it difficult for our students to attend series classes," she says.

The specialty classes offered include many that focus on cooking problems and basic techniques including pastry, food processor cooking, how to get your money's worth at the meat counter, sausage making, wok cooking, and microwave cooking.

Helen, a home economist, has been teaching at the secondary level and in adult education for 11 years. Sally Pace, an instructor at the school, is a home economics teacher who has specialized in microwave cooking. "We like to do things that make cooking easier. We think cooking should be fun. It is not necessarily confusing or complicated if you know the basic techniques," Helen says.

Classes at the school are lecture/demonstration and are limited to 15 students.

Brochure available   Fees: low

Marion Cunningham's Cooking Classes

1147 Northgate Road
Walnut Creek, California 94598
415/934-3332

Personal cooking that tastes good and looks beguiling and artless is the forte of Marion Cunningham, Walnut Creek.

"Personal cooking shows the flavor of an individual hand at work, and in my cooking and teaching I encourage the sharing of oneself more fully," Marion says. Marion, who has been teaching for 10 years, says in the past the biggest trouble she has seen with entertaining is "a misconception that entertaining should be impressive, rather than pleasing. But now I think the trend is more to making people comfortable in our homes with food that is welcoming and not in any way imposing. I often suggest a supper menu of three courses that is utterly simple so that the cook can relax, is happier and entertains more happily and freely."

Although not formally trained, Marion was entrusted with the revision of a classic American cookbook, *The Fannie Farmer Cookbook,* which took her four years of "loving, careful work." Her revision will be published in summer 1979 by Knopf. Marion says she has been cooking for over 40 years. During the last 12 years she has taken lessons from professionals and non-professionals here and in Europe. She is a West Coast associate of James Beard and has assisted and taught with him for four years.

Marion's classes are lecture/demonstration and are limited to 15 students. Classes are available for out-of-town students.

No brochure available   Fees: moderate-high

Peppercorn Gourmet Goods

& Cooking School, Inc.

2040 Broadway #100
Boulder, Colorado 80302
303/449-5847

Variety is the spice of life and there's plenty of variety in the classes at the Peppercorn Cooking School, Boulder. Lebanese cuisine, French pastry, vegetarian cooking, wok cookery, and desserts au naturel (without sugar) are but a few of the specialty classes offered. All classes are taught in the evening, are full participation, and are limited to 10 students.

Barbara David co-owner, is a home economist who has taught at the secondary school level. Her partner is Doris Houghland, who has been a restaurant manager and is writing a vegetarian cookbook. Other instructors at the school include Susan Aiello, who studied at the Kushi Institute in Boston; Bill Fore, chef at one of Boulder's finest restaurants; and Douglas Kouri, who is Lebanese and taught in Oregon before coming to Colorado.

Brochure available   Fees: low

World of Cuisine Cooking School

3095 South Trenton
Denver, Colorado 80231
303/751-4256

The World of Cuisine Cooking School is an integral part of a gourmet cooking club that features a members' store, special dinners, catering services, a foods boutique specializing in prepared gourmet foods to take home, and discounts at food-related businesses.

The cooking school part of this venture is directed by Marcia Fox, who has been a caterer for eight years. Marcia has studied in Italy, France, and New York. Most of the classes are taught by Marcia with "occasional guest instructors in certain specialty areas."

All classes at the school are participation only and are limited to eight to 10 students. The schedule lists several specialty classes as well as classes in the cooking of Provence, Mexican cooking, and Italian cuisine from Tuscany.

"Anyone can cook," Marcia says. "Everyone can learn new techniques. Beginners and cooks of 20 years' experience prepare food side by side. The rewards are great."

Brochure available   Fees: low-moderate
(club membership additional)

peppermill

Coeur D' Alene Mall Annex
Coeur D' Alene, Idaho 83814
208/664-2926

Described by its teachers as "a small school, in a small town," the Peppermill in Coeur D' Alene offers personalized classes in many topics, from using the microwave to French, Italian, and Chinese cooking. These courses are taught by five instructors, each with his or her own specialty.

The instructors' backgrounds are diverse. Two are caterers, one lived and taught in the Far East, another is a home economist who interned with *Sunset* magazine, one took an advanced class at La Varenne in Paris, and another studied the use of microwave cooking long before microwave ovens were available to the public.

One day each month the school offers a wine tasting class that is a six-course, six-wine dinner with a discussion of each wine as it is served. All classes are lecture/demonstration and are limited to 10 students.

The philosophy behind this school is that cooking is a natural activity that can be enhanced by love and sharing.

Brochure available   Fees: low

Creative Cooking Center

14631 S.E. McLoughlin
Milwaukie, Oregon 97222
503/653-5544

Microwave cooking from basics to specialties is the focal point of the Creative Cooking Center in Milwaukie. Owners Clare Acker and Darlene Yount have been associated with a major microwave distributor, teaching others how to demonstrate the microwave oven. Both have home economics training.

In addition to the basic microwave cooking class, the school offers instruction in cooking wild game, preparing Oriental and Mexican foods, and making candies with the microwave oven. The school also sells microwave accessories.

Brochure available   Fees: low

Greb's

5027 N.E. 42nd Street
Portland, Oregon 97218
503/284-7023
503/284-0083

"Quality, not quantity" is the motto at Greb's, a 10-year-old cooking school, kitchen accessory shop, and remodeling business in Portland and Gresham. The school offers "a small number of carefully selected courses taught by a small number of carefully selected culinary experts."

Manager Victoria Greb, the third generation of her family to be involved with the company, has studied with James Beard. Her staff includes Josef Kara, a graduate of the Culinary Institute of America, who is a chef and restaurateur. Marie Kuehnel, who takes annual trips to Italy to work with Marcella Hazan, is a resident instructor. Jenny Kim, a native of Canton, teaches 14 styles of Chinese cuisine. Wayne Quinnell is a teacher and chef. Virginia Israelit, a native of Texas, teaches Mexican cooking and other specialties. Tom Morris is a former wine steward and is said to "have tasted around the globe."

Classes at the school reflect the staff's interests and backgrounds, but include also special cook-and-picnic classes, tours to a local herb farm and vineyard, and classes in wine appreciation. All classes are full participation and are limited to six students.

Brochure available   Fees: low

14603 N.E. 20th Street
Bellevue, Washington 98007
206/641-4520

The sun may fade in the evening, but not the cooking activity at the Sunshine Kitchen Company, Bellevue. With more than 29 specialty classes and 17 series classes, cooking there might well be a round-the-clock phenomenon.

Some of the school's more unusual offerings include a 10-week professional chef's course and other classes with such intriguing titles as Strawberries, Strawberries, Strawberries; Entertaining on a Shoestring; and The Angling Gourmet. The school has two locations, one in Bellevue and one in Seattle. All registrations are made at the Bellevue address.

Susan Bradley, the school's coordinator, has a background in classical French cuisine and has studied with several French chefs. She is apprenticed to Chef Gerard Paratt at Gerard's Relais De Lyon restaurant in Bellevue. She has taught for four years and is considered the school's resident baker. Susan directs a staff of a dozen teachers with varying backgrounds. It includes chefs, home economists, cookbook authors, and well known local cooks.

The Sunshine Kitchen Company has both lecture/demonstration and participation classes. All classes are limited to 10 students.

Brochure available   Fees: low-moderate

Yankee Kitchen School of Cookery

10108 Main Street
Bellevue, Washington 98004
206/455-0614

A varied class schedule that includes a Heart and Health course is the fare at the Yankee Kitchen School of Cookery. Director Nancy Lazara is a diploma graduate of the Cordon Bleu, London, and worked professionally in a restaurant before opening her own cooking school. After two years she merged her school with a cookware shop owned by her mother.

The backgrounds of the school's instructors are as varied as the courses it offers. Nancy Varriale is an educator who learned Italian cooking from her mother. Her classes focus on the cuisine of Northern Italy. Ellen Mohl and Steven Paul are graduates of the Culinary Institute of America. Other teachers include a home economist who specializes in microwave cooking and specialists in Mexican and Russian cuisines.

Some of the classes at The Yankee Kitchen School of Cookery are one, two, or four sessions in length, while others are series of six weekly classes. The school sponsors tours to London to study at the Cordon Bleu.

Brochure available   Fees: moderate

SHARON'S KITCHEN

2852 80th S.E.
Mercer Island, Washington 98040
206/232-7710

"Good food in its finest form" is the goal of Sharon Kramis, owner/director of Sharon's Kitchen in Mercer Island. Sharon, a home economist, has worked for *Sunset* magazine, has taught cooking at The Bon in Seattle, and has been a "devoted student of James Beard for the past six years."

The staff at Sharon's Kitchen includes Marian Yih, who started her own cooking school in Hong Kong in 1968 and has had her own television program; Alba Maccarrone, a local authority on Italian food; Ellie Schuck, an experienced teacher and demonstrator of microwave cooking; and Marcel Foster, a master baker from Switzerland who has had his own bakery for 30 years and is currently teaching baking to professional chefs. Sharon also draws upon other local talent for specialty classes that include sessions about cheeses and lessons in making Italian sausages.

Classes at Sharon's Kitchen are mostly lecture/demonstration with limited participation, and have a maximum of 16 students each. The school sponsors several study trips, including an excursion to Vancouver, British Columbia, and a fall tour of California's Napa Valley. Special classes for out-of-town students are available upon request.

Brochure available   Fees: moderate

Lorraine Arnold's International Kitchen

2201 N.E. 65th Street
Seattle, Washington 98115
206/524-4004

French and Italian cuisines and French pastry are the focal point of classes taught at Lorraine Arnold's International Kitchen, Seattle.

Lorraine Arnold, owner/director, was trained as a chef in New Orleans. She has written for *Seattle* magazine and has had her own television show. She has been in business for 16 years. Before opening her school in 1976, she taught at community colleges in her area and had classes in her home.

Jean Benjamin, instructor at the school, was born in Holland and trained as a pastry chef there and in Germany. He has worked as a pastry chef in Europe and in New York City, most recently at Luchow's. He has also taught at community colleges in New York and Seattle.

"Our classes are taught with a view to expanding a student's knowledge of basic techniques and of each cuisine's own particular style," Lorraine says. "We stress building a foundation of 'what goes with what' and then creating your own dishes. Recipes are only a guideline and cooking is an art—and a joy."

Classes taught at the school include two levels of French cuisine, French pastry, Northern and regional Italian cooking, and occasional specialties including soups, bread, and creole cookery. Most classes are lecture/demonstration and are limited to 12 students.

The school arranges for its students to dine in restaurants as a group and hosts student parties about once a month.

The International Kitchen has special concentrated classes for out-of-town students and will assist with travel and hotel arrangements.

Brochure available   Fees: moderate

Karen Gregorakis Creative Cookery and Catering

5604 17th Avenue N.E.
Seattle, Washington 98105
206/523-9823

"Attentive cookery belongs to the arts," says Karen Gregorakis, owner/director of Karen Gregorakis Creative Cookery and Catering in Seattle. At her in-home school, which she plans to move soon to larger quarters, Karen teaches full participation classes to six students at a time.

The school's repertoire is presented in a repeating group of eight classes—four representing the cuisines of France, Italy, Greece, and Spain and Mexico; three on specialty topics such as seafoods and vegetables of the Pacific Northwest; and one intriguing class called Posh Picnics.

Karen's formal education was in social work. "I am a former psychiatric social worker who began my professional food career four years ago when I decided to become a cheese expert. Though I am not formally trained, my instruction is dedicatedly professional and represents not only thousands of hours of research over the years, but an exciting culmination of intuitive/genetic culinary talents and belief in self."

Through her school Karen communicates to students that cooking is a "creative endeavor that can provide satisfying artistic talents for so many people who might otherwise feel stilted, stifled, and stymied."

The best cooking, she believes, "involves not fancy gadgets, not necessarily prolific instruction, but rather impeccably fresh ingredients and sensitivity to self and others."

Brochure available   Fees: high

House of Rice
4112 University Way N.E.
Seattle, Washington 98105
206/633-5181
206/633-0738

"Our goal is to bring our culture to people through food," say Henry and Edna Matsubu, owner/directors of the House of Rice Oriental Cooking School, Seattle.

The 16-year-old school offers classes in the cuisines of China, Japan, East India, and Indonesia. Cantonese cooking, however, receives particular emphasis. The school offers beginning, advanced, special advanced, and gourmet classes in the foods of Canton. All classes are lecture/demonstration and are limited to 12 persons.

Jane Wong Lewis, a home economist, teaches Cantonese cooking. Mei Yea Liao, who teaches northern Chinese and Taiwanese cooking, has a certificate from Wei Chuan Cooking School in Taipei, Taiwan. Other instructors are Sharmia Batra, who teaches Indian cooking; Hideko Kanzaki, who teaches Japanese cooking; and Louise Svilainis, who teaches Indonesian cooking.

The school is associated with a gourmet food and gift shop.

Brochure available   Fees: low

La Cuisine School of Cooking

7812 Lake City Way N.E.
Seattle, Washington 98115
206/522-6718

Although it just opened in 1979, La Cuisine School of Cooking in Seattle is "a full-time school whose only reason for being is the quality teaching program we are developing," according to Bruce C. Weller, owner/director.

"We want to cater to the professional as well as the dilettante—to all who are seeking professional training from professional people," he concludes.

Bruce is a former university professor of sociology who brings a background in both fine cooking and education to the school. He earned a grande diplome from La Varenne, Paris, where he was a teaching assistant (stagiaire) working with the master chefs as a translator and student liaison. He also holds a certificate from the Cordon Bleu in Paris. He teaches three levels of French cuisine: foundations, intermediate, and advanced.

Maunena (Mauny) Carter Kaseberg, the other full-time instructor at the school, also specializes in French cuisine as well as in specialty cooking with the food processor. Like Bruce, she was a teaching assistant at La Varenne, and is a candidate for the grand diplome of that school. She has worked as an apprentice to a Seattle pastry chef.

Most classes at La Cuisine are demonstration and are limited to 20 students. Participation classes will be limited to eight students. Special concentrated classes for out-of-town students are planned for the summer months.

Brochure available   Fees: high

Listed Cooking Schools

Arizona
Parisian Kitchen
6760 East Camino Principale
Tucson, Arizona 85715
602/886-5223

California
Virginia Hjelte
P.O. Box 676
Belvedere, California 94920
415/937-0555

Judith Kane Jeanson
140 North Hamilton Drive
Beverly Hills, California 90211
213/659-8572

Marinette Georgi Cuisine Minceur
2315½ Rose Street
Berkeley, California 94708
415/848-8736

Joyce Esersky Goldstein
2515 Etna Street
Berkeley, California 94704
415/843-1074

Frazier Farms Cooking School, Creative Cuisinieres
13th and Center City Parkway
Escondido, California 92025
714/745-2141

Mission Gourmet Cookware
165 Anza Street
Fremont, California 94538
415/657-8062

Lenore Bleadon
170 Rancheria Road
Kentfield, California 94904
415/461-0988

Peter Formosa—Cooking with Consciousness
428 San Benito Avenue
Los Gatos, California 95030
408/354-8704

Hayward School of Cookery and Catering
3710 Fletcher Drive
Los Angeles, California 90065
213/257-3438

Lesands Cooks
1139 Chestnut Street
Menlo Park, California 94025
415/325-1712

The Cookery at the Cove
c/o The Village Cookery
17 Orinda Way
Orinda, California 94563

Helen Cassidy Page School of Cooking
144 Melville Road
Palo Alto, California 94301

The Cooking Craze
609 San Anselmo
San Anselmo, California 94960
415/459-1488

Kitchen Liberation
Mission Valley Center West
824 Camino Del Rio North, Suite 403
San Diego, California 92108
714/299-4040

Emalee Chapman
405 Davis Court
San Francisco, California 94111
415/397-8088

Charcuterie Cooking School
25 Buena Vista Terrace
San Francisco, California 94117
415/431-0211

Jenny Chen Cooking School
175 Villa Terrace
San Francisco, California 94114
415/863-5765

Flavors of India
1242 44th St. Avenue
San Francisco, California 94122
415/752-1995
415/752-9195

Rosemary Hinton
34B Hill Street
San Francisco, California 94110
415/285-6482

Hyde and Green Company
1898 Hyde Street
San Francisco, California 94109
415/441-2130

Marlene Levinson Cookery
55 Raycliff
San Francisco, California 04115
415/921-4060

Larry Negri Cooking School
1715 Castro Street
San Francisco, California 94131
415/285-6058

La Cucina Italiana
207 McNear Drive
San Rafael, California 94901
415/456-8921

Marscell Rodin
P.O. Box 1094
San Rafael, California 94902

Le Kookery Cooking School
13624 Ventura Boulevard
Sherman Oaks, California 91423
213/995-0568

Papagayo School of Mexican Cooking
155 Jamaica Street
Tiburon, California 94920
415/435-3389

Janice Lowry
14 San Antonio Court
Walnut Creek, California 94958
415/937-0587

Connecticut
Ron Buebendorf
44 West Putnam
Greenwich, Connecticut 06830
203/869-7139

Florida
Kettles Culinary Supplies
1074 South Florida Avenue
Lakeland, Florida 33803
813/688-0130

The Kitchen Shoppe
431 East Zarragossa Street
Pensacola, Florida 32501
904/434-0065

Georgia
Bailee's Best
107 E. Jones Street
Savannah, Georgia 31401
912/234-4178

Illinois
Tin Pan Galley
271 St. Clair Square
Fairview Heights, Illinois 62208
618/632-1210

Le Petit Bedon
1319 West Devereux
Peoria, Illinois 61614
309/692-4524

Kansas
The Back Burner
6964 West 105th Street
Overland Park, Kansas 66204

Tin Pan Galley
3700 East Douglas
Wichita, Kansas 67208
316/684-9651

Minnesota
Rosa Isleib
18316 Woolman Drive
Minnetonka, Minnesota 55343
612/474-3716

La Bonne Cuisine
6716 Samuel Road
Edina, Minnesota 55435
612/944-2485

TH'RICE
1086½ Grand Avenue
St. Paul, Minnesota 55105
612/225-0513

New Jersey
Irene Feigelis
2 Palisades Court
Cresskill, New Jersey 07626
201/568-6480

The Ginger Tree
183 Kinderkamack Road
Emerson, New Jersey]7630

Joan Hoffman's School of Cooking
63 Horizon Terrace
Hillsdale, New Jersey 07642

La Cuisine
396 Franklin Avenue
Wyckoff, New Jersey 07481
201/891-4161

Chingwan Tcheng's Chinese Cooking
40 6th Street
Cresskill, New Jersey 07626
201/567-5310

New York

China Institute of America
125 East 65th Street
New York, New York 10021
212/744-8181
In Julie's Kitchen
1527 Weaver Street
Scarsdale, New York 10583
914/723-8870
International School of Cooking
143 West 94th Street
New York, New York 10025
212/749-5000
Mattimore Cooking School
Oak Place
Croton-on-Hudson, New York 10520
914/271-3142
The Mandarin Inn
Peter Wong
14 Mott Street
New York, New York 10002
Anne Sekely School for Cooking
229 East 79th Street
New York, New York 10021
212/744-0500
Scuola Italiana di Cucina of the America-Italy Society
667 Madison Avenue
New York, New York 10021
212/838-1560

North Carolina

Ecole de Cuisine Lafayette
P.O. Box 53445
Fayetteville, North Carolina 28305
919/484-0652

Ohio

Drannon's Gourmet Cooking School
Aledo Drive
Dayton, Ohio 45430
513/426-6316
Good Things
2390 East Main Street
Columbus, Ohio 43209
614/237-8668
Pandenomium
19300 Detroit Road
Rocky River, Ohio 44116
216/331-0964

Mr. Pots & Pans, Inc.
986 West Centerville
Centerville, Ohio 45459
513/434-6635

Oklahoma

Winifred Cowen
344 East 29th Place
Tulsa, Oklahoma 74114
918/747-6000
The Fair Culinary Shop
5201 A South Sheridan
Tulsa, Oklahoma 74145
918/663-8422
Sue Schempf
1215 East 20th Street
Tulsa, Oklahoma 74120
918/585-5023
Tin Pan Galley
144 Woodland Hills Mall
Tulsa, Oklahoma 74133
918/252-1212

Oregon

The Food Experience
525 S.W. 12th Street
Portland, Oregon 97205
Richard Nelson
1151 S.W. King Avenue
Portland, Oregon 97025
503/227-0254

Tennessee

The Cooks' Nook Inc.
4004 Hillsboro Road
Nashville, Tennessee 37215
615/383-5492

Texas

Batterie De Cuisine Inc.
4360 Westheimer on Mid Lane
Houston, Texas 77027
713/961-1373
Edible Arts
7230 Mason Dells Drive
Dallas, Texas 75230
214/361-7902
Edmond Foulard at Foulards'
10001 Westheimer Road
Houston, Texas 77027
713/789-1661

Inn at Brushy Creek
Round Rock, Texas 78664
Sharon Oswald
1136 Berthea
Houston, Texas 77026
713/528-3661
Nancy Parker
1615 Walworth Street
Greenville, Texas 75401
214/455-6723

Virginia
The Kitchen Barn
1600 Hilltop West Executive Center
Virginia Beach, Virginia 23451
803/422-4777

Washington
Esther Chen's Chinese Cooking School
5230 University Way N.E.
Seattle, Washington 98105
206/524-3575
The Good Wife
17171 Bothell Way N.E.
Seattle, Washington 98155
206/363-1343
Mary Pang's Chinese Cooking School
811 7th Street
Seattle, Washington 98104
206/622-3524

Wisconsin
The Postilion School of Culinary Arts
775 North Jefferson
Milwaukee, Wisconsin 53202
414/276-4141
The Postilion School of Culinary Arts
615 Old Pioneer Road
Fond du Lac, Wisconsin 54935
414/922-4170

Professional Schools

California Culinary Academy
215 Freemont Street
San Francisco, California 94105
415/543-2764

Culinary Institute of America
Route 9
Hyde Park, New York 12538
914/452-9600

New York City Community College
School of Hotel and Restaurant
Management

300 Jay Street
Brooklyn, New York 11201
212/643-8595

New York Institute of Dietetics
154 West 14th Street
New York, New York 10011
212/675-6655

The Restaurant School
2129 Walnut Street
Philadelphia, Pennsylvania 19103
215/561-3446

Have Whisk Will
Travel—Traveling Cooks

Rick Bayless (Mexican/Latin American)
P.O. Box 7214
Ann Arbor, Michigan 48107
313/434-5458

**Black's Gourmet Cooking School on
Wheels (International/Natural Foods)**
153 East Main Street
Northville, Michigan 48167
313/349-0447
313/478-5771

Marion Conlin (Classical/International)
1200 on the Mall #616
Minneapolis, Minnesota 55402
(612) 339-2280

Phillip Brown (Meats)
1141 Armada Drive
Pasadena, California 91103
213/681-7849

Biba Caggiano (Italian)
1411 46th Street
Sacramento, California 95819
916/455-7208

Flora Chang (Chinese)
6544 Andasol Avenue
Van Nuys, California 91406
213/343-2823

**Flo Braker European Pastry Instructor
and Consultant (Pastry)**
1441 Edgewood Drive
Palo Alto, California 94301
415/327-0221

**Shirley Corriher (Southern/Simplified
International)**
3152 Andrews Drive N.W.
Atlanta, Georgia 30305
404/233-0923

Michael De Vidts (tailored to the group)
2-C Hanover House
147 15th Street N.E.
Atlanta, Georgia 30361
404/881-0009

Josephine Gatan (Chinese/French)
2030 Fairburn Avenue
Los Angeles, California 90025
213/474-0995

**Bess Greenstone (International/Eastern
European)**
3571 Valley Meadow Road
Sherman Oaks, California 91403
213/788-0628

Kenneth Hom (Regional & Classic Chinese)
P.O. Box 4303
Berkeley, California 94704
415/843-5579

Sheilah Kaufman ("Fearless and Fussless")
10508 Tyler Terrace
Potomac, Maryland 20854
301/299-5282

Caroline Kriz (Contemporary/International)
100 East Walton
Chicago, Illinois 60611
312/751-2655

Barbara Malone (Microwave/Food Processor)
P.O. Box 8155
Coral Springs, Florida 33065
305/752-1721

Rosemary Manell (French)
41 Beach Road
Belvedere, California 94920
415/435-0354

Katie Milhiser (Sweets)
85 La Salle
Piedmont, California
415/655-5757

Judith Olney (French)
1500 Forest Hills Plaza

Durham, North Carolina 27707
919/489-1018

Jacques Pepin (French)
214 Durham Road
Madison, Connecticut 06443
203/245-4846

Joan Polin (Kosher)
7700 Woodlawn Avenue
Melrose Park, Pennsylvania 19126
215/635-4135

Barbara Tropp (Chinese)
970 Greenwich Street
San Francisco, California 94133
415/441-2124

Paula Wolfert (Moroccan/Nouvelle Cuisine)
145 East 84th Street
New York, New York 10028
212/734-3684

Diana Rossen Worthington (French/International)
P.O. Box 24AA1
Los Angeles, California 90024
213/476-1081

Judy Vance (International)
717 South Stone
LaGrange, Illinois 60525
312/354-6196

Appetizers

Rillettes
(Pork Spread)
(Denise Schorr, Massachusetts)

What Frenchman is not familiar with this most universal of delicatessen products? Every province, township and village in France has its own variety of Rillettes, a meat pate used either as an appetizer or as an hors d'oeuvre. Rillettes from les charcuteries of Normandy are of rabbit meat; from Angers, of goose. But the most acclaimed Rillettes come from Le Mans and Tours, cities in the valley of the Loire. They are made from pork and goose meat combined and just plain pork, respectively.

The Rillettes which follows is my adaptation of a recipe from an old friend, whose family for generations had lived in the Province of des Deux-Sevres, just south of the Loire. It is made from pork, which is always available. We like it because it is less greasy than most Rillettes.

It has a rather coarse, stringy texture, not smooth like a liver pate. Some fat will be apparent as it cools, but do not remove it, for this would change the personality of this provincial delicacy.

This pate may be made in advance, as it will keep well up to several weeks refrigerated and may also be frozen. It makes a distinguished hors d'oeuvre to have on hand for large or small gatherings.—Denise Schorr

Ingredients: for 3 to 3½ cups cooked and well packed; serves about 30 as an hors d'oeuvre

2½ to 3 lb. pork butt with bone
3½ cups cold water
1 tsp. salt
10 turns of black pepper mill, medium grind (a scant ¼ tsp.)

½ tsp. dried thyme
1 large garlic clove, peeled
1 large bay leaf
1 whole small yellow onion (about ¼ pound) peeled

Ingredients: for 6 cups cooked and well packed; serves about 60 as an hors d'oeuvre

4 to 4½ lb. pork butt with bone
4½ to 5 cups cold water
1½ to 2 tsp. salt
15 turns of black pepper mill, medium grind (a heaping ¼ tsp.)

1 tsp. dried thyme
2 large garlic cloves, peeled
2 bay leaves
1 whole medium-size yellow onion (about ½ pound) peeled

Method:
The butt is that part of the pork shoulder nearest the neck. It may be found already deboned, in which case ask the butcher for the bone, as it adds extra flavor to the final product. However, it is always a little more expensive when purchased with the bone removed. This process can be done in the home kitchen easily; all that is required is a little patience and a good, sharp knife.

To debone: Cut through meat to the bone all along length. Slowly, inch by inch, sever meat from bone with a scraping motion of the knife, and pull the meat away with the other hand. That's all there is to it.

Next, cut meat into thin 2-inch strips, ½-inch wide or into 2-inch cubes. Combine all ingredients, including bone, in a 4-to-6-quart pot (a Dutch oven is good). Bring to a boil. This will take from 15 to 20 minutes. Set lid ajar, and simmer 5 hours. (In 3 hours meat is edible, but in the additional hours of simmering, it will take on more of the flavor of the seasonings.) Liquid should be nearly evaporated when done.

Check from time to time to assure that it is simmering gently and stir with a wooden spoon. Meat should not stick to pan bottom.

Remove bay leaf and bone, then mash meat with wooden spoon. When cool, store in glazed earthenware, stoneware or glass containers. If there is any liquid left, pour over packed pate.

To Serve: Remove Rillettes from refrigerator at least one hour before serving so that it will be easy to spread.

For an hors d'oeuvre, spread Rillettes on crackers or small rounds of rye bread. It also makes a delicious appetizer accompanied by crusty French bread.

Chicken Liver Paté
(The Restaurant School, Pennsylvania)

1 lb. butter
1 lb. onions peeled and sliced thinly
4 cloves garlic, peeled and smashed
5 medium red Delicious apples, cored
  and thinly sliced
2 bay leaves
1 tbsp. thyme
1 tbsp. basil
½ cup brandy
3 lb. chicken livers washed
  and cleaned
6 tbsp. flour

4 egg yolks
2 cups heavy cream
3 tbsp. sugar
3 tbsp. salt
1 tsp. white pepper
1 4-6 qt. mixing bowl and wisk
2 (3 qt.) earthenware terrines or
  casseroles
1 large roasting pan to hold the
  casseroles
Water
Aluminum foil

Melt butter in large brazer over low heat and saute onions, garlic, apples, bay leaves, thyme, and basil until onions are clear and apples soft. Add to this mixture the livers and allow them to absorb the butter just coloring them but not cooking them through. Flame the livers and preceding ingredients in brandy. Put the mixture through the fine blade of a meat grinder. Make a paste of the flour and egg yolks and slowly combine with the cream so there are no lumps. Combine the liver and cream mixtures and force through a sieve into a mixing bowl. The mixture will be quite soupy. Be sure to leave any grainy parts in the sieve so the paté has a silky texture. Combine well with the wisk and add salt, pepper and sugar. Adjust seasoning and pour into the earthenware terrines. Rap them on the table so there are no air bubbles in the mixture. Cover the terrines with aluminum foil and place in roasting pan. Pour water into the roasting pan so that it comes ⅓ up the side of the terrine and bake in a preheated 350-degree oven for 45 minutes to 1 hour. The patés are done when they have first set and have no cracks on the top. To test them slightly shake the terrines. The mixture should be a mass but slightly shaky to the touch much like a custard. Cool and refrigerate. They keep at least a week and are better several days after making. The insides of the terrines when served will have a slight pink tinge. The patés are scooped out with spoons or an ice cream scoop and placed on a bed of Boston lettuce and watercress. The portions may be accompanied by any of the following: black bread, wheat thins, or toast, cornichons, chopped onions, sieved eggs, or madiera gele.
The terrines must be tightly covered with a clear food-wrap after each serving and refrigerated. The texture of this dish is much like a mousse or foie gras.
Yields 30 servings.

Shrimp or Crab Meat Paté
(Ursula's Cooking School, Georgia)

4 oz. cream cheese, room temperature
2 oz. butter, room temperature
1 inch anchovie paste
1 tbsp. dry onion
1 tbsp. cocktail sauce
2 tsp. lemon juice
½ tsp. lemon pepper

½ tsp. prepared horseradish
½ tsp. Worcestershire sauce
12 oz. cooked shrimp or crab meat, chopped
1 hard-cooked egg, chopped fine
2 tbsp. parsley, chopped fine

Mix all the ingredients except egg and parsley together with mixer until creamy.
Add salt to taste. Shape into ball.
Mix egg and parsley together and coat ball. Refrigerate ball a minimum of 2 hours or overnight. Serve with wheat crackers.

Ham Mousse-Paté
(The Lillian Haines School of Culinary Arts, California)

1½ lbs. cooked ham
¾ lb. veal
1 cup soft breadcrumbs
¼ cup milk
⅓ cup butter

½ cup heavy cream, whipped
3 egg yolks
½ tsp. chopped parsley
3 egg whites, stiffly beaten

Grind the veal and ham together. Soak the breadcrumbs in milk, then squeeze dry. Cream the butter. Add squeezed breadcrumbs, egg yolks, salt, white pepper, chopped parsley and ground meat and mix well. Fold in the beaten egg whites and whipped cream.
Grease and flour a 5-cup form and fill three-quarters full with mixture. Cover the form and place in a pan of hot water. The water should come two-thirds of the way up the sides of the form. Cook for one hour on the top of the stove, keeping the water at simmer. Add more hot water as necessary.
NOTE: This is a great hot dish served with a salad for lunch, as a Country Paté on a buffet, or as a first course for dinner. Also, this is great served cold...and freezes well.

Copyright 1979 by Lillian Haines, C.E.C.

Cha Gio Ga
(Spring Rolls)
(Cuisinier, Connecticut)

Cha gio is the most popular dish in the Vietnamese cuisine, for rich and poor alike. Usually it is filled with pork and crab, but a combination of any meat or seafood can be used. They can be used as appetizers or as a main dish.

Filling:

2 oz. cellophane noodles, soaked in warm water for 10 minutes, and cut into 1-inch pieces

1 lb. raw chicken breast, cut into thin strips

2 tbsp. tree ear, soaked in warm water for ½ hour, finely chopped

3 cloves garlic, chopped fine

3 shallots, chopped fine

½ lb. crabmeat, fresh, frozen or canned

½ tsp. black pepper

Combine all of the above ingredients in a bowl, mixing well with hands. Set aside.

Wrapper:

20 round rice papers (banh trang)

4 eggs, beaten

2 cups of vegetable oil

Cut rice paper rounds into quarters. Using a pastry brush, paint beaten egg over the entire surface of each paper, working on several at a time. In a few seconds the papers will soften and become flexible. Place 1 teaspoon of filling along the curved edge of the paper in a rectangular shape. Roll once, then fold over the sides to enclose the filling; then continue rolling. The beaten egg will not only make the wrapper flexible but will also hold it together. Pour the oil into a frying pan and place the spring rolls into the cold oil. Turn heat to moderate and fry for about 30 minutes or until they are a golden brown. Remove from pan and drain on paper towels.

The spring rolls can be served on a platter with a bowl of nuoc cham or they can be accompanied by a vegetable platter, in which case a spring roll is placed on a lettuce leaf together with a slice of cucumber, a sprig of coriander and a sprig of mint. Each diner is given a small bowl of nuoc cham into which the lettuce-wrapped spring roll is dipped.

Spring rolls can be completely cooked, frozen and reheated in a 350-degree oven or partially cooked ahead one day, refrigerated, and the cooking completed the next day.
Yield: 80

Nuoc Cham

No Vietnamese meal is served without nuoc cham, a hot, tangy sauce to be sprinkled on food as desired. Using fish sauce as a base it is a flavor enhancer without peer.

2 cloves garlic

4 dried hot chili peppers or 1 fresh chili pepper

5 tsp. of sugar

Juice and pulp of ¼ lime

4 tbsp. fish sauce

5 tbsp. water

Place garlic, peppers and sugar into a mortar and pound into a paste. Add the lime juice and pulp and combine with the paste in the mortar. Add the additional ingredients and use as required.

If you do not own a mortar and pestle, mash the ingredients with the back of a spoon. If done in a blender, the sauce is never of the right consistency. Nuoc cham can be made in larger quantities and stored in the refrigerator for about one week.

Quiche Lorraine
(Creative Cookery, Texas)

6 slices bacon
½ cup grated cheese
2 cups half and half
1 tbsp. flour

4 eggs
1 unbaked pie shell
Ground nutmeg
Ground cayenne pepper or Tabasco

Fry bacon until partly done, then drain and cut into pieces. Cut Swiss cheese in julienne pieces. Line a 9-inch quiche pan with dough. Sprinkle bacon and cheese to cover bottom of crust.
Combine the eggs, flour, half and half, pinch of nutmeg, a few grains of cayenne pepper or a squirt of Tabasco and white pepper. Beat well. Place lined quiche pan on baking sheet. Pour egg mixture over bacon and cheese. Bake in preheated 375-degree oven for 35 minutes. To test before removing from oven, place a point of a knife in middle of quiche; if knife comes out dry, quiche is done.

To prepare in advance:
Line pastry shell with bacon and cheese. Mix rest of ingredients together for custard. Refrigerate separately. Let stand at room temperature before combining and baking. Serves 6.

Souffle Roulade Rousse
(La Cuisinique School of Cookery, Ohio)

I find that cooks like ideas, therefore may I suggest an improvization of a time-consuming recipe given to me by a charming hostess.

Use your favorite jelly roll recipe and eliminate all but 1 tbsp. of sugar.

After baking, roll in towel until ready to fill.

Fill jelly roll with equal parts of cheese (cream or farmer's or a combination—Breakstone's preferred), and sour cream (Breakstone's preferred), into which has been folded red or black caviar to the individual taste and budget.

Garnish with chopped chives or scallions, hard cooked egg yolks and whites, caviar, sour cream and lemon twists or wedges.

Serve sliced with garnishes and lemon zest flavored iced Vodka.

Servings depend upon size of jelly roll and appetites of guests, and whether it is served as an appetizer, luncheon main course, or fish course.

Boursin Cheese Quiche
(Marlene Sorosky's Cooking Center, California)

Flaky Pastry:

1¼ cups all-purpose flour
¼ tsp. salt

¼ lb. plus 2 tbsp. butter, cold and
  cut into 10 pieces
3 to 5 tbsp. ice water

In a medium bowl or food processor fitted with the steel knife, mix flour, salt and butter until crumbly. Add ice water; mix until dough is thoroughly moistened. Place on a flat surface and knead into a ball. Wrap in wax paper and refrigerate several hours or until cold enough to roll. On a lightly floured surface, roll out dough to fit into an 11-inch quiche pan with a removable bottom. Refrigerate for at least 30 minutes to rest the gluten in the flour. Line pastry with foil. Fill to the top with rice or beans. Bake at 425 degrees for 10 minutes. Carefully remove foil containing rice or beans. Cool.

Filling:

1 cup (4 oz.) Swiss cheese, shredded
¼ cup chopped green onions
¼ cup chopped ripe olives
1 small tomato, seeded and diced

3 eggs
½ cup whipping cream
1 (5 oz.) pkg. Boursin spiced cheese

Sprinkle prebaked crust with ¾ cup of Swiss cheese. Sprinkle green onions, olives and tomato over Swiss cheese. In a medium bowl, mix eggs, cream and Boursin cheese. Pour over vegetables. Sprinkle with remaining ¼ cup Swiss cheese. Bake in bottom third of oven at 375 degrees for 35 minutes or until puffed and golden brown. Let stand 5 minutes before cutting into wedges. Makes 8 servings.

To Make Ahead:
Flaky pastry may be frozen in a ball or may be frozen or refrigerated several days after it is prebaked. Filling may be made several hours ahead, but should not be put into the pastry or baked until ready to serve.

Variations:
Crab or shrimp may be substituted for the tomato.

Beet Top Cheese Pie (Quiche)
(Zona Spray Cooking School, Ohio)

Inspired by the Italian Easter Pie Genovese. A nice dish when beets are going wild in the garden. No one guesses the filling ingredients. Good for an appetizer or main dish. Can be made without prebaking the crust but baking time is increased.

Double recipe Pate Brisee (pie crust dough)

2 lb. beet greens
2 tbsp. butter
¾ tsp. salt
Good grind fresh allspice
2 tbsp. oil
¼ cup minced chives
¼ cup minced fresh marjoram, parsley, lemon-balm or basil
½ cup fresh grated Parmesan cheese

4 slices lightly smoked or unsmoked bacon
1 onion, minced
Fresh ground nutmeg
1¼ lbs. Ricotta cheese
1 cup milk
½ cup whipping cream
3 eggs
2 tbsp. flour
Salt, pepper

Roll & Bake Crust: Roll dough 1/8" thick. Line 13-inch loose bottom quiche pan with dough; extend edges up sides to make a good retainer. Chill. Bake blind 12-15 minutes until set in 425-degree oven. Cool.

Prepare vegetables: Wash greens, spin dry and chop finely or chop in food processor using on-off motion. (A blender liquefies the leaves.) Put 2 tablespoons butter in bottom of large saucepan, then chopped greens and sprinkle with salt and allspice. Cover, cook 4-5 minutes until wilted; turn greens once or twice to cook evenly. If liquid remains in pan bottom, raise heat and cook briefly to evaporate moisture. Or drain in sieve, pushing gently with spoon to remove liquid.

Toss greens in bowl with oil, herbs, Parmesan cheese, salt and pepper to taste.

Prepare cheese filling: Fry bacon until crisp, remove bacon, crumble. Saute onion briefly in drippings until translucent; season with salt, pepper and a dash of fresh ground nutmeg. Toss onion and bacon with beet tops.

Place ricotta, milk, cream and eggs in food processor bowl. Whirl until smooth. Season with ½-¾ teaspoon salt, more pepper (or cayenne) and nutmeg. Add flour and whirl just to blend. Pour over beet tops. Fold together. Smell or taste and adjust seasonings.

Fill & Bake: Pour filling into baked shell. Bake in preheated 400-degree oven for 15 minutes, then at 350 degrees 20-30 minutes or until custard is set and slightly puffy. Remove quiche from pan, cool on cake rack. Serve warm or room temperature. Can be reheated.

Variations: If filling is left over, fill little tart shells or bake without a crust in ramekins. Recipe makes one 13-inch quiche, two 9-inch quiche or one 9-inch quiche and about 12 individual-size quiche.

Soups

Bisque D'huitres
(Oyster Bisque)
(Forty Carrots School of Creative Cookery, Tennessee)

This may seem like a great deal of work for a simple bowl of soup, but once you have tasted it it's easy to forget how much work went into it.

3 tbsp. olive oil
1 to 1½ lb. shrimp, unpeeled
¼ cup Cognac
1 small onion
1 stalk celery
1 carrot
4 shallots, minced
1 clove garlic, crushed
1 bay leaf
2 tbsp. fresh chopped parsley
½ tsp. each dried thyme & oregano

4 tbsp. tomato paste
½ cup dry white wine
1 cup fish stock (or ¼ cup each clam
   juice and canned chicken broth.)
½ tsp. salt
Pinch each black and cayenne pepper
1 cup heavy cream
½ cup half and half
24 oysters
8 tbsp. whipped cream
6 tbsp. softened butter

Heat the oil in a large heavy pan over medium high heat. (The pan should have a big enough surface area on the bottom so that the shrimp form no more than one layer while being sauteed.) Add the shrimp and cook quickly, tossing gently, until they have turned pink (3 to 5 minutes). Drain and reserve the pan juices. Return the pan to the heat and add the Cognac. At this point you may flame the Cognac, although I feel that a nicer flavor is achieved by simply allowing the shrimp to steam in the Cognac as the alcohol is evaporated. When the strong Cognac fumes have ceased (or the flame is extinguished) empty the shrimp and Cognac into a second bowl and peel the shrimp, reserving the shells.

Cut the onion, carrot and celery into brunoise (small dice). Return the oil to the pan and when it is hot add the vegetables and saute until tender, but not browned. Add the parsley, shallot, garlic, bay leaf, oregano, thyme, tomato paste and wine. Raise the heat and again allow the alcoholic fumes to cook off. Add the stock and reserved shells and allow the soup to simmer about 20 minutes. Strain the soup. Take out ½ cup of the carrot, onion and celery mixture (avoid getting shrimp shells mixed in with this mixture). Using the fine blade of a food mill or the steel blade of a food processor, grind the shrimp meat and ½ cup vegetables. Add this to the strained soup.

Mix together the shrimp soup, salt, peppers, cream and half and half. Heat this thoroughly, but do not let it boil or it may get a slightly burned taste. Just before serving add the cleaned oysters and allow them to cook just until they float to the surface. In each serving bowl put 1 tablespoon whipped cream and ¾ tablespoon softened butter. Pour in the Bisque, allowing each person 3 oysters. Serve immediately.

8 servings.

Basic Beef and Vegetable Soup

(Charie MacDonald, Illinois)

14 cups degreased beef stock
1 cup sliced meat from beef stock
2 cups vegetables from beef stock
½ cup barley
¼ cup corn

¼ cup peas
¼ cup carrot, finely chopped
¼ cup celery, finely chopped
Salt, pepper to taste

The stock:

1 lb. meaty beef shin bone
1 lb. veal knuckle bone,
   broken into 2″ pieces
5 lb. lean or old bones (bones that
   have been used in previous stock pot)
7 qt. water
1 tbsp. salt
1 bay leaf

10 peppercorns
15 sprigs parsley
2 onions, sliced
2 large carrots, sliced
2 stalks celery with leaves, sliced
2 lb. tomatoes, quartered
1 cup rolled oats

For light brown colored stock—In a 16 quart stock pot place bones that have not been cooked before (new bones) with salt. Cover with water. Bring to a boil, about 50 minutes. Remove scum.

For dark brown colored stock—In a 12″ x 8″ roasting pan place new bones (bones that have not been previously cooked), 1 carrot and 1 onion. Bake at 450 degrees for 60 minutes, turning the bones and vegetables to expose all surfaces. Discard fat. Remove the bones and vegetables to the stock pot. Deglaze the pan with 2 cups of water. Place this liquid with the remaining 6½ quarts water in the pot. Add salt.

Add old bones and rest of ingredients to light or dark brown stock. Simmer the pot until the liquid has reduced by one-third, about 4 hours. Allow the pot to cool slightly for easier handling, then strain out the stock. Degrease.

Slice the meat from the bones, discarding fat. Save 2 cups of the vegetables for puree. Separate bones, saving the new bones for your next pot.

Making the soup:

Puree the 2 cups vegetables with some of the degreased stock. In a 5-quart saucepan place the stock, pureed vegetables, sliced meat, barley, corn, peas, carrot and celery. Simmer slowly for twenty minutes or until vegetables and barley are cooked. Taste and season with salt and pepper.

Note: Soup will reduce and thicken as it reheats. Soup freezes well for 3 months.

Chilled Curried Carrot Soup
(Continental Cooking, New York)

½ stick butter or margarine
1 large onion chopped (1 cup)
1 lb. carrots, pared and sliced
¾ tsp. curry powder
1 thin strip lemon peel

1 can chicken broth
1½ tsp. salt
¼ tsp. pepper
1 cup light cream

Melt the butter in a large saucepan. Saute onion and carrots until onion is tender (about 5 minutes). Add the curry powder and lemon peel, cook 3 min. longer. Pour the chicken broth into a 1-quart measure and add enough water to make 1 quart of liquid, add to onion and carrot mixture. Bring to boiling, lower heat, cover and simmer for about 20 minutes or until carrots are tender. Remove from heat and cool slightly. Puree the soup in an electric blender. Pour into a large bowl. Stir in salt, pepper and cream. Cover and chill for at least 4 hours.
Serves 6.

Tomato Potato Potage
(Judith Bell's Cooking Kitchen, Inc., Minnesota)

¼ cup butter
3 onions, sliced
1 carrot, sliced
Pinch of sugar
1 tsp. salt
Dash of ground pepper
2 potatoes, sliced
4 cups cold water

4 cups canned Italian tomatoes, drained
3 tbsp. tomato paste
½ tsp. baking soda
1 cup heavy cream
Finely chopped parsley, chives or celery tops for garnish

Saute onion and carrot in butter. Add sugar, salt, pepper, potatoes, tomatoes, tomato paste and water. Simmer, partially covered, 1 hour. Put through food mill or puree with food processor.
Add baking soda and cream. Taste and adjust seasonings. Bring to serving temperature. Taste and adjust seasonings. Garnish and serve.
Serves 8.

Split Pea Soup
(The Natural Gourmet Cookery School, New York)

1½ cups green split peas
6 cups water
1 medium yellow onion

1 carrot (medium)

2 parsley sprigs
1 tbsp. tamari soy sauce (obtainable in health food stores)
Sea salt to taste

Wash split peas, put them in a large soup pot with the water over a high flame, uncovered. Peel the onion, cut in quarters, add. Scrub the carrot, cut in large chunks, add with parsley sprigs. Lower flame to minimum, cover, let simmer for 1 hour. Then add tamari soy sauce, salt, simmer another 5 minutes. Mash the carrot pieces with a fork, then serve.

Pork, Cellophane Noodles and
Szechuan Preserved Kohlrabi Soup
(Madame Grace Chu, New York)

2 oz. dried cellophane noodles
¼ lb. lean pork
¼ cup dried mushrooms
¼ cup Szechuan kohlrabi
¼ cup bamboo shoots

2 tbsp. pickled cabbage (optional) if not
  used add 1 tsp. salt
1 green onion, green part only
4 cups chicken stock

Soak mushrooms in warm water for ½ hr. Drain and cut into fine shreds. Cut the pork, half frozen, into matchstick-sized shreds. Soak cellophane noodles in hot water for 15 minutes. Drain and cut into 2" lengths. Rinse Szechuan kohlrabi and cut into fine shreds. Shred the bamboo shoots and chop the pickled cabbage into ¼" pieces. Slice green onion top into ¼" pieces. Bring the stock to boil. Add pork shreds and stir a few times with chop-sticks. Add mushrooms, kohlrabi, pickled cabbage and bamboo shoots and bring to boil. Boil for 2 minutes. Add cellophane noodles. When the soup boils again, add green onion and serve hot.

Creme Olga
(A green-onion and mushroom soup)
(Gourmet School of Cooking and Entertaining, California)

2 to 3 bunches green onions
¾ lb. mushrooms
1 stick unsalted butter (¼ lb.)
4 cups chicken stock or bouillon
1¼ cups half and half

1 cup whipping cream
Salt
White pepper
Cayenne
2 tbsp. flour

In a heavy saucepan melt the butter. When it foams add the green onions, diced fine, including the green part. Add 1 teaspoon salt and ½ teaspoon white pepper. Cover the pan and cook slowly for 10 minutes—do not brown.
Remove the pan from the heat and stir in 2 tablespoons flour. When mixture is smooth, add 4 cups chicken stock. Stir over heat until the soup boils. Turn heat down and simmer, uncovered, for 10 minutes.
Wash and dry well ½ pound of the mushrooms. Slice finely, stems and all, and add to soup. Immediately whirl in a blender, a little at a time, and then return the soup to the pan.
Add the half and half to the soup, reheat gently. When hot, add the remaining mushrooms (washed, dried and sliced thin) to the soup.
Serve at once in warmed soup bowls. Pass a bowl of whipped cream seasoned with a bit of salt and cayenne pepper.

Hungarian Gulyas Soup

(Epicure School of Fine Cooking, New Jersey)

1 medium onion, chopped
¾ lb. beef, diced small
1½ tsp. Hungarian paprika
Pinch of caraway seeds,
  mashed with a spoon
Pinch of marjoram
Clove of garlic
  lanced with a toothpick

1½ tsp. flour
2 tsp. tomato paste
4 cups beef stock or veal stock if
  available (this can be made from
  boullion base, cubes, powder or liquid,
  such as Campbell's)
1 medium potato, diced small
Salt

Saute onion in butter until golden brown in a heavy 6-8 quart stock pot. Add meat and spices. Cook until meat is lightly browned. Sprinkle with flour. Add tomato paste and stock. Boil slowly, 1-1½ hours. Add potatoes and continue cooking until potatoes are done, about 20 minutes. Let soup stand off the fire. Remove garlic and skim off most of the fat. Correct seasoning with salt. Bring back to a boil for serving.
Serves 6-8.

Breads

Chive Biscuits
(The Baker's Rack, Kentucky)

6 cups all-purpose flour
¼ cup double-acting baking powder
¼ cup sugar
¼ cup chopped chives or ⅓ cup
  frozen chopped chives

2 tsp. salt
1 tsp. baking soda
2 cups shortening
About 1¼ cups buttermilk

In large bowl with fork, mix well first 6 ingredients. With pastry blender or two knives, used scissor-fashion, cut shortening into flour until mixture resembles coarse crumbs. Stir in 1¼ cups buttermilk until mixture is just moistened. (If dough is too dry, add ¼ cup more buttermilk.) Preheat oven to 400 degrees. Turn dough onto well-floured surface. With floured hands, knead dough 8 to 10 times until smooth. With floured, stockinette-covered rolling pin, roll dough into ¼" x 10" rectangle about ½" thick; cut into 2" squares. With pancake turner, place on large cookie sheets, about ½" apart. Bake 13 to 15 minutes until golden. Makes 3 dozen.

Challah (Braided Egg Bread)
(What's Cooking, Maryland)

2 pkgs. yeast
6 tbsp. sugar or honey
1 cup warm water
2 tbsp. oil

½ cup egg yolks (5-6)
1½ tsp. salt (rounded)
5 cups unbleached flour
Poppy seeds
1 egg yolk

Mix together the first three ingredients and allow the yeast to "proof." Add oil and eggs and mix well. Add three cups of the flour and mix well again. Add 1 cup more flour and turn out on a floured board to knead, adding the last cup of flour as needed. Knead until smooth and elastic.
Place in a greased bowl. Turn to grease bottom and sides and cover. Let dough rise 1½ hours until doubled in bulk. Punch dough down and divide into 2 parts. Divide each part in three and braid. Place in loaf pan or on cookie sheets and brush with oil. Cover and let rise 45 minutes to 1 hour until doubled in bulk. Brush with a beaten egg yolk mixed with 2 tbsp. water, and sprinkle with poppy seeds. Bake at 350 degrees for 20 minutes. Makes 2 loaves or 2-2½ dozen rolls.

Whole Wheat Bread
(Marilyn Myers' Kitchen, Arkansas)

1 loaf:

1 package dry yeast
½ cup water
1 tsp. sugar
½ cup bulgarian cultured milk
   (buttermilk)
1 tbsp. unsalted butter

1 tbsp. salt
1 cup unbleached white flour
1 large egg
¼ cup water
2½ to 3 cups whole wheat flour

Dissolve the yeast in ½ cup warm water (110-115 degrees). Add 1 tablespoon sugar, stir, and set aside in a warm spot until bubbles appear on the surface.

Gently warm the cultured milk in a saucepan. Add the unsalted butter and salt and stir to dissolve. Remove from heat and cool, if necessary, to the temperature of the yeast mixture. Put 1 cup of unbleached white flour in a warm bowl. Stir in the yeast and milk mixtures until no lumps of flour remain.

Lightly beat 1 egg with approximately ¼ cup warm water. When combined the liquid should equal ½ cup.

Add the egg/water mixture to the sponge and gradually mix in the 2½ to 3 cups of whole wheat flour. When a rough dough has formed, turn the dough out onto a floured board. Knead the dough 10-15 minutes, adding as little additional flour as possible to prevent the dough from sticking to the board. The dough should be resilient and firm.

Place the dough in a clean, buttered bowl, turning it around so that all sides are lightly coated with butter. Cover the bowl with plastic wrap and set in a warm spot (about 85 degrees) until the dough has doubled in bulk.

Punch down the dough, turn it out onto a board, and knead lightly for a couple of minutes. Let rest about 5 minutes covered with plastic wrap.

Shape the dough into a loaf and place in a buttered loaf pan (4½ " x 8½ ").

Again, set in a warm spot until the dough has doubled in bulk.

Bake in a 450-degree oven for 10 minutes. Turn oven down to 375 degrees and bake another 30-35 minutes.

Remove from the oven and turn the loaf out onto a wire rack to cool. The loaf should rest on its side and will have a hollow sound when tapped on the bottom.

Entrees

Tamale Pie
(The Cooking School, Texas)

2 lb. ground beef, preferably
    chili grind
2 large onions, chopped
2 cloves garlic, minced
2 tbsp. salad oil

1 green pepper, finely chopped
1 cup celery, finely chopped
1 (6 oz.) can tomato paste
3 tbsp. chili powder
½ tsp. cayenne

Mush:
1 cup cornmeal or Masa Harina
1 tsp. salt
3 cups cold water

Brown meat, onions and garlic in oil. Skim off 2-3 tablespoons oil and meat liquid to be used in the mush. Add other vegetables and simmer 10 minutes. Add tomato paste and seasonings, simmer about 1 hour.

Mush: In saucepan mix cornmeal with cold water, add oil and liquid reserved from meat. Add salt and pepper to taste. Cook 20 minutes.

Line the bottom of an ovenproof 3-quart casserole with the mush. Add the meat and vegetables and top with a thick layer of the mush. Bake at 350 degrees in a pan of hot water for 1½ to 2 hours.

Double the mush recipe if you like more meal on top.

Serves 8.

Caroline's Steak Au Poivre
(Caroline Kriz, Illinois)

4 rib eye steaks, ½ inch thick
Freshly ground white pepper
1 to 2 tbsp. sweet butter (depending
    upon fat content of steaks)
½-1 tbsp. olive oil

Salt to taste
½ cup dry vermouth
1 cup whipping cream
About ½ tsp. crushed tarragon

Press pepper into both sides of steaks. Let stand about 15 minutes. Heat butter and oil in 12-inch frypan until sizzling hot. Add steaks, cook over medium high heat about 3 minutes per side or to desired doneness. Remove to warm platter, salt to taste, keep warm while making sauce.

Add vermouth to drippings in pan. Bring to a boil, reduce by half. Add whipping cream, stir and reduce to thicken slightly. Add tarragon, stir, cook 1-2 minutes. Spoon over steaks. Serve immediately.

Serves 4.

Copyright 1978 Caroline Kriz

Filets Stuffed with Horseradish in a Madeira Sauce

(Anne Byrd's Cookery, North Carolina)

6 beef filets, 1 inch thick

6 tbsp. horseradish, grated,
  or prepared horseradish

2 tbsp. butter or olive oil

Salt and pepper

1½ cups Madeira sauce, hot

Cut a horizontal slit in the side of each filet. The slit should be about 1″ wide. Insert the point of a knife into the slit and cut a pocket in the center of the steak. Fill with 1 tablespoon of the horseradish.

In a saute pan, melt the butter over very high heat. Add the meat, leaving space between the pieces to allow steam to escape. Saute for about 3 minutes. Turn the filets and cook for about 3 more minutes (or longer if you want a filet more done than medium rare). Season. Serve topped with Madeira Sauce made from the brown sauce below. Serves 6.

Basic Brown Sauce
(makes 1 cup)

3 tbsp. butter

1 medium onion, minced

1 medium carrot, diced

1½ tbsp. flour

2 cups beef stock or canned beef broth

2 cloves of garlic, minced

Bouquet Garni

2 tsp. tomato paste

¼ tsp. pepper

Salt

Saute the onion and carrot in the butter for about 5 minutes. Off the fire, blend in the flour. Return to the fire and cook the roux for about 10 minutes or until it is brown. Remove the pan from the heat and stir in the stock, blending well. Add garlic, bouquet garni, tomato paste, and pepper. Return to the heat and bring to a boil. Reduce the heat, cover the pan, and cook slowly for about 2 hours. The mixture should be reduced to half its original volume. Strain and salt if necessary.

Madeira Sauce

½ cup Madeira
2 tbsp. cognac
1 recipe Basic Brown Sauce, hot

Boil the Madeira and cognac, reducing it to ¼ cup. Stir this into the hot Basic Brown Sauce. Reduce if necessary to thicken.

Hamburger Wellington

(Junior Chef's Kitchen, Maryland)

1 cup ground beef

1 tsp. chopped parsley

1 tsp. vegetable oil

1 tbsp. Parmesan cheese

1 tsp. water

½ beaten egg

¼ tsp. pepper

1 Pepperidge Farms pastry shell
   (defrosted)

Mustard, onion or mushroom for filling

With a fork, lightly mix all of the ingredients together slowly, carefully and thoroughly in a bowl.

Put a heavy cast-iron skillet on the burner and heat it until it is very hot. Don't add oil or butter to it.

When the skillet is hot, sprinkle salt on it. About 1 rounded tablespoon will do.

Roll the hamburger between your hands to make a round, flat shape (not too flat or too big). Place the hamburger on the salted part of the skillet.

Let the meat cook for about 3 to 5 minutes (medium to well done).

Turn it over with a spatula and cook 3 to 5 minutes on the other side.

Remove the hamburger from the skillet and make a little cut in the middle with a knife to see if it's done the way you like it.

*Chill the hamburger in the refrigerator for about 30 minutes to 1 hour.

With a floured rolling pin, roll a pastry shell to measure a rectangle, 1 inch wider than the hamburger and 2 times longer than the hamburger.

Place the hamburger on the lower half of the pastry.

Spread mustard, onion, or mushroom on top of the hamburger.

Wet the edges of the pastry with water and fold the top ½ of the pastry over the hamburger. Make the edges meet.

With the tines of a fork, gently press the sides of the pastry together.

Place the Wellington on a greased baking sheet and brush the top with milk or beaten egg.

Slide the baking sheet into a preheated 450-degree oven for 10 minutes and then lower the temperature to 350 degrees for about 20 to 30 minutes.

Serves one.

Lemon Lamb Lawry's

(Lawry's California Center, California)

2 tsp. Lawry's Lemon Pepper Marinade
1 cup water
2 tbsp. salad oil
2 lb. ground lamb, shaped into 16 balls*
1 large onion, sliced
1 tbsp. olive oil

½ cup lemon juice
1 tsp. Lawry's Seasoned Salt
1½ lb. fresh green beans, cut in
1-inch pieces
1 tsp. oregano, crushed
¼ cup pine nuts

Combine Lemon Pepper Marinade and water. Let it stand while browning the lamb. Heat salad oil in an electric skillet at 375 degrees. Brown lamb balls on all sides; add the onion and saute. Add the olive oil; carefully stir the lamb balls and onion to coat. Add the water, lemon juice, Seasoned Salt, green beans and oregano. Cover and simmer at 200 to 225 degrees for 1½ hours, stirring occasionally to prevent sticking. If needed, an additional ¼ cup water may be added during cooking. Serve over buttered noodles.
Makes 6-8 servings.
*2 pounds boneless lamb, cut in 1-inch cubes may be used in place of ground lamb.

Shaslik

(Russian Lamb Kebab)

(The Happy Baker, Tennessee)

1 leg or shoulder of lamb
3 cloves of crushed garlic

For marinade:
1 cup olive oil
2 tbsp. red wine vinegar
1 tbsp. basil
1 tsp. rosemary, crushed

1 tbsp. coarse salt

¼ cup chopped parsley
1 tbsp. freshly ground pepper
1 cup red wine

Remove fat from the lamb and slice meat into 2″ square cubes. Rub in crushed garlic-salt mixture. To make marinade: Combine remaining ingredients and blend well. Place lamb cubes in the marinade and refrigerate, covered, for 24 hours. Arrange lamb on skewers. Light charcoal briquettes in the grill, hibachi, or smoker stack. Smoker can also be used without the lid. Place a few wood chips on fire to add smoked flavor. Turn skewers often until nicely brown and crusty on the outside but still pink and juicy in the middle. Marinade can be used for basting while the Shaslik is cooking.
Serves 6-8.

Lamb Shanks-Madras Curry
(Alice M. Perlmutter, New York)

½ cup peanut oil
8 trimmed lamb shanks
5 tbsp. flour
2 tbsp. madras curry powder
1 cup Sauterne

2 tsp. salt
¼ tsp. freshly ground pepper
2 cloves garlic, mashed
1 onion, finely sliced
½ cup blanched peanuts

In wide, deep pot heat oil and brown shanks well. Remove. Into drippings over heat cook flour and curry for 3 minutes. Add wine, stirring constantly until smooth and thickened. Add seasoning and onions. Cook for 2 minutes then add shanks. Cover tightly and simmer for 1 hour. Serve. Garnish with fresh parsley or coriander and peanuts. Rice or bulgur is the starch accompaniment.

Loin of Pork Vouvray
(The Jean Brady Cooking School, California)

1½ cups Vouvray wine
20 large pitted prunes
2 boneless loin pork roasts (center cut) totaling 3½ lbs., tied together at 1- to 2-inch intervals to make a single round roast with a ready made pocket
3 tbsp. butter
2 tbsp. oil

6 tbsp. Cognac
1¼ cups beef stock or bouillon
1 cup heavy cream
2-3 tbsp. elderberry jam or jelly
2 tbsp. orange juice
Salt and pepper to taste
Beurre manie, made with 4 tbsp. flour and 4 tbsp. butter

Pour wine over prunes and let soak one hour. Preheat oven to 375 degrees. Using a wooden spoon handle, push as many prunes as you can into the cavity of the roast. Reserve remaining prunes. Heat butter and oil in a skillet large enough to hold the roast. Brown the roast on all sides. Warm Cognac and ignite while pouring over the roast. Roast in oven, uncovered, to an interior temperature of 160 to 165 degrees. Remove roast to heated platter and allow to rest at least 15 minutes. Meanwhile, in the skillet, combine the stock or boullion with the wine from the prunes, the heavy cream and jam or jelly. Deglaze pan and reduce liquids to ⅔ volume. Add remaining prunes. Add orange juice and season with salt and pepper. Whisk beurre manie into the sauce, 1 tsp. at a time, to thicken. Spoon some of the sauce over roast and carve into one inch slices. Fan three slices in front of roast to serve and pass remaining sauce.
Notes: If your butcher is your friend he will place your marinated prunes between the roasts and tie them in for you. Pork is a difficult meat to buy. Know where they sell the best, so that you will serve a tender, succulent roast. Roast should not be fatty (in the past, when pigs were fed garbage, pork was fat) but pour off any accumulated fat before deglazing the pan with the wine and cream mixture.

Mandarin Sweet and Pungent Pork

(Joanne Hush Cooking School, Connecticut)

1 lb. lean pork, cut into 1" cubes

Batter:
1 egg, lightly beaten
1 tbsp. dry sherry
1 tbsp. cornstarch
2 tbsp. flour
½ tsp. salt

4 cups peanut oil
2 tbsp. peanut oil
2 medium carrots, sliced, parboiled
8 medium broccoli flowers, parboiled

1 small can pineapple chunks, saving
  the juice
½ tsp. ginger, minced
½ tsp. garlic, minced

Sauce:
1 cup chicken broth and pineapple juice
  combined
3 tbsp. sugar

3 tbsp. rice vinegar
1 tbsp. soy sauce
3 tbsp. tomato catsup

1 tbsp. cornstarch dissolved in 2 tbsp.
  water

Combine batter and add pork. Set aside 30 minutes. Heat 4 cups oil and fry pork at 375 degrees for 8 minutes. Drain and set aside. Add 2 tablespoons oil to a heated wok. Add ginger, garlic; stir, then add vegetables. Stir and add sauce and bring to a boil. Add cornstarch and stir until thickened. Pour sauce over pork before serving.

Yang Chow Fried Rice

4 cups cold cooked rice
½ cup diced, cooked ham
¼ cup frozen peas, thawed

¼ cup scallions, chopped
2 eggs, scrambled

Sauce:
2 tbsp. black soy
¼ cup chicken broth
1 tbsp. sherry

½ tsp. salt
4 tbsp. peanut oil

Add 4 tablespoons peanut oil to heated wok. Stir-fry vegetables 1 minute. Add rice and eggs and stir thoroughly. Add sauce and heat for about 3 minutes.

Pork Loin Normande
(Cook's Corner, Inc., Connecticut)

1 tbsp. butter	3 tbsp. Calvados
1 tbsp. oil	1 tbsp. flour
2 pork tenderloins (1½-2 lb.) or 1 loin of pork	1½ cups chicken stock
	Salt and pepper
1 medium onion, sliced	¼ cup heavy cream
2 tart apples, pared, cored and sliced	Bunch of watercress

In a saute pan heat the oil and butter and brown pork on all sides. Remove it, add the onion and cook until soft but not brown. Add the apple and continue cooking until apple and onion are golden brown. Return the pork to the pan, pour the Calvados over and flame. Stir in the flour, add the stock, salt and pepper, and bring to a boil. If using tenderloins cover and cook—at a simmer—40 to 50 minutes on top of the stove, until the meat is tender, stirring sauce occasionally. If using loin of pork bake in 350-degree oven for 2 hours, or until tender, stirring sauce occasionally.

Remove the pork, slice it and arrange it on a platter and keep it warm. Remove onion and apple from sauce and puree them or put them through a strainer. Return to saucepan and reduce to a coating consistency. Add the cream, bring to a boil and taste for seasonings. Pour the sauce over the pork and garnish with watercress.

Serves 6.

Scallopine al Carciofe
(Creative Cooking, Maryland)

1½ to 2 lb. pink veal, sliced very thin	6-8 mushrooms, sliced
	1 pkg. frozen artichokes, thawed and drained
½ cup flour	¼ cup beef stock (use Bovril)
Dashes of: cayenne, nutmeg, dry mustard, sugar, msg, sage	½ tsp. tomato paste
2 tbsp. butter	½ cup dry Marsala
2 tbsp. olive oil	3 tsp. flour
2 tbsp. Cognac	1 tbsp. currant jelly
	½ cup grated Parmesan cheese
	¼ tsp. salt
	Pinch black pepper
	½ tsp. oregano

Trim off any fat from veal and cut into serving-size pieces. Place each piece between wax paper and pound with a mallet to about 1/8″ thickness. Place flour in a bowl, add dashes of herbs, pinch of salt and black pepper. Mix. Flour the pounded veal. Using a large skillet, heat butter and olive oil. Brown pieces of veal on both sides, quickly. Pour over flaming Cognac. Remove meat to platter and keep warm. Deglaze pan, add mushrooms and artichokes and brown slightly. Add beef stock (Bovril), and tomato paste and mix carefully. Dissolve flour in Marsala and add to skillet, stirring constantly until thickened. Add jelly and correct seasonings. Place meat in a heatproof casserole and smother with artichokes and mushrooms. Pour sauce over all. Sprinkle with cheese and oregano. Bake at 375 degrees until lightly browned. This takes about 15 minutes. Watch carefully and do not let dry out.

Sliced Braised Veal with Ham & Mushroom Puree

(Carol's Capers, New Jersey)

2 lb. top round of veal, barded
Salt and ground pepper
½ lb. boiled ham, sliced 1/16″ thick
2 large onions, sliced
1 clove garlic, minced
2 shallots, minced
1 large carrot, cut in
   ½″ pieces for chopping

½ cup dry white wine
1 cup veal or beef stock
1 tbsp. tomato paste
Bouquet garni
1 tsp. dried savory, crumbled
½ tsp. dried thyme, crumbled
1 tbsp. Cognac

Gently brown veal in heavy Dutch oven. Remove meat. Drain off accumulated fat.

Place medium slicing disc in food processor. Slice onions and add to Dutch oven. Change to steel blade knife. Start machine. Drop garlic through feeder tube and mince. Then add carrots and process to a course chop. Empty basket into Dutch oven and saute with onions until vegetables are softened and lightly browned. Return meat to pan and heat. Deglaze with white wine and reduce to ½. Add stock, tomato paste, bouquet garni, savory and thyme. Bring to a slow boil. Cover and simmer on top of stove or in a 300-degree oven for 1 to 1¼ hours or until meat is fork tender. Remove veal and bouquet garni from pan and allow to cool. Reserve celery from bouquet garni. Add to other vegetables.

Degrease gravy. Puree vegetables with meat juices until very smooth in processor fitted with steel blade knife. This will have to be done in 2 or 3 batches. Empty into a saucepan. Add Cognac. Bring to a slow boil and simmer 5 minutes. Adjust seasonings. Set aside.

Mushroom Puree:

½ lb. mushrooms, finely chopped
2 tbsp. chopped parsley
2 tbsp. butter
1 tbsp. flour

½ cup milk
Salt and ground pepper
Nutmeg to taste

Fit processor with steel blade knife. Chop mushrooms (½ at a time). Empty basket. Add parsley and chop. Set aside.

Melt butter in a heavy skillet. Add mushrooms and saute on a high flame until liquid evaporates. Reduce flame, stir in flour, blending well. Cook slowly for 1 minute. Add milk, bring to a slow boil, stirring until smooth and thickened. Add parsley and seasonings. Set aside.

TO ASSEMBLE:

Spoon a little sauce on the bottom of a large oven-to-table platter.

Cut veal into 1/8″ slices. Remove string and barding before slicing.

Place a slice of veal on platter. Spread with 1 tablespoon mushroom puree. Top with a piece of ham cut approximately the same size as veal. Mask with sauce. Repeat with overlapping layers of veal, mushrooms, ham and sauce, ending with a slice of veal. Tuck any small pieces of veal underneath. Spoon remaining sauce on top. Cover *loosely* with foil. *MAY STAND SEVERAL HOURS AT THIS POINT.

Bake in a 350-degree oven, 20 to 25 minutes or until sauce starts to bubble and meat is heated through. Baste occasionally. Serve at once with mushroom garnish.

Mushroom Garnish (optional):

Fit processor with thin slicing disk. Process ½ lb. mushrooms into thin slices. Melt 2 tablespoons butter in a heavy skillet. Quickly saute mushrooms until slightly wilted. Sprinkle with a little lemon juice, salt and pepper. Spoon down center of veal just before serving.

Tony Bommarito's Chicken Grand Marnier
(The Pampered Pantry, Missouri)

2 double chicken breasts, boned
    and skinned
Flour
Butter
Zest from 1 orange

Juice from 1 orange
⅓ cup Grand Marnier
¾ cup heavy cream
Nutmeg
Salt and white pepper

Remove the zest from large orange, being careful to peel off only the orange-colored outer skin, without any of the bitter white part. Slice this in thin julienne strips. Place the strips in the Grand Marnier to marinate. Remove juice from orange and set aside.

Dust the chicken breasts lightly with flour. Sauté in a heavy pan in melted butter until just golden brown. Do not over-cook as it results in a dry piece of meat.

Add the Grand Marnier and orange zest and simmer a few minutes, turning the chicken to absorb the flavor.

Add the heavy cream and simmer slowly to reduce a bit. When it thickens, add enough orange juice to make the sauce a good consistency.

Add a few grinds of fresh nutmeg, white pepper and salt to taste.

May be garnished with thin orange slices.

Serves 4.

Moo Goo Guy Pen
(Katherine M. Chin R.D., Maryland)

2 cups white and/or dark chicken meat
2 slivers fresh ginger root
2 bunches Chinese bok toy
1 bunch celery heart
8 to 10 small Chinese dried mushrooms
    cut in half (soaked in water
    first)

½ cup sliced bamboo shoots
½ cup sliced waterchestnuts
24 fresh snowpeas
1 tbsp. cooking oil

Mixture for gravy:

2 tbsp. cornstarch in ½ cup tap water
2 tsp. dry sherry wine
1 tbsp. salt
1 tsp. sugar

1 tbsp. thin soy sauce
Dash of pepper
Dash of sesame seed oil

Filet chicken meat; then cut filets into pieces about 2″ long and 1″ wide. Slice bok toy diagonally; slice celery heart diagonally. Snap off tips of fresh snowpeas. Wash vegetables and drain off water. Have ingredients within easy reach. Heat wok; add oil and allow to become hot. Put in fresh ginger root; then add chicken; add bok toy, celery, mushrooms, bamboo shoots and waterchestnuts. Note: small amount of liquid will appear from the vegetables. Allow ingredients to simmer for 1 to 2 minutes. Cover wok and let simmer for another 1 minute. Uncover. Approximately ¾ cup of liquid should have accumulated. Then add snowpeas. Have liquid come to a rolling boil before pouring in the gravy mixture. Pour this mixture in slowly while stirring gently the ingredients. Liquid mixture is now thickening. Add dash of sesame seed oil and stir once again. Delicious with hot white rice.

Serves 4 to 6.

Supremes Saute
(The Classic Cook, Pennsylvania)

½ tsp. salt
¼ tsp. freshly ground pepper
1 cup flour
4 large chicken breasts, boned
4 tbsp. butter
½ tsp. dried thyme

½ tsp. dried basil
2 scallions, finely chopped
⅔ cup dry white wine
1 can (6 oz.) sliced mushrooms, drained
3 tbsp. finely chopped fresh parsley

Combine the salt, pepper and flour in a shallow dish and dust the chicken breasts well. In a large, heavy skillet melt the butter. Over medium-high heat saute the supremes until golden brown, turning them frequently and adding more butter if necessary. Sprinkle all remaining ingredients, except mushrooms, evenly over supremes. Cover tightly and simmer for 30 minutes. Add drained mushrooms and continue cooking until chicken is fork tender and no liquid remains. Serves 4.

Poulet Saute a la Provencal
(La Bonne Cuisine, California)

1 roasting chicken, jointed
8 sprigs thyme
8 slices lean bacon
2 tbsp. butter
2 tbsp. oil
1 large onion, chopped

4 medium-sized tomatoes
1 tbsp. flour
1 cup dry white wine
1 clove garlic
Salt and Pepper

Garnish:
Finely chopped parsley
Rounds of French bread, fried in oil

Remove the skin from the chicken. Lay a sprig of thyme on each joint and wrap with a slice of bacon. Tie with a piece of thin string. Heat butter and oil in a saute pan or skillet until hot and saute each joint until it is a rich brown color. Remove the chicken and quickly fry the onions, add the tomatoes which have been skinned, seeds removed and cut into shreds. Sprinkle in the flour. Mix well and then pour on the wine. Add the garlic crushed with a little salt and seasoning. Bring to a boil. Add the browned chicken joints. Cover and simmer gently on top of the stove for 30 minutes or in 350 degree oven until tender.
Place the chicken joints in a warm serving dish, removing the string. Place the pan over a high heat and reduce the sauce until the consistency of thin cream. Adjust the seasonings, pour sauce over the chicken. Garnish with the French bread and dust thickly with the finely chopped parsley.
Serves 4-5.

Copyright La Bonne Cuisine 1972.

Sliced Filet of Duck with Oranges and Grapes
(Judith Ets-Hokin Culinary Institute, California)

4 oranges
4 duck breasts and thighs (deboned)
Unsalted butter
4 ounces (½ cup) glace de viande

2 small bunches seedless grapes
Salt
Pepper

Note: Glace de viande: a reduction of brown stock until it reaches a thick gelatinous glaze.

Remove the zest from 4 oranges. Peel and section them, reserving the juice. Saute in a five-quart saute pan the fileted breasts and thighs of 2 ducks, turning frequently until browned, no more than 5 minutes total. Meat should be pink. Remove filets to a carving board and let rest. Pour off the fat and add the reserved orange juice and 4 ounces glace de viande and the orange zest. Deglaze the pan and reduce the sauce. Remove the skin and fat from the duck meat and slice into thin slices across the grain. Saute 2 handfuls seedless grapes in 2 tablespoons butter for 1 minute. Add the grapes to the sauce with the orange sections. Season with salt and pepper. Place a piece of thigh and breast meat in the center of a warmed plate. Spoon the sauce and fruit over the meat. Serves 8.

Curried Chicken with Fresh Peaches
(Hurrah!, Ohio)

4 whole chicken breasts, split
2 tbsp. butter
1 tbsp. oil
1 onion, chopped
1 heaping tbsp. curry powder
1 heaping tbsp. flour
2 cups chicken stock
  (canned or fresh)
1 clove garlic, pressed
1 cup boiling water
2 tbsp. grated coconut

2 tbsp. chopped almonds
½ lemon, juice only
1 tbsp. sugar
1 tsp. cornstarch
¼ cup whipping cream
2 fresh peaches, peeled and sliced or
  canned white peaches
6 cups cooked rice

Wash and dry chicken. Heat 1 tablespoon butter and 1 tablespoon oil in a large pan and saute chicken until golden brown. Remove from pan. Saute onion in same pan until clear, add curry, cook 2 minutes. Add remaining butter and flour and cook for 2 minutes. Add warm stock and garlic. Simmer 15 minutes. Return chicken, cover pan and cook until chicken is tender, about 25 to 30 minutes.

Remove chicken. Strain sauce. Add "nut milk" to it. (The nut milk is made by putting the coconut and almonds into boiling water, removing from heat, soaking one hour and straining). Mix lemon juice with sugar and cornstarch and add to sauce. Wipe out pan and return chicken to it. Stir cream into sauce. Add peaches and spoon over chicken. Reheat slowly. Serve over rice. Garnish with parsley.
Serves 6-8.

Chicken Celestine Bonniers

(Annemarie's Cookingschool, New York)

3 whole chicken breasts, boned,
  skinned and cut in half
4 tbsp. margarine
1 tsp. vegetable oil
Juice of 1 lemon
Salt and pepper
1 tsp. rosemary

½ cup shallots, finely chopped
2 cups fresh mushrooms, thinly sliced
½ clove garlic, put thru garlic press
½ cup dry white wine
½ cup chicken broth (Campbell's)
2 tbsp. parsley, finely chopped
1 tsp. flour mixed with 1 tsp.
  margarine

Sprinkle the chicken with lemon juice and let marinate for 5 minutes, then season with salt, pepper and the rosemary.

In a heavy saute pan heat the margarine and oil and brown the chicken breasts on both sides, remove from the pan and put aside. Add the shallots and mushrooms and saute for about 4 minutes, stirring constantly, then add the garlic, wine and chicken broth. Return the chicken breasts, bring to a boil and simmer for 20 minutes. Add the parsley and thicken the sauce with the flour and margarine mixture.

Serves 4.

Poulet Aux Ecrevisses
(Chicken Breasts with Shrimp)

(Alma Lach Cooking School, Inc., Illinois)

2 whole chicken breasts
2 cups seasoned chicken broth
1 lb. jumbo shrimp, cleaned
  and deveined
1/8 lb. butter
1 tbsp. minced shallots
1 clove garlic, put through press
3 tbsp. Cognac

¼ cup chicken broth
Salt to season
White pepper to season
¼ tsp. sugar
Pinch saffron threads
2 tbsp. Madeira
3 egg yolks
¾ cup whipping cream

Put chicken breasts into cold broth. Bring to a boil. Turn off heat, cover and let stand off the heat for 15 minutes. Do not let the meat boil.

Split shrimp lengthwise in half. Saute in butter with shallots and garlic until they turn pink, or for about 2 minutes. Pour Cognac over and set aflame. Lift shrimp from skillet to a plate.

Add wine, broth, some salt and pepper and the sugar, saffron threads and Madeira. Reduce by half. Strain into a clean pan.

Remove skin from chicken and debone. Cut into chunks about the size of the shrimp. Add chicken and shrimp to the strained sauce. Heat to a boil.

Combine yolks and cream and mix well. (This is called a liaison.) Remove chicken and shrimp from heat. Pour the egg-cream mixture into the chicken-shrimp and stir. Return to a very low heat and carefully heat until the sauce is hot. Do not let it boil or it might curdle. Serve with rice pilaf and a green salad.

Serves 6.

Chicken With Chestnuts
(Murray Hill School of Cooking, New York)

3 tbsp. vegetable oil
3 tbsp. butter
25 small white onions, peeled
25 chestnuts (approx. 1 lb.)
1 chicken cut into 8 serving pieces
   (or cut-up chicken parts)
Salt
Pepper

2 tbsp. flour
1 cup chicken broth (canned)
2 tbsp. tomato puree
½ tsp. thyme
2 cloves of garlic
½ cup dry white wine
½ to 1 cup heavy cream

Drop the onions into a pot of boiling water for 1 minute, drain and peel. This is easiest to do if one starts by cutting off the root.

In a heavy 4-quart pot melt the butter together with the oil. Saute the peeled onions until they start to brown. Shake the pan occasionally to prevent them from burning. Remove onions and reserve.

While the onions are browning, cut a cross on top of each chestnut with a small sharp knife and put them in a saucepan with water to cover. Bring to a boil and simmer 10 minutes. Remove a few chestnuts at a time and while still hot peel off the outer hard skin and inner peel. If they are too difficult to peel return to hot water for a couple of minutes. Reserve chestnuts.

Dry the chicken pieces, salt and pepper them and brown in the same pot as onions; if necessary add some more butter. When the chicken pieces have a nice golden color, powder with flour, add hot chicken broth and scrape up any brown bits on bottom of pan. Add the tomato puree, thyme, whole garlic cloves and the white wine. Cover the casserole and bring to a slow simmer; after 10 minutes add chestnuts and onions, and ¼ cup heavy cream. Continue simmering the chicken until tender, about 40 minutes total cooking time. Add the cream ¼ cup at a time as needed to maintain enough liquid. The sauce should not be too thin. Correct seasoning if necessary and serve.

Serves 4-6.

Baked Stuffed Fillet

(Ann Mariotti's Cooking School, New York)

½ cup olive oil
6 thin slices of filet (flounder or sole)
12 raw shrimp, chopped
½ onion, chopped
1 stalk celery, chopped
3 tbsp. Swiss cheese, chopped
1 hard cooked egg, chopped

2 tbsp. parsley, chopped
2 tbsp. tomato sauce
¾ cup bread crumbs
6 tooth picks
6 pieces raw onions
6 pieces of bay leaf

In a large frying pan put ¼ cup oil. Cook onion and celery until soft. Add shrimp. Cook until shrimp is slightly pink. Do not overcook. Remove from heat. Add cheese, egg, parsley, tomato sauce and ¼ cup of bread crumbs. Mix well.

Divide the mixture evenly on the fillet slices and spread. Roll jelly-roll style and fasten with a toothpick. Secure the toothpick with a piece of bay leaf on one side and a piece of onion on other side.

Roll each piece of fillet in the remaining oil and then in the remaining bread crumbs. Place close together in a small baking dish. Bake for 30-35 minutes at 350 degrees.
Serves 6.

Caribbean Crepes Surprise

(Cooking Under Glass, Tennessee)

2 cups cream
1½ to 2 cups flaked coconut
¼ cup butter
3 tbsp. cornstarch
½ to 1 tsp. salt, or to taste

½ lb. shrimp, cooked
¼ to ½ lb. fish fillets or crab,
        cooked and flaked
12 crepes

Combine cream and coconut and bring to a boil. Let mixture stand at least half an hour. Drain through a sieve, pressing and squeezing on the coconut to extract all of the cream. Refrigerate or freeze coconut for later use. Reserve cream.

Melt butter in saucepan and blend in cornstarch. Add coconut-flavored cream and cook till thickened. Season. Reserve half of sauce (about 1 cup) for topping. Add seafood to the remaining sauce to make filling. Spoon filling into centers of crepes and roll. Place seam side down in an oven-proof, shallow baking dish.

Thin remaining sauce with 1 or 2 tablespoons milk, and spoon over filled crepes. Bake at 400 degrees for 10-15 minutes, or until bubbly. Fills 12 crepes. Garnish with paprika, Parmesan cheese, or toasted coconut.

Bass Poche "Baumaniere"
(Sue Lyon's Essencial Cooking School, New Jersey)

1 qt. fish fumet, strained
1 (3 lb.) striped bass
½ cup olive oil
1 tbsp. crushed, dried basil
½ peeled and seeded tomato
½ clove of garlic, crushed

A few thyme leaves
Pinch of crushed fennel seeds
Small piece of bay leaf
Juice of 1 lemon
Fresh chopped parsley

Place the striped bass in a fish poacher or in a large roasting pan. Pour fumet over fish so that it almost covers it. You may add equal parts white wine and water to raise the level. Bring liquid to the barest simmer and allow to "shiver" covered about 30 minutes. When the fish is done, the eye will become opaque, but you should flake the thickest part to see if the fish easily comes away from the bone. Lift out the fish and place it on a large deep platter. Allow it to cool to room temperature. (If you plan to serve the fish cold, prepare the following sauce as you prepare the fish. If you plan to serve it warm, make the sauce the day before so it will be ready.)

For sauce: Combine the rest of the ingredients except the chopped parsley and mix well. Heat to serving temperature. Pour over the fish. Sprinkle chopped parsley over the fish just before serving. For ease in serving you might want to remove the skin, head and tail of the fish before placing on serving platter.

Fried Oysters (Ch'ao Seng-Huo)
(The Mandarin Cooking Class, California)

2 jars medium-sized fresh oysters
(approximately 3½ cups)

Flour
Cottonseed oil

Batter:
1 cup flour
1 egg
1 cup cornstarch
2 tbsp. cottonseed oil
1 cup cold water

1 heaping tsp. baking soda
1½ tbsp. white vinegar
1 tsp. sesame oil
½ tsp. salt
Splash of wine

Prepare batter, beating with whisk until smooth. Add a little more water if too thick. (This is also a good batter for shrimp.)

Place oysters in a bowl. Add a handful of flour and toss to draw out sand and other impurities. Rinse with water once or twice, then drain. Poach oysters for 1 minute in boiling water. Remove with strainer and put into cold water for 1 minute. Drain.

Meanwhile, heat oil over high temperature until bubbling. Roll oysters in flour. Then cover with batter and deep fry 5 to 6 minutes. Turn from time to time until golden brown. Deep fry 3 to 4 minutes if oysters are small. Serve with catsup and hot mustard.

Baked Stuffed Fish
(Culinary Arts, Maryland)

Stuffing:

½ cup finely chopped shallots
2 tbsp. sweet butter
¾ cup finely chopped mushrooms
   (Duxelles)
1 egg beaten with ¼ cup milk

1 cup fresh bread crumbs
¼ cup finely chopped parsley
1 tsp. thyme
Dash of nutmeg
Salt and pepper

Fish:

2 medium-to-large striped bass, salmon,
   lake trout, rock, etc.
Salt and pepper
6 tbsp. sweet butter

¾ cup dry white wine
2 tbsp. lemon juice
4 parsley sprigs

Sweat shallots with butter (do not brown). Add the mushrooms and cook them until they have evaporated all excess liquid. Add 1 tablespoon of dry Madeira if desired. Combine the *duxelles* with the egg/milk mixture. Add crumbs, parsley, thyme, salt, pepper, and nutmeg. Taste for seasoning. Cool.

Season the fish with salt and pepper, and stuff it loosely. Sew up the opening with a *trussing* needle and strong thread or string.
Place heavy aluminum foil in the bottom of a roasting pan and place the fish on top. Dot with 4 tablespoons of the butter. Add the wine, lemon juice, and parsley springs.
Bake in a 400-degree oven for about 35 minutes, or until the fish flakes easily with a fork. Remove to a warm serving platter, remove the foil and thread, and strain the sauce into a saucepan. Swirl in the remaining 2 tablespoons of butter, pour the sauce over the fish and serve.

Serves 10.

Copyright Culinary Arts 1977

Fijiian Baked Fish Isa Lei
(Gloria Olsen, Tennessee)

A specialty of the Isa Lei Hotel in Suva, Viti Levu, Fiji Islands.

6 fillets of turbot, cod, red snapper,
   or pompano, skinned
1½ cups cream, light or heavy
1½ cups unsweetened coconut

2 tbsp. butter
1½ tbsp. cornstarch
1½ tsp. salt

Place fillets in a 9″ x 13″ baking dish which has been buttered. Bring cream and coconut to a boil and let stand ½ hour. Strain, pressing hard to extract all the juice. Discard coconut. Make a roux with butter and cornstarch, add coconut milk, and cook until thick. Season, pour over filets, and bake in a 350-degree oven about ½ hour, or until golden. Serves 6.

Trota al Piatto (Trout Cooked on a Plate)
(Giuliano Bugialli Cooking Classes, New York)

A special way to cook filleted trout. The fillets are put on oven-proof plates with a little wine, lemon juice, and olive oil, then the plate is placed over a steaming stockpot. While simple to prepare, the presentation of this fish generally provides a touch of drama, and the result is delicious.

4 brook trout (about 2 lb.)	**¼ cup dry white wine**
4 or 5 sprigs Italian parsley	**2 tsp. olive oil**
Juice of ½ lemon	**Salt and freshly ground white pepper**

Wet your hands, then cut off the heads and tails of the trout with a knife. Open stomachs to clean out the viscera. With a boning knife, extend each stomach opening down to the tail end, to open the fish completely, then insert the point of the knife alongside the backbone at the head end. Move the knife downward to the tail end. Repeat the procedure on the other side of the bone, then lift the bone out.

Coarsely chop the parsley and set it aside.

Put the lemon juice in a small bowl, along with the wine, olive oil, and salt and white pepper to taste. Stir very well with a wooden spoon.

Oil 4 ovenproof plates and on them place the trout fillets, with their skins on. Pour the liquid in the bowl over the trout and sprinkle the chopped parsley on top, then wrap the plates completely in aluminum foil.

Put a large quantity of water in 4 saucepans and set them on the heat. When the water reaches the boiling point, lower the flame to a simmer and place the plates on top of the saucepans. Let the fish steam for 16 to 18 minutes.

Remove the plates from the saucepans, carefully unwrap the foil, and serve immediately. Serves 4.

Baked Clams Arregenata
(Chef Ralph Varketta, Florida)

1 cup plain bread crumbs	**Salt, pepper, Accent to taste**
1 tbsp. grated Parmesan cheese	**½ cup olive oil**
¼ cup chopped parsley	**12 cherrystone clams**
1 clove crushed garlic	**4 lemon wedges and 4 parsley sprigs**
1 tbsp. oregano	

In 2-quart bowl mix all ingredients except clams, lemon and parsley.

Wash, open, loosen clams.

Cover each clam with liberal amount of bread mixture, pack well.

Place stuffed clams on baking sheet and add 1/2 cup of white wine or clam broth or water to pan.

Bake at 400 to 425 degrees for 15 to 20 minutes or broil for shorter period (12-15 minutes). Garnish with lemon wedge and parsley sprig.

Serves 4 as appetizer, 2 as main course.

NOTE: After preparing clams, they can be frozen until needed—thaw before using. Or refrigerate until needed.

Whole canned or minced clams can be used if fresh are not available.

For easy shucking or opening of clams, wash well, place in plastic bags and freeze until needed. Upon thawing clams will open. Proceed as for fresh.

Stuffed Florida Red Snapper
(Bobbi & Carole's Cooking School, Inc., Florida)

1 3-lb. red snapper, head and tail left on, butterflied

Stuffing:

3 tbsp. minced shallots

4 tbsp. butter

1 clove minced garlic

1 tbsp. chopped parsley

8 oz. white crabmeat

1 lb. shrimp (8 oz. chopped for stuffing,
   8 oz. whole for garnish)

3 slices bread, soaked in water and
   squeezed out

Salt and pepper

1 cup mirepoix: ⅓ cup each chopped
   onions, carrots and celery

2 cups fish stock or white wine

Melted butter to brush on fish

Lemon slices for garnish

Parsley for garnish

Saute shallots in the butter until limp. Add garlic, parsley, crabmeat, ½ lb. chopped shrimp and bread. Cook over medium heat for 10 minutes. Season stuffing with salt and pepper. Season fish inside and out with salt and pepper. Stuff fish. Close opening using poultry lacers. Fold a piece of aluminum foil into 3 layers making sure it is 3 inches longer than the fish at both ends. Oil the strip and place it in a buttered baking dish. Place fish on strip surrounded by mirepoix. Brush the fish with melted butter. Cover the tail with foil. Pour in enough fish stock or wine to cover the bottom of the pan. Bake in a 375-degree oven for 35 minutes, basting often. Place the fish on serving platter, using foil as a lifter. Garnish with whole cooked shrimp, parsley, lemon slices and an olive for the eye.
Fish is done when the flesh at the backbone is opaque and flakes easily when poked with a fork.
Serves 6.

Jing Yue—Kwangtung Province Fish
(Irene Wong's Great Asia Cooking School, Texas)

1 2-lb. fresh fish (sea bass is traditional)
   with head and tail

1 tsp. salt

2 slices ginger

1 green onion

⅓ cup oil

⅓ cup light soy sauce

Wash, scale and remove entrails from the fish if the fish man did not do it. Dry and place in a deep plate. Salt the fish. Slash with a knife in two places on both sides. Shred ginger and green onion. Set aside. Make sure the water is boiling before you put the fish in to cook, so you can time from that point. Set fish on plate on rack, cover and steam 20 minutes. Before the fish is ready, heat the oil to HOT. Take the plate out of the steamer, pour off liquid in plate, scatter the shredded ginger and green onion over the fish. Drizzle the soy sauce, then the hot oil, on the puffing fish. The sizzle always brings people into the kitchen. Serves 4. Substitution: Use 1½ lbs. fish fillet (any kind). Do not salt the fish. Steam 10 minutes. Follow all other directions. You may reduce the oil poured on the fish, since its primary purpose is to sear the fish skin. For fewer calories, you may omit the oil, steaming the fish with soy sauce and scattering the green onions and ginger slivers at the end before serving.

Pizza alla Napolitana

(Culinarion, Illinois)

1 package active dry yeast
¼ cup warm water
½ tsp. salt

1 cup warm water
3 cups flour
3 tbsp. olive oil

Dissolve yeast in warm water; let stand until bubbly. Combine flour and salt in large bowl; make a well in the center. Add the yeast mixture and water and 3 tablespoons oil. Stir until combined. Knead until smooth (10 minutes).
Let rise in warm place. Punch dough down; divide into 2 portions. Spread in 2 well-oiled pans. Cover with choice of filling below.
Bake at 400 degrees until golden and crusty.

Pizza Margherita:
1 lb. Italian-style tomatoes, chopped
1 lb. Mozzarella cheese, shredded
2 to 3 tsp. oregano
Salt and pepper
3 to 4 tbsp. olive oil

Pizza Napolitana:
1 lb. Italian-style tomatoes, chopped
1 lb. Mozzarella cheese, shredded
1 can anchovy fillets
Basil
Oil-cured olives, pitted
Oregano
Olive oil

Sausage Jambalaya

(Lee Barnes Cooking School and Gourmet Shop, Louisiana)

1½ lb. hot or smoked sausage
1 large onion, chopped
1 green pepper, chopped
4 stalks celery, chopped
2 cloves garlic, minced
1 (1-lb.) can of tomatoes, drained

2 cups rice
3¾ cups chicken stock*
2 cups smoked ham, cubed
4 green onions, chopped
¼ cup parsley, chopped
Tabasco, salt, pepper to taste

In a covered Dutch oven, saute sausage and remove. In same oil, saute onions, green pepper, and celery. Add the rice. Stir to coat rice with oil. Add tomatoes, garlic, and ham. Add stock. Bring to a boil. Cover and let simmer 30 minutes.
Add sausage, green onions, parsley. Season to taste. Cover and cook 10 more minutes.
Serves 6-8.

*Chicken Stock:
1 small chicken
1 veal knuckle
3 qt. water
1 onion, quartered
2 carrots, chopped

2 stalks celery, chopped
1 bay leaf
10 peppercorns
Salt

Place chicken and veal knuckle in water. Bring to a boil and skim surface. Add remaining ingredients. Simmer half-covered 3 hours, strain, cool, refrigerate. Remove fat once it has solidified.

Jambalaya
(The Chef's Connection, Indiana)

1 or 2 strips bacon, chopped
Vegetable oil
1 cup chicken (raw, cut in 1″ pieces)
1 cup ham cut in 1″ pieces
2 lb. Andouille (Cajun sausage) French or Italian mild, or any sausage with garlic may be substituted. Poach sausage in wine and chicken broth for 30 minutes.
1 (1-lb.) can Italian plum tomatoes (chopped-drained-reserve liquid)
1 cup onions, chopped
1 cup green peppers, cut in ½″ pieces
1 cup raw hard rice
2 garlic cloves, minced
1 bay leaf, crushed
1½ tsp. salt
2 tsp. paprika

¼ tsp. cayenne pepper
¼ tsp. thyme
¼ tsp. black pepper
1 tsp. chili powder
1/8 tsp. ground cloves
¼ tsp. dried basil
1/8 tsp. mace
3 tbsp. dried parsley *or* handful fresh
2½ cups liquid (which consists of any old broth you have around-chicken, beef, pork, sausage broth, reserved tomato liquid, wine—a combination of these with salt and pepper (lightly) should cook down about 1 hour.

Fry bacon and remove from skillet. Pour in oil (so that there is ½ grease and ½ oil). Saute onion, garlic and ⅓ of the peppers. Remove to casserole. Saute raw rice until barely golden. Remove to casserole. Add all other ingredients to casserole except the liquid. Mix and let set a few hours. Then pour in the broth until it's ¼″ above jambalaya. Cover. Bake in 350-degree oven 1¼ hours or until rice is soft. Try to keep liquid ¼″ above at all times until near the end. You don't want it too moist or too dry. Add liquid if necessary. ½ hour before done, add the reserved green peppers. (Turn oven to warm and this will hold a couple hours).
Serves 8-10.

Vegetables

Frittata Di Carciofi e Patate
(Artichoke and Potato Frittata)
(Loni Kuhn Cook's Tour)

Frittati can, of course, be made with practically any combination of vegetables—beans, broccoli, zucchini, peppers, peas, etc.

8 cooked artichoke bottoms or 1
    package frozen artichoke hearts,
    thawed
2 cups cold boiled potatoes
¼ cup butter
¼ cup olive oil
1½ tsp. salt
1 tsp. freshly ground pepper

1 cup sliced onions
2 to 3 cloves garlic, minced
¼ cup chopped parsley
1 tsp. oregano
¼ tsp. Thyme
6 beaten eggs
½ cup freshly grated Parmesan cheese

If using the frozen artichoke hearts, cut in half. Slice the artichoke bottoms. Heat the butter and oil in a heavy 10-inch frying pan. Add the salt and pepper, onion and garlic, and cook, stirring about 5 minutes over medium heat. Turn heat high and when the pan sizzles, add the artichokes and potatoes, stirring gently. Add the herbs and eggs, lifting the vegetables to urge the egg to the bottom of the pan. Turn the heat very low and cook about 12 minutes without stirring or until egg is set. Sprinkle top with cheese and place under broiler until brown.

Braised Celery
(The Cooking School, Alabama)

Allow ¾-1 cup celery per person. Strip the leaves from the stalks, and if there are strings remove them. Cut in slices or in thin julienne strips about 2 to 3″ long and about ½″ wide. Place celery in a heavy saucepan with tight-fitting cover. Add water or chicken broth to cover saucepan bottom, cover and steam over medium heat 10-12 minutes, or until the celery is crisply tender. Add butter and braise for several minutes. Season to taste.

Aubergines Provencal
(Eggplant-Tomato Casserole)
(John Simmons Cooking School, Tennessee)

1 medium size eggplant	Oregano flakes
4 tomatoes	¼ cup freshly grated Parmesan cheese
Salt and pepper	

Cut eggplant in half, peel and cut into ¼″ slices. Peel tomato and slice. In a quart casserole, arrange a layer of eggplant; sprinkle with salt and pepper. Arrange a layer of tomatoes; sprinkle with salt, pepper, oregano flakes that you have crushed finer with your fingers, and cheese. Repeat layers until casserole is full, ending with cheese on top. Cover and bake in 400-degree oven 30 to 40 minutes or until eggplant is tender. Test eggplant for doneness with a long pronged fork or icepick.

Sesame Eggplant
(Margaret Spader Chinese Cooking School, New York)

This is a cold vegetable dish that can be prepared several hours ahead of a meal. The texture is soft, but a sprinkling of finely slivered ginger root and toasted sesame seeds adds flavor and texture.

1 medium eggplant (about 1½ to 2 lb.)	1½ tbsp. light soy sauce
2 scallions, finely minced	3 tbsp. sesame seed oil
2 tsp. slivered ginger	Toasted sesame seeds*

Wash eggplant. Dry well. Cut it in half lengthwise and place in a steamer. Steam 15 to 30 minutes, depending on the size. It should be soft when pierced with a fork. Cool and tear into shreds 3 x ½ inches.

Sprinkle scallion and ginger shreds over the shredded eggplant. Cover and refrigerate.

Mix soy sauce and sesame oil. 15 minutes before serving, drizzle over eggplant and let come to room temperature. Sprinkle with toasted sesame seeds.

Serves 4 to 6 persons.

*To toast sesame seeds: heat a small skillet over medium heat. Add sesame seeds and stir constantly. The seeds will become shiny as oil is released, then turn brown. Stirring facilitates even browning.

Green Beans Bernaise
(The Happy Baker, Tennesses)

2 lb. fresh snap beans
1 tsp. salt
2 tsp. sugar
12 slices of lean bacon

6 scallions, including the green tops,
    cut in ¼ inch slices
6 tbsp. parsley, chopped
4 tbsp. butter, preferably clarified

Leave the beans in long pieces with the ends trimmed off. Blanch in boiling water with the salt and sugar for 10 minutes. Quickly drain and refresh in cold or ice water. Meanwhile, bake the bacon at 400 degrees in the oven until crisp. This is better than frying. Drain the bacon well on thick layers of paper towel. Snap into little pieces and set aside. Melt the 4 tbsp. butter in a large skillet over low heat and add the sliced scallions and the chopped parsley. Cook until the scallions are wilted. Now add the green beans and the bacon and parsley and toss together. Season with freshly ground black pepper and serve.
Serves 6-8.

Leek Pie (variation on a flamiche)
(Les Deux Gourmettes, Maryland)

1 9" pie shell, unbaked
2 lb. leeks, 6-8 medium
9 oz. lean bacon
6 oz. cream cheese

6 tbsp. heavy cream
2 eggs
Salt and pepper

Slit, wash and cut leeks in small pieces. In a heavy skillet, saute the diced bacon for a few minutes, then add the leeks and simmer, covered, for about 1 hour.
Add the cheese, the cream and the eggs, salt and pepper.
Pour into the pie shell and bake at 425 degrees for 30 minutes.

Crocchettine Di Patate
(The Italian Kitchen Cooking School, New Jersey)

2½ lb. potatoes
3 eggs, beaten
4 tbsp. Locatelli cheese, grated
½ tsp. parsley, chopped
2 tsp. salt
¼ lb. salami, diced

¼ lb. mozzarella, diced
1 egg, beaten for coating
1 cup bread crumbs
¼ tsp. salt
¼ tsp. pepper
1 cup olive oil

Wash potatoes and place in a 3 qt. saucepan with enough water to cover and 2 tsp. salt. Boil until fork tender, drain and cool. Peel off skin and mash potatoes. Beat in 3 eggs, salami and mozzarella, grated cheese, parsley and dash of pepper. Mix thoroughly. In a separate dish mix bread crumbs, salt and pepper together. Break off pieces of potato mixture and shape into balls or 3″ long cigars. Dip into egg then into bread crumbs, coating evenly. Heat oil in heavy skillet. Place 6-8 balls in hot oil, cook 4-6 minutes or until golden brown. Turn to brown on the other side.
Makes 24.

Potato Souffle with Caviar Sauce
(Jerome Walman Cooking School, New York)

4 baking potatoes
1 stick butter (sweet), melted
1 egg

Salt, pepper, fresh dill
Sour cream
Red caviar

Bake well-scrubbed and dried potatoes in 400-degree oven 1 hour, until done (45 minutes, if smaller potatoes).

Cool potatoes, scoop out pulp and put in food processor. Add the egg. With processor running, slowly add the butter, then the dill. It will have the appearance of a thick hollandaise. Fill skins. This much can be done in advance and refrigerated. Place in buttered baking dishes and bake at 400 degrees about 20 minutes, until hot, browned on top and risen.

Top with sour cream (2 tablespoons) and 1 teaspoon red caviar and serve in baking dishes. Russian Vodka, Champagne or a full bodied white wine is excellent with this.

Four main course servings, or 8 first course servings if half of each potato is used.

Sweet Potatoes Parmesan
(La Cuisine, Texas)

3 lb. large sweet potatoes
6 tbsp. butter
½ cup heavy cream

⅓ cup freshly grated Parmesan cheese
Salt & white pepper to taste
Grating of fresh nutmeg

Wash the sweet potatoes and bake them on the oven rack at 400 degrees for about 40 minutes. The potatoes are done if tender when pierced with a small, sharp knife.

Peel the potatoes while they are very hot and force them through a ricer or food mill in order to give a light, fluffy consistency and to hold back any strings. Combine the potatoes with 4 tablespoons butter, salt, pepper and nutmeg to taste. Butter the bottom and sides of a 6-cup Charlotte mold with the remaining 2 tablespoons butter. Line the bottom of the mold with a round of carefully fitted waxed paper. Pack the potatoes firmly into the Charlotte mold, pressing with a wooden spoon. The dish may be prepared a day in advance and refrigerated at this point.

Bake uncovered in a 350-degree oven for 30-40 minutes.

To serve, unmold the potatoes onto a heated serving plate. In a chilled mixing bowl, whip the cream lightly until it becomes the consistency of a light sauce. Pour the cream over the potatoes and sprinkle with Parmesan cheese. Place under a broiler until golden and bubbly. Serve immediately. Serves 8.

Ratatouille Nicoise
(Tante Marie's Cooking School, California)

¼ cup olive oil
2 medium green peppers, sliced
1 cup sliced onion
2 cloves garlic, crushed
2 tbsp. oil
2 medium zucchini, cut in 1 inch cubes

1 medium eggplant, cut in 1 inch cubes
4 medium tomatoes, peeled,
   seeded and quartered
Salt and pepper
2 tbsp. chopped parsley

In a large skillet, saute the green pepper and onion and the garlic about 5 minutes, remove. Add 2 tbsp. oil to the pan and saute the zucchini and eggplant until tender, about 5 minutes. Remove. Return the vegetables to the pan in layers: first the pepper and onion mixture, then the zucchini and eggplant mixture, then the tomatoes. Season each layer with salt and pepper and sprinkle with chopped parsley. Simmer, covered, over low heat 2 minutes basting occasionally. Remove cover and cook 15 minutes longer, basting occasionally. Serves 6-8.

Salade "La Belle Pomme"

(La Belle Pomme, Ohio)

Betty Rosbottom says, "This lovely salad was a special treat on a recent visit to Paris. I sampled the dish in a small restaurant and asked the owner how it was made. She shared with me the list of ingredients. The following recipe is an adaptation of La Belle Pomme."

8-10 cups shredded cabbage (1½ medium heads). The cabbage should be cut by hand into long julienne strips or put through a food processor using the standard slicing blade. It should *not* be grated finely.
¾ lb. best-quality baked or boiled sliced ham cut in julienne strips

¾ lb. Gruyere cheese cut in julienne strips
4 tbsp. parley, chopped fine
1-2 truffles, very finely chopped (optional)
Salt/pepper to taste
Lettuce leaves (Boston or Bibb)

Roquefort Vinaigrette Sauce:

1 tbsp. Moutarde de Meaux (available in food specialty stores) or Dijon mustard can be substituted
1-2 cloves garlic, peeled and minced
½ cup red wine vinegar

1½ cups olive oil
¼-⅓ cup roquefort or bleu cheese
Salt/pepper to taste

Combine mustard, salt and pepper and garlic in bottom of a large bowl. Gradually add in olive oil, beating constantly. Add crumbled roquefort cheese until incorporated and mixture is smooth.*

Add shredded cabbage, julienne ham and cheese strips and mix well. Add chopped truffles and chopped parsley. Correct seasonings and serve each portion on a bed of lettuce.

This is a very beautiful salad and can serve as a first course for a formal meal or can be used for very nice buffets. We used it to accompany a lobster souffle last winter in one of our classes.

*The salad dressing may be prepared in a food processor. Add mustard, vinegar, salt, pepper, garlic and roquefort and process til smooth (about 10 seconds). Gradually add olive oil until well blended.

Desserts

Baked Cranberries
(Madame Colonna's School of Cooking, Virginia)

1 lb. raw cranberries
1½ cups sugar
¼ to ½ cup orange liqueur (Grand
   Marnier or Triple Sec)

Wash cranberries but do not dry them. Place in a covered baking dish and sprinkle with the sugar. Cover with aluminum foil, pressing the foil tightly against the top and sides of the berries inside the baking dish. Cover dish with lid and bake at 375-degrees for 45 minutes. When cool, remove cover and foil. Add the orange liqueur. Before baking remember that no extra water is used except that which clings to the berries after washing and draining.

Almond Roll
(Look & Cook, New Jersey)

6 eggs, separated
¾ cup sugar
1 cup finely ground almonds
   (about 4 oz.)

1 tsp. baking powder
½ tsp. almond extract

Grease a 15″ x 10″ pan and line it with waxed paper. Grease waxed paper generously. Preheat oven to 350 degrees. Beat the egg yolks with sugar until pale and thick. Add the almonds, baking powder and almond extract and mix until blended. Beat egg whites with a pinch of salt until stiff and fold into the egg yolk mixture. Pour into the prepared pan and spread evenly. Bake 15 minutes. Remove from oven and turn over onto a kitchen towel dusted with confectioners' sugar. Carefully peel off the waxed paper. Roll cake in towel and allow to cool.
When cool, unroll gently and spread cake with Cream Filling. Gently roll up again and using the aid of the towel, roll cake on serving platter and chill until ready to serve.

Cream Filling:
Beat till stiff—
1½ cups heavy cream
½ tsp. almond extract
2 tbsp. confectioners' sugar

Pistachio Pastry Rolls (or real Baklava)
(Andreés Mediterranean Cooking School, New York)

Syrup:
1 cup sugar
1 cup water
1 tbsp. lemon juice
1 tbsp. orange blossom water

Rolls:
1 package fillo dough
½ cup samna, melted (samna is Mid-Eastern clarified butter)
1½ cups pistachio nuts
¾ cup sugar
1 tbsp. orange blossom water

Prepare syrup by cooking all syrup ingredients except orange blossom water for 10 minutes or until the consistency of spun honey. Add orange blossom water, cook 2 more minutes, let syrup cool and refrigerate.

Put pistachio nuts in blender, add sugar and chop coarsely. Put mixture in a bowl and add orange blossom water. Mix thoroughly.

Take three whole sheets of fillo dough, butter the top one. Place about 2-3 tablespoons of nut mixture at the bottom edge of sheets and roll, very tight in a cigar-like fashion. Place in pre-buttered baking dish, all rolls side by side, tightly fitting. Cut in 2″ segments with a sharp knife. Brush left-over butter on top of rolls. Bake 25 to 30 minutes in 350-degree oven, or until golden.

Pour cold syrup over hot baklava. Best prepared early in the morning, or the day before it is to be served.

Makes 4 dozen 2″ rolls.

Tarte Bourdaloue aux Poires
(Antonia Allegra Griffin School of Cooking, California)

1 pate brisee*, unbaked, lining a
    drop-bottom tarte pan
½ cup + 1 tbsp. granulated sugar
2½ oz. (½ cup) slivered almonds,
    ground in blender
2 tbsp. flour
3 tbsp. melted butter

1 egg
1 egg yolk
3 tbsp. heavy cream (not beaten)
1½ tsp. almond extract or Kirsch
5 pears, poached and cut in half or
    1 can (1 lb. 13 oz.) pears,
    drained
Apricot preserves

Preheat oven to 425 degrees. In a bowl, blend all ingredients except the pear halves. Pour the almond-egg-cream (actually a light frangipane) into the unbaked pate brisee. Arrange the pear halves on top of the filling. Bake 25 minutes. The filling will become quite dark, mahogany colored. Remove the tarte from pan and brush with glaze of strained apricot preserves and water. Serve at room temperature.

Serves 8.

*pie crust dough

Gingerbread Waffles with Lemon Custard Sauce
(L'Ecole de Cuisine, Arkansas)

¼ cup butter
½ cup dark-brown sugar
½ cup dark molasses
2 eggs, separated
1 cup milk
2 cups flour

1½ tsp. baking powder
1 tsp. cinnamon
1 tsp. ginger
¼ tsp. cloves
¼ tsp. salt

Cream the butter and brown sugar together. Beat in, on medium speed with an electric mixer, the egg yolks and molasses. Beat in milk. Sift together the flour, baking powder, cinnamon, cloves, ginger and salt. With clean, dry beaters, beat the egg whites until very stiff. By hand, stir the sifted dry ingredients into the creamed mixture, then fold in the beaten whites. Cook on a preheated waffle-gridded iron. Makes 4 sets.

Lemon Custard Sauce:

3 eggs
¾ cup sugar
¼ cup fresh lemon juice

1 tsp. grated lemon peel
Dash of salt
2 tbsp. melted butter

With an electric mixer, beat together the eggs and sugar until thick and lemon-colored. Add the lemon juice, grated peel, salt and butter. Beat together well. Pour this mixture into the top of a double boiler and cook, stirring, over simmering water, until thick. It will coat a spoon and fall off the spoon with "plops" rather than a long, slow slide. This sauce may be served warm or cool. It may be prepared ahead, refrigerated and re-heated over boiling water in the double boiler for serving hot. It will "stiffen" quite a bit when refrigerated. Serves 8. Waffles may be frozen and reheated directly on oven rack briefly to heat through. Do not freeze Lemon Custard Sauce.

Walnut Meringue Cookies
(Cooking With Mady, New York))

5 egg whites at room temperature
1 tsp. vanilla extract
¼ tsp. cream of tartar

1 cup sugar
¾ cup finely chopped walnuts

Whip egg whites by hand or machine until frothy. Add cream of tartar, sugar (one tablespoon at a time) and one teaspoon vanilla. Whip on medium-to-high speed until whites are shiny and peaked. Fold in chopped walnuts. Drop by teaspoonsful on baking sheet coated with butter and flour. Bake at low preheated over 180-190 degrees for 1¾ hours or until dried. Store in dry covered container. Meringues will keep for months.
Makes 25-30 meringues.

Lime Curd Tarts
(The Peppermill, Idaho)

Pastry:

1 cup flour
1 tbsp. sugar
6 tbsp. butter

1 egg yolk
1 tbsp. water

In a bowl mix flour and sugar. With pastry blender or with fingers, cut in the butter until the mixture resembles cornmeal. Add yolk and water, mix well, gather into a ball, cover and chill for about 1 hour. Roll dough between sheets of waxed paper until as thin as pie dough. Cut into rounds and press into tart tins. Prick bottoms and bake in a 375-degree oven for about 15 minutes or until browned. Cool and remove from tins.

Filling:

4 eggs
1 cup sugar
½ cup lime juice

1 tbsp. lime peel, grated
½ cup butter

Beat eggs until light and stir in the rest of ingredients. Cook over medium heat, stirring, just until mixture boils. Remove from heat and cool. When cooled, spoon into tart shells and decorate with a sprig of mint. Shells can be baked and frozen for up to 3 months. Simply thaw at room temperature. Filling can be covered or not while cooling and after filling as it will not crust.

Not-Quite-Classic Creme Brulee
(Potpourri School of Cooking, Pennsylvania)

1 quart heavy cream
4 cinnamon sticks
½ cup sugar

8 egg yolks
Light brown sugar

Two days ahead: Put the cream, cinammon sticks and sugar in a saucepan. Stir over medium heat to dissolve sugar, then bring to the boil. Cover and refrigerate overnight.
One day ahead: Bring the cream to the boil again. Whisk the egg yolks. Fish the cinnamon sticks out of the cream and slowly add the cream to the yolks while whisking. Pour the custard through a strainer 10 times, then pour into a dish which can take heat and cold and which can be brought to the table. The custard should not be too deep—a 7½" x 13" Pyrex dish is a good size.
Set the custard dish in a larger pan and add hot water about half way up the custard dish. Bake in a preheated 325-degree oven for about 35 minutes, or until the custard is barely set. Cool, then chill overnight.
A few hours before serving: Fill a pan with ice and set the custard dish on the ice. Adjust your broiler rack so that the top of the dish will be 4-5 inches from the heat, and pre-heat the broiler. Put light brown sugar through a sieve and cover all the custard about 1/4" deep. Set the whole apparatus under the broiler just long enough for the sugar to begin to melt. Watch constantly that it does not burn. Refrigerate to harden.
To make a more traditional Creme Brulee, omit cinnamon sticks and reduce sugar to 1/4 cup. Add two teaspoons vanilla to the custard mixture before baking.

Flan de Prunes

(Cooking-With-Class, Inc., New York)

Preheat oven—375 degrees.

½ cup butter
1 cup sugar
1¼ cups flour
½ tsp. salt
½ tsp. cinnamon

¼ tsp. baking powder
1 lb. fresh plums
   halved & pitted
1 egg
Approx. ½ cup heavy cream

Cream butter and sugar until fluffy. Add rest of dry ingredients and mix as you would for pie crust. Reserve ⅓ cup of mixture.
Press mixture into and up the sides of an 11″ tart pan.
Arrange plums in a single layer over crust, skin side up. Sprinkle with ⅓ cup reserved mixture and bake for 15 minutes.
While baking, beat egg slightly and add cream.
Pour egg mixture over plums after baking 15 minutes, and return to oven for about 25 minutes or until knife comes clean.
Cool, then cut into serving pieces.
Serve warm or cold.
Serves 6-8.

Creme Glace au Caramel

(Frozen Caramel Mousse)

(Truffles, Georgia)

Best made one day or at least 2½ hours ahead.

For Two:
2 egg yolks
⅓ cup sugar

¾ cup heavy cream
¼ tsp. vanilla extract

Beat egg yolks until they whiten.
In a small saucepan boil sugar and one tablespoon water to make golden-brown caramel syrup. At the same time, bring ½ cup of water to boil. Remove caramel from heat. Pour the boiling water over immediately, being careful not to spatter. Stir and return to boil to dissolve caramel, scraping bottom of pan to collect it all.
Beat the caramel, a little at a time, into the egg yolks. Whip hard until the mixture is creamy. Set bowl over ice cubes and continue to whip while the mixture thickens and cools. Set aside.
Whip the cream with vanilla over ice cubs. Remove some of the whipped cream for decoration. Fold the remaining into the caramel mixture. Pour into ice cube tray. Freeze for at least two hours or until set.
To serve, spoon mousse into chilled dishes and decorate each serving with some of the whipped cream and a crystallized violet.

Apple Mousse—Mousseline De Pommes

(A La Bonne Cocotte, New York)

For the caramel:
½ cup sugar
4 tbsp. water
1 tbsp. corn syrup
The Creme Chantilly (see recipe)

For the mousseline:
2 lb. Cortland or MacIntosh apples
(about 8 apples)
¼ cup water
⅓ cup sugar
8 tbsp. unsalted butter (room temperature)
4 tbsp. apricot preserves
4 eggs

Make a caramel for the mold: melt the sugar, water, and syrup in a heavy saucepan over medium high heat—do not stir. Bring to a boil and heat to 320 degrees. Be careful not to burn the caramel.

Quickly pour the caramel into a ring mold (1 qt.) and coat the mold all over by tipping it in all directions (use pot holders to hold the mold).

Peel, core and slice the apples and cook with ¼ cup water over high heat until they turn into a near-puree. Stir constantly with a wooden spoon. Preheat oven to 400 degrees.

Add the sugar, butter, and apricot preserves and cook for 5 more minutes, stirring all the while.

Pass the mixture through the fine blade of a food mill or through the food processor.

Cook the puree for another 5 minutes more over high heat so that it thickens a bit. Remove from heat and allow to cool for 5 minutes.

Beat 4 eggs well with a fork, add them to the cooled mixture, and mix well. Pour the mixture into the caramel-lined mold.

Place the mold in a water bath of hot water which is about ⅔ the depth of the pan. Poach for 45 minutes to one hour. The Mousseline will be golden brown on top when done.

Remove from oven and allow to cool 5 minutes. Then turn the ring mold upside down onto a serving platter. Wait about 30 minutes to unmold. Chill. Best done the day before your party.

Serves 8.

The Creme Chantilly:
1 cup heavy cream
2 tbsp. Grand Marnier
¼ cup superfine sugar

Put your mixing bowl in the freezer for 10 minutes. The colder it and the cream are, the lighter will be the Chantilly.

Start whisking slowly and speed up gradually. As soon as the cream starts to thicken sprinkle in the sugar and beat until fairly firm, add the liqueur. Be careful not to beat the cream into butter.

Serves 8.

Chocolate Mousse Roulade

(The Perla Meyers Cooking School, New York)

Roulade:

2 squares semi-sweet chocolate

1 to 2 tbsp. espresso
    or strong coffee

6 eggs, separated

¾ cup sugar

¼ cup unsweetened, powdered
    cocoa (generous)

Pinch of salt

Mousse:

4 ounces Maillard chocolate

2 tbsp. espresso or strong coffee

⅓ cup butter, broken into pieces

2 egg yolks

3 egg whites

1½ tbsp. sugar

Confectioners' sugar for sprinkling

Preheat the oven to 375 degrees. Butter a jelly roll pan (10″ x 15″). Line bottom and sides with one long piece of waxed paper. Butter and flour the paper. Set aside.

In the top of a double boiler melt the chocolate with the coffee. Set aside to cool slightly.

In a bowl beat the yolks for 4 to 5 minutes until light lemon colored. Add half the sugar and continue to beat at high speed for an additional 5 minutes until very thick. On lowest speed add the melted chocolate and then the cocoa, beating only until smooth.

In a large bowl, beat the whites with the salt until they begin to thicken. Add the remaining sugar and continue beating until the whites hold a shape and are stiff but not dry. Fold the whites and chocolate together. Turn into prepared pan, handling lightly. Spread level and place in the oven.

While the cake is baking (about 25 to 30 minutes) wet and wring out a smooth kitchen towel. When top of cake springs back when lightly touched, remove from oven. Working quickly cut around sides of cake if it is sticking to sides of pan and turn out onto prepared towel. Carefully peel off waxed paper and starting at long side, roll the cake and towel together. Place on a rack to cool. It must be completely cool to fill.

The Mousse

While the cake is baking, prepare the mousse. In the top of a double boiler, melt the chocolate and coffee together. Remove from the heat and set aside to cool slightly. Then whisk in the butter in bits, making sure the mixture is not too hot to melt the butter. Let it cool completely until it is the texture of thick cream.

When the mixture has cooled, stir in the yolks, one at a time until thoroughly blended.

Beat the whites until they are thick and foamy. Add the sugar and continue beating until they hold a shape and are stiff but not dry. Fold the whites and chocolate mixture together and chill in the refrigerator until the mousse is quite thick yet spreadable.

Unroll the roulade. Spread generously with the mouse and roll up again. The roulade may be refrigerated at this time for a short while to solidify, or for several hours. Remove from the refrigerator at least ½ hour before serving. Sprinkle with confectioners' sugar and slice on the angle for serving.

Mousse au Chocolat
(Cordon Bleu de Paris, New York)

4 oz. semi-sweet chocolate
4 tbsp. butter (unsalted)

4 egg yolks
4 egg whites

Place chocolate and butter in a sauce pan, and allow to melt over low heat.

Remove pan from heat and stir in egg yolks until chocolate thickens. Pour into large mixing bowl.

Beat egg whites until stiff.

Fold half of stiff whites into chocolate with whisk. Add remaining whites and fold in with rubber spatula.

Pour mousse into serving bowl or individual cups or glasses. Refrigerate for 2 hours to set. Serve cold.

Serves 6.

Mousse a l'Orange
(Florence Simon School of Gourmet Cooking, Texas)

3 egg yolks
¾ cup sugar
1/8 tsp. salt
1 tbsp. unflavored gelatin
2 tbsp. cold water
2 tbsp. orange flavored liqueur
   (Cointreau or Grand Marnier)
1 cup fresh orange juice
1 tbsp. cornstarch

3 tbsp. grated orange peel
   (Note: Grate orange peel before
   squeezing for juice.)
3 egg whites, beaten until stiff
   but not dry
½ cup heavy cream, whipped
Crystalized violets for garnish
½ tsp. orange flavored liqueur
   (Cointreau or Grand Marnier)

Beat egg yolks with sugar and salt in bowl until they are light and lemon colored.

Sprinkle gelatin over cold water and orange liqueur to soften, 3-4 minutes. Add orange juice, cornstarch and grated orange peel. Heat the orange juice mixture just to the boiling point and add it to the egg yolks, beating briskly, and continue to beat the custard until it is thickened, 5-7 minutes. Allow to cool.

Fold in *egg whites and ½ of the whipped heavy cream. Pour or spoon the mousse into individual 5-ounce parfait or stemmed wine glasses. Chill the mousse and serve it topped with orange liqueur-flavored whipped cream. Garnish with crystalized violets.

Note: It takes about 5 medium oranges to make 1 cup juice.

*Trick: Beat egg whites at room temperature to effect greater lift.

Gateau Chez Nous
(La Cuisine Cooking Classes, Massachusetts)

1 cup ground walnuts
½ cup flour
6 eggs
1 cup sugar
1 tbsp. vanilla extract
1 cup Kirsch syrup

2½ cups heavy cream
8 oz. semi-sweet chocolate, melted and cooled
2 tbsp. pulverized espresso coffee grounds (yes, grounds)

Line an 11″ x 16″ jelly roll pan with waxed paper. Set aside.

In a bowl combine the walnuts and flour and mix well. In large bowl of mixer, place eggs and sugar and beat on high speed until tripled in bulk and very thick. Fold in the nut mixture. Pour into prepared pan and bake at 350 degrees for 20 minutes or until golden. Cool. Cut the cake into three strips lengthwise. Brush strips with the Kirsch syrup.

Whip the cream until thick and gently fold in the melted cooled chocolate and coffee grounds.

Spread cream on a cake layer, top with another cake layer, top with more cream and finally add the last layer. Frost the entire cake with the cream. Save some to pipe out rosettes on top of the cake. Chill 2 hours before serving.

12 to 16 servings.

Cheese Cake
(Jean Sparks Cooking School at Lawrens, Alabama)

Crust:

1 package graham crackers
¼ lb. butter cut into 6 or more pieces

⅓ cup confectioners' sugar
¼ tsp. cinnamon

With metal blade of food processor in place process graham crackers until they become fine crumbs. Add butter, sugar and cinnamon and process until butter is absorbed into crumbs. Press crumb mixture into bottom of a greased 8-inch spring form pan.

Cake:

Rind of 2 oranges
Rind of 2 lemons
3 (8-oz.) packages cream cheese
4 large eggs

1 tsp. vanilla
1 scant cup sugar
2 tbsp. sour cream
¼ cup half and half cream

Put orange and lemon rind into processor bowl with metal blade and process until finely grated. Add 1 package of cream cheese, cut into pieces, and 1 egg. Process until smooth, then add another package cream cheese and 1 egg. Repeat once more, then add final egg, sugar, vanilla, sour cream and cream. Process until thoroughly mixed. Pour into prepared pan and bake in preheated 350-degree oven for about 1 hour and 15 minutes or until center does not quiver when pan is shaken. Let cool in pan, then refrigerate. Cheesecake is usually better when prepared a day in advance.

This may be topped with ½ pint sour cream to which ¼ cup sugar and 1 teaspoon vanilla have been added. Spread with topping as soon as cake is removed from oven.

Ricotta Cheesecake Roman Style
(Bocconotti di Ricotta alla Romana)
(The Renaissance Chef Cooking School, Washington, D.C.)

Pastry:
2¼ cups flour, sifted
½ cup superfine sugar
   (castor or bar sugar)
¼ tsp. salt
Pinch cinnamon
1 tsp. orange rind, grated

¼ cup plus 1 tbsp. butter, cold
¼ cup plus 1 tbsp. lard, cold
3 eggs, lightly beaten

Pastry:
Sift together flour, sugar, salt and cinnamon into a large bowl. Add orange rind. Add cold butter and lard and cut into flour mixture. Add eggs and mix well. Form into a ball. Wrap dough in waxed paper and chill for 1 to 2 hours in refrigerator.

Filling:
1 lb. Ricotta cheese
½ cup superfine sugar,
   (castor or bar sugar)
Pinch salt

5 egg yolks, lightly beaten
1 tbsp. cinnamon
½ cup candied fruits, finely chopped

Filling:
Press Ricotta through a fine sieve or cheesecloth into a large bowl. Beat until smooth. Add sugar, salt, egg yolks, cinnamon and candied fruit and mix well.

Glaze:
2 tbsp. lard, melted
1 egg yolk, slightly beaten
1 tbsp. sugar

Final Preparation:
Take ⅔ of dough and place on a floured surface. Roll out into a large circle to fit an 8-inch pie plate. Place dough sheet into pie plate. Prick bottom with fork. Add filling.
Roll out remaining dough until large enough to cover. Cover filling with dough. Crimp edges of dough.
Mix melted lard, egg yolk and sugar together in a small bowl. Brush glaze over dough. Prick a few holes on top of dough. Bake in 350-degree preheated over for 1 hour or until firm and brown. Remove from oven and cool. Serve at room temperature.

Serves 8.

German Apple Cake
(International Cuisine, Inc., Pennsylvania)

Crust: 1-2-3 Dough

1 egg

1 cup sugar

2 cups butter or margarine

3 cups flour

Combine ingredients quickly to a pastry consistency—do not overwork the dough. Let rest in refrigerator for a while. Grease and flour a 9-inch springform pan. Press dough into pan, covering the bottom and reaching about halfway up the sides. Recipe makes enough dough for 2 cakes.

Filling:

4-5 large baking apples

½ cup heavy cream

Juice of 1 lemon

2 eggs

1 tbsp. cornstarch

Apricot glaze

1 cup sour cream

½ cup sugar or less, depending on
    the apples

Few drops of vanilla

Breadcrumbs

Peel apples, core and cut in half. Cut small strips crosswise on top of the apples to score them. Sprinkle the bottom of the crust with the breadcrumbs to form a thin, even layer. Place the apples in the pan, rounded side up. Fill in the spaces with pieces of apple. Mix the rest of the ingredients together and pour over the apples. Bake in a preheated 375-degree oven for 1 hour to 1½ hours or until the apples are tender and the filling set. Cool slightly and paint the top with melted apricot glaze.

Gateaux Par Avion
(Par Avion, New York)

1 yellow cake baked in tube pan. Slice into 3 or 4 layers. Sprinkle each layer with Drambuie.

Praline Cream:

2 cups whipping cream

2 tbsp. confectioners' sugar

1 tsp. vanilla

1 cup praline powder

Whip the cream until stiff. Fold in sugar, vanilla and praline powder.

Praline Powder:

Melt 1 cup sugar in a skillet over low heat, stir constantly. When the sugar has turned to liquid and light brown, stir in 1 cup almonds or hazelnuts. Pour onto a buttered platter. When it is cool, pulverize in food processor.

French Icing:

2 cups sifted confectioners' sugar

¼ cup sweet butter

1 egg

1 tsp. vanilla

Blend flour and butter. Beat in egg and vanilla, mix till smooth. If frosting is too thick, add 1-2 tablespoons milk. Place mixture over hot (not boiling) water 10-15 minutes.

Fill each layer with Praline Cream.

Frost top layer with French Icing. Decorate with nuts, candied fruit, or decorate with decorator's frosting.

Carrot Cake

(Epicurean Gallery, New York)

2 cups flour	2 tsp. baking powder
1¾ cups sugar	1 tsp. salt
1¼ cups oil	4 eggs
2 tsp. cinnamon	½ cup chopped pecans
2 tsp. baking soda	3 cups (1 lb.) finely grated carrots

Grease and flour 3 (9-inch) layer cake pans.
Preheat oven to 350 degrees.
Mix oil and sugar together. Beat in eggs one at a time. Add dry ingredients.
Fold in carrots and nuts. Divide evenly in 3 pans and bake for 30 minutes.
Remove from pans and cool on racks. Cut each layer in half horizontally so there are 6 layers. Frost layers with following icing. Stack them and ice top of cake, leaving sides uniced.

Cream Cheese Icing:

8 oz. cream cheese
½ lb. butter
1 (16-oz.) box confectioner's sugar
1 (6-oz.) can crushed pineapple, well drained
1 tsp. vanilla

Cream softened cheese and butter. Add confectioner's sugar a little at a time and beat until all is absorbed and fluffy. Add vanilla, fold in crushed pineapple. Chill for ½ hour before using.
NOTE: This cake freezes very well even after it is iced.

Apple Madeleine Cake

(Persimmon Tree Cooking School, Illinois)

4 apples (Golden Delicious work well)	1 cup flour
1 cup sliced almonds	½ cup margarine or butter, melted and cooled
3 large eggs	1 tsp. grated lemon rind
1 cup sugar	1 tbsp. lemon juice

Peel and core apples. Cut in half crosswise and lay in a buttered 9″ x 13″ baking dish. Leave a space between the apples. Top each apple with sliced almonds. Put eggs in top of double boiler over simmering water and gradually beat in the sugar with an electric mixer or a large whisk. Beat until the egg volume has doubled and the batter is light, thick and pale yellow. Remove from heat and fold in the flour completely before folding in the butter, lemon juice and rind. Spoon batter over and around each apple. Bake in a 350-degree oven for 40 minutes or until golden brown. This is nice served warm with whipped cream or ice cream. Serves 4-6.

Gateau Au Rum Chocolat (Rum Cake)
(C. Steele Kitchen, Arizona)

Multi-layered cake sandwiched with rum-soaked candied fruit and macaroon crumbs.

1 cup butter	1½ cups sifted flour
1 cup superfine sugar	½ cup milk
1 egg	3 egg whites
3 egg yolks	2 tsp. baking powder

Preheat the oven to 350 degrees. Butter an 8-inch springform cake pan. Cream the butter in the mixer until it is light and fluffy. Add the sugar and again beat until light and fluffy. One at a time, beat in the egg and egg yolks. When the mixture is very light, alternately beat in the sifted flour and milk little by little. In a separate bowl, beat the egg whites to soft peaks with a wire whisk or rotary beater. Fold them into the flour mixture, then fold in the baking powder. Put the mixture into the pan and bake 40 minutes, or until the cake is firm to the touch and just begins to shrink away from the sides of the pan. Remove the cake from the oven. Turn it out of the springform mold and cool it on a wire rack.

Filling:

4 cups coarse macaroon crumbs	1 cup rum
1½ cups mixed glaceed fruits (cherries, citron, orange, lemon peel), finely chopped	3 tbsp. red currant jelly

Combine the macroon crumbs and glaceed fruits in a bowl with the rum. Let the mixture stand until all the rum is absorbed.

Lightly butter an 8-inch springform cake pan. Slice the cake horizontally into ½″ layers. Put a layer in the bottom of the springform mold. Cover it with a little of the filling. Sandwich the whole cake, alternating layers of cake with filling, and ending with a layer of cake on the top. Cover the cake with foil and put a gentle weight on the top. Chill the assembled cake in the freezer 2 hours, then turn it out onto a cake rack. Melt the jelly in a little pan, and brush it all over the cake.

Remove cake from pan to serving platter. Ice with Chocolate Rum Butter Cream.

Icing (Chocolate Rum Butter Cream):

8 oz. dark sweet chocolate	3 egg yolks
1¼ cups granulated sugar	½ tsp. cream of tartar
¾ cup water	¾ lb. sweet butter, creamed
3 tbsp. rum	until light and fluffy

Cut the chocolate into pieces and put in a small heavy pan with 4 tablespoons water and the rum. Stir over low heat until the chocolate is melted (do not cook any longer). Let the chocolate cool. Beat the egg yolks in the mixer until stiff. In pan cook the sugar, cream of tartar, and ½ cup water until the syrup forms a thin thread between the finger and the thumb (225 degrees). Slowly pour the hot syrup over the beaten yolks, beating all the while and continue beating until the mixture is thick and cool. Gradually add the creamed butter and beat well. Then beat in the cooled melted chocolate.

Serves 12.

Pommes Bourgeoise

(The Every Day Gourmet Cooking School, Massachusetts)

6 cooking apples
1½ cups water
½ cup dry white wine
¾ cup sugar

A piece of vanilla bean
Custard, recipe below
Macaroon crumbs or toasted almond
  slivers
Coarse sugar

Core, peel and cut the apples in half, from stem to base. Boil water, wine, sugar and vanilla bean for three minutes. Remove the vanilla bean. (It may be washed and reserved for another use.) Poach the apple halves until tender. Leave them in the syrup until cool.

Prepare the custard:

½ cup sugar
3 tbsp. cornstarch
3 tbsp. flour

2 cups milk
4 beaten egg yolks
1 tbsp. brandy or rum, or 1 tsp. vanilla

Blend with a wire whisk in a heavy saucepan: sugar, cornstarch, flour and milk. Stir, over low heat, until it boils. Pour a little of the mixture onto the egg yolks, beating with a whisk as you pour. Add egg mixture to the saucepan and, stirring constantly, bring again to a boil, slowly. Add brandy. Cool slightly before using.

Place the apples, cut side up, in an oven-proof dish. Coat each one with the custard. Sprinkle with the macaroon crumbs and some sugar. Set aside until needed. (May be made as much as a day ahead.)

Bake at 450 degrees for 5 to 10 minutes, until glazed. Serve warm.

Copyright 1978 Sheila Elion

Microwave

Medley of Western Vegetables
(Microwave Cooking Center, California)

1 large zucchini squash	1 green pepper
1 large crookneck squash	1 small cauliflower
1 large summer squash (pattypan)	2 bunches broccoli
3 large fresh mushrooms	1 cube butter (may use less)
1 red pepper	Garlic salt and seasoned pepper to taste

Slice squashes into rounds about ¼" thick. Break cauliflower into flowerets. Cut broccoli into flowerets, leaving some of the stem. Slice mushrooms. Cut peppers into strips. Select a large round platter that will fill the entire microwave range cavity. Place broccoli in circle around outside of platter. Place cauliflower inside of broccoli. Arrange other vegetables in center, alternating for color. Melt butter in small measuring cup, and pour lightly over vegetables. Season vegetables with garlic salt and pepper. Cover with plastic wrap and cook 5 minutes, just until vegetables are fork tender. Remember they will continue to cook for a few minutes. Vegetables should be crisp, Oriental style.

Utensil - 12" round platter

Zucchini Pizza
(Microwave Kitchen Shop, Indiana)

3½ cups grated zucchini	½ cup grated Mozzarella cheese
3 eggs, beaten	½ cup grated Parmesan cheese
⅓ cup all-purpose flour	1 tbsp. fresh basil or ½ tsp. dried
Desired pizza toppings: tomato sauce, mushrooms, green pepper, cooked meat, etc.	Salt and pepper

Salt zucchini lightly; let stand for 15 minutes. Squeeze out the excess moisture. Combine with the other ingredients; spread in an ungreased 9" x 13" glass baking dish. Microwave on HIGH 6-8 minutes or bake at 350 degrees for 20-25 minutes, or until firm.
Top with favorite pizza topping. Sprinkle with grated cheeses. Heat until cheese is melted; microwave 1-2 minutes or place in oven at 350 degrees for 10-15 minutes. Serve hot. Serves 4-6.

Crown Vegetable Mold
(Microwave Center, Inc., Illinois)

1 lb. fresh green beans
4 large carrots
1 summer squash, sliced into ¼-inch slices
1 medium zucchini, sliced into ¼-inch slices
1 cup Brussels sprouts
1 cup fresh cauliflower

½ cup peas, fresh or frozen
⅓ cup butter or margarine
8 medium potatoes, peeled and cubed
¼ cup butter or margarine
1 package (3 oz.) cream cheese
¼ tsp. salt
½-¾ cup milk

Clean the green beans and carrots and cut into uniform lengths. Arrange the carrots, beans, squash, zucchini, Brussels sprouts, cauliflower and peas on a round 12-inch glass or plastic tray, cover and microwave on HIGH for 10-12 minutes or until tender. Salt lightly and allow to stand uncovered. Spread sides and bottom of 2 quart casserole with ⅓ cup butter or margarine. Chill the casserole. Cover the potatoes with plastic wrap and microwave on HIGH for 14-16 minutes. Let stand 5 minutes. Beat until smooth with ¼ cup butter, the cream cheese, salt and milk. Around the outside edge of the bottom of the buttered and chilled casserole, make a border with the cooked peas. Make a circle of overlapping slices of summer squash and zucchini. Fill center with remaining peas. Carefully spread layer of mashed potatoes over arranged vegetables. Stand beans and carrots upright alternately side by side to make a fence around buttered sides of casserole dish. Cover beans and carrots with mashed potatoes, being careful to press sides firmly so that potatoes fill spaces between. Arrange layer of cauliflower, then zucchini, summer squash and Brussels sprouts in center. Cover with remaining potatoes. Microwave on HIGH for 8-10 minutes. Let stand for 10 minutes before inverting on serving platter. Serves 10-12.

Roast Chicken with Sauerkraut
(Everything Microwave, Ohio)

1 (3 to 4 lb.) roasting chicken
1 to 2 cups sauerkraut
¼ cup butter

Paprika
Poultry seasoning

Sprinkle body cavity with salt and pepper. Fill cavity lightly with sauerkraut. Tie legs together and wings to body. Place chicken, breast side down, on microwave roasting rack in 2 qt. (12″ x 7″) glass baking dish.
Melt butter on MED. HIGH (70% power) about 30 seconds. Brush outside of chicken with melted butter, sprinkle with paprika and poultry seasoning.
Microwave on full power ½ of total cooking time (9 minutes per lb.). Turn breast side up, brush with melted butter, sprinkle with paprika and poultry seasoning.
Microwave on full power for second half of cooking time or until microwave meat thermometer registers 170 degrees. Let stand, covered with foil, 5 to 10 minutes before serving.
Serves 4-6.

Applesauce
(Shirley Waterloo Culinary Instruction, Illinois)

2 lb. tart cooking apples, about
  6 or 7 medium
½ cup water

½ cup sugar
1 vanilla bean, split in half
1 tbsp. lemon juice

Pare, core and quarter apples. With slicing disk in place, insert apples in tube of food processor with cut side against slicing blade. Slice, using medium pressure. Place in glass bowl. Add water, sugar and vanilla bean. Cover with glass lid or waxed paper. Microwave for 12 minutes on HIGH or until apples are very soft. Stir once or twice during cooking. Remove vanilla bean. Add lemon juice. Taste and adjust seasonings.

Serve warm or cold as a meat accompaniment or dessert.

About 3 cups.

Chicken In Cellophane
(Microwave Oven Workshop, California)

3 breasts of chicken, split
  and boned (6 pieces)
1 cup bread crumbs
½ cup grated Parmesan cheese
1 tsp. paprika
Salt and white pepper

¼ lb. butter or margarine, melted
6 squares of cellophane*
2 tsp. cornstarch
1 cup chicken broth
¼ cup dry white wine or dry Vermouth

Melt butter.

Mix bread crumbs, cheese, salt and pepper together.

Dip breasts into butter, then roll in crumb mixture.

Sprinkle with paprika (outside of breasts) and place the paprika side down on cellophane.

Fold as for envelope and place folded side on Pyrex cook & serve platter. Place on outside rim of platter.

Bake in microwave oven for 3 minutes (3 half breasts). Six pieces cook for 7 minutes.

Bring chicken broth to boil, mix cornstarch with 2 tablespoons of wine. Add rest of the wine and cook until clear.

Pour over chicken just before serving.

*Cellophane is different from plastic wrap and must be used.

Miscellaneous

Basil Sauce Chez Mimi
(Chez Mimi, Iowa)

This is delicious on sliced tomatoes and onions and equally good on green beans as a marinade. It is based on the classic Italian Pesto Sauce, which uses fresh basil.

Although you could use dry basil, I do not recommend it. I suggest getting fresh basil and freezing it in olive oil and then completing the recipe as you are ready to use it. It freezes very well. Do not add the lemon juice or vinegar as it becomes stronger on sitting or freezing and could ruin the sauce.

1 cup fresh basil leaves, torn into
   small pieces and loosely packed
6 tbsp. good olive oil
1/8 tsp. salt
Freshly ground pepper (about 8 twists)

2 tbsp. wine vinegar or
   lemon juice or a combination
1 large clove garlic, mashed
2 tbsp. freshly chopped parsley
1 tsp. heavy cream (optional)

Crush the basil in a mortar & pestle or use a food processor or blender. If using a machine, add the olive oil with the basil leaves and parsley.

Add the vinegar or lemon juice and whisk together.

Add the salt, pepper and garlic.

Add the oil, slowly at first and whisk well.

Add the cream and taste and correct seasoning.

If using this with tomatoes, layer the tomatoes and add some sauce. Add another layer of tomatoes until all is used up. Marinate at room temperature for an hour or two. Tomatoes taste much better if they are not ice cold. However, you may marinate in the refrigerator, but remember to take out about ½-1 hour before ready to eat.

This also may be served with green beans—simply toss the hot vegetable with this dressing, cool and serve.

Serves 6-8 (¾ cup sauce).

Copyright 1978-Chez Mimi Cooking School

Cold Gooseberry Soup

(Elizabeth B. Germaine Cookery Demonstrations, Minnesota)

2 cups water
⅓ cup sugar
8 whole cloves
2-inch stick of cinnamon
Juice of 1 lemon

3 egg yolks
⅔ cup whipping cream
1 (16 oz.) can gooseberries
2 tbsp. brandy
Needleshreds lemon rind

Combine water, sugar, cloves, cinamon, and lemon juice in pan. Bring to the boil, stirring until sugar is dissolved. Remove from heat.

Beat egg yolks lightly with cream. Drain gooseberries. Mix gooseberry juice into cream mixture and add to pan. Return to heat, stir until boiling. Remove from heat and strain into bowl. Add gooseberries and brandy. Cover and chill.

Before serving, garnish with needleshreds of blanched lemon rind.
Serves 4-6.

Tahini

(Wholistic Nutrition Center, Wisconsin)

1 cup raw fresh sesame seeds
½ cup natural vegetable oil
¾ cup water
3 garlic cloves, mashed
1 tsp. sea salt

½ tsp. ground cumin
½ tsp. turmeric
Dash cayenne
Juice of 3 lemons

Blend sesame seeds, vegetable oil, and water. Add garlic cloves, sea salt, cumin, turmeric, and cayenne. To this mixture, slowly add the lemon juice. Blend until well mixed. Makes 2 cups.

This salad dressing is also delicious mixed with cooked legumes. Serve as is or mix with plain yogurt or water.

Avocado Supreme

½ cup plain yogurt
1 peeled avocado
1 tbsp. or more chopped onion
3 tbsp. pure lemon juice

1 tsp. apple cider vinegar
¼ tsp. sea salt
Garlic (optional)

Blend on low speed until well mixed. Makes 1 cup.

Thanksgiving Stuffing
(For a 6-10 pound turkey)
(Helen Worth Enterprises, New York)

Thanks to today's packaging you can buy giblets and livers without buying the bird, meaning you can have giblet gravy too. This stuffing also makes an excellent accompaniment for entrees such as roast pork and veal chops and, of course, is perfect for roast chicken.

¾ cup butter or margarine
1 tsp. paprika
2 tsp. dried thyme
2 tsp. dried marjoram
1½ cups celery (about 2 large branches), diced
Turkey giblets and liver, ground

8 sprigs parsley, ground
1 medium onion, ground
2 eggs, beaten slightly
8 cups stale bread (about 16 slices)*
¼ tsp. salt
1/8 tsp. fresh-ground pepper

In large skillet melt butter or margarine. Add paprika and herbs and cook over low heat, stirring as necessary, until aromatic, about 2 minutes. Add celery and simmer uncovered 5 minutes. Add giblets, parsley, and onion. Cover and cook over low heat, stirring as necessary, until red color disappears, about 5 minutes. Remove from heat, add eggs, and mix well.

Choose white bread, whole wheat, or a combination. Do not remove crusts. Pull into ½-inch pieces and place in colander. Hold under running hot water briefly until moistened and squeeze dry. Mix with other ingredients and season to taste. Stuff a bird or pile lightly into a casserole. Score top of casseroled stuffing like a checkerboard and sprinkle with paprika. Bake in preheated moderate (350-degree) oven until browned and crusty, about 45 minutes. Makes 12 servings.

*Bread should be almost brittle-dry.

Noodles
(Colonial Cooking School, Oklahoma)

3 egg yolks
1 whole egg
3 tbsp. cold water

½ tsp. salt
1¾ cups sifted unbleached flour

Beat the yolks and the whole egg until very light. Beat in the cold water and the salt. Stir in the flour and work in a kneading motion with the heel of your hand. Divide the dough into 3 parts. Roll out each piece as thin as possible (paper thin) on a lightly floured board. Place on a towel until dough is partially dry. Roll up dough as for jelly roll. With a sharp knife, cut into strips of desired width. They may be cut into squares for soup. Shake out the strips and spread out on a large tray to dry for several hours before using or storing. Noodles will keep for two weeks in the refrigerator or may be frozen in a tight container. Cook noodles in rapidly boiling, salted water for 5 minutes before adding to soup or using as a side dish.

Ruth's Rice and Fruit Dressing
(Ruth's Kitchen, Illinois)

¼ lb. butter
1 med. onion, chopped
1 cup sliced fresh mushrooms
2 tbsp. slivered almonds
4 cups cooked rice
    (leftovers are fine)

1 tbsp. raisins, plumped
2 tsp. salt
Pepper to taste
½ tsp. thyme
1 (11 oz.) can mandarin oranges, drained

Melt butter in large skillet.
Add onions and mushrooms and cook over medium high heat until onions are transparent.
Add almonds and cook a moment longer.
Add rice, raisins, salt, pepper, thyme and mandarin oranges.
Reduce heat to medium low and continue heating and stirring until thoroughly heated, about 5 minutes.
Taste for salt and pepper, adding more if needed.
This goes very well with poultry that has a fruit sauce. Also goes well with pork and ham.
Serves 6-8.

Risotto Milanese
(Lynne Kasper's Cooking School of Denver)

2 to 3 tbsp. butter
1 medium onion, minced
2 cups long grain or Avorio rice
½ cup dry white wine
6 to 8 cups rich homemade chicken
    stock

½ tsp. saffron, crumbled
Salt and freshly ground pepper
1 cup freshly grated Parmesan cheese
½ lb. mushrooms, sliced and fried in
    2 tbsp. butter

In a heavy 3- to 4-quart casserole, saute onion in butter until soft and transparent. Stir in rice and saute until rice starts to appear chalky. Bring chicken stock to a boil and stir in saffron. Pour 1 cup of boiling stock into rice and stir. Simmer over medium or medium-low heat, stirring until stock is absorbed (do not let rice burn). Repeat this process, adding the wine also, until rice is tender but not mushy-soft. Mixture should be creamy but not soupy. Do not cover pot and do not try to steam rice. Stir in mushrooms and cheese. Season to taste.
Serves 6-8.

Schools Index

Levinson, Marlene, Cookery, 129
Lirio, Jack, Cooking School, 116
Look & Cook, 14
Louisiana Cooking School, 61
Lowry, Janice, 129
Lyon, Sue, Essencial Cooking School, 11

Malone, Barbara, 133
Mandarin Inn, The, 130
Mandarin Salon de Cuisine, The, 117
Manell, Rosemary, 133
Marinette Georgi Cuisine Minceur, 128
Mariotti, Anne, Cooking School, 11
Marique School of French Cooking, 45
Mary Kathryn's Gourmet Kitchen, 108
Mason, Carol, Food Originals, 5
Matter of Taste, A, 97
Mattimore Cooking School, 130
Mayer, Paul, Cooking School, 118
Mexican Cooking Classes (Diana
    Kennedy), 42
Meyers, Perla, International Kitchen
    School, 45
Microcookery Center, Inc., 81
Microwave Cooking Center, 103
Microwave Kitchen Shop, 89
Microwave Oven Workshop, 108
Milhiser, Katie, 133
Mission Gourmet Cookware, 128
Mr. Pots & Pans, Inc., 130
Monique's, 79
Moore-Betty School of Fine Cooking, 46
Muffoletto, Anna, Cordon Bleu of New
    York, Ltd., 46
Murray Hill School of Cooking, 47
Myers, Marilyn, Kitchen, 55

Napercurean House, Inc., 85
Natural Gourmet Cookery School, The, 40
Negri, Larry, Cooking School, 129
Nelson, Richard, 130
New York City Community College, 132
New York Institute of Dietetics, 132

Ojakangas, Beatrice, Country Cooking
    School, 92
Olney, Judith, 133
Oriental Food Market and Cooking
    School, 80
Oswald, Sharon, 131

Page, Helen Cassidy, School of Cooking, 128
Pampered Pantry, The, 95
Pandemonium, 130
Pang, Mary, Chinese Cooking School, 131
Pan Handler, The, 88
Papagayo School of Mexican Cooking, 129
Par Avion Pantry, 28
Parisian Kitchen, 128
Parker, Nancy, 131
Parrish, Marlene, Teaches Cooking, 18

Pepin, Jacques, 133
Peppercorn Cooking School, Inc., 122
Peppermill, 123
Perfect Pan, The, 112
Perlmutter, Alice M., Cooking School, 31
Persimmon Tree, 80
Polin, Joan, 133
Postillion School of Culinary Arts, The
    (Fond du Lac, Wis.), 131
Postillion School of Culinary Arts, The
    (Milwaukee, Wis.), 131
Potpourri School of Cooking, 15
Proper Pan Cooking School, 86

Quan, Constance, Cooking School, 23

Renaissance Chefs Cooking School, The, 6
Restaurant School, The, 132
Rodin, Marscelle, 129
Rowantree Farm, Cooking School, 31
Ruth's Kitchen, 83

Schempf, Sue, 130
School of Contemporary Cooking, 47
Schorr, Denise, 27
Scuola Italiana di Cucina of the American-
    Italian Society, 130
Sekely, Anne, School for Cooking, 130
1770 House Cooking School, The, 29
Sharon's Kitchen, 125
Silo Cooking School, The, 22
Simmons, John, Cooking School, 65
Simon, Florence, School of Gourmet
    Cooking, 75
Sorosky, Marlene, Cooking Center, 120
Spader, Margaret Chinese Cooking
    School, 48
Spray, Zona, Cooking School, 98
Steele, C., Kitchen, 69
Stock Pot, The, 56
Sunshine Kitchen Co., 124

Tahnk, Jeanne, Gourmet Kitchen, Inc., 27
Tante Marie's Cooking School, 118
Taylor, Emilie, Meat School, 13
Taylor, Suzanne, Cooking Classes, 25
TH'RICE, 129
Tin Pan Galley (Fairview Hts., Ill.), 129
Tin Pan Galley (Kan.), 129
Tin Pan Galley (Lake Bluff, Ill,), 84
Tin Pan Galley (Okla.), 130
Tropp, Barbara, 133
Truffles Gourmet Cooking School, 58

Ursula's Cooking School, 59
Urvater, Michele, 49

Vance, Judy, 133
Varketta, Ralph, Cooking School, 55
Von Welanetz Cooking Workshop, The, 106

Recipe Index